Slavery as Salvation

SLAVERY

AS

SALVATION

THE METAPHOR OF

SLAVERY IN PAULINE

CHRISTIANITY

DALE B. MARTIN

YALE UNIVERSITY PRESS

NEW HAVEN AND LONDON

Published with assistance from
the Mary Cady Tew Memorial Fund.

Designed by Sonia L. Scanlon.
Set in Janson with Optima display type by
The Composing Room of Michigan, Inc.
Printed in the United States of America by
Vail-Ballou Press, Binghamton, New York.

Library of Congress Cataloging-
in-Publication Data
Martin, Dale B., 1954–
    Slavery as salvation : the metaphor of
slavery in Pauline Christianity /
Dale B. Martin.
        p.   cm.
    Includes bibliographical references.
    ISBN 0–300–04735–5 (alk. paper)
      1. Slaves—Biblical teaching.
2. Salvation—Biblical teaching.
3. Sociology, Biblical.   4. Bible. N.T.
Epistles of Paul—Criticism,
interpretation, etc.   I. Title.
BS2655.S55M37   1990
227'.06—dc20   90–12224
                                        CIP

The paper in this book meets the guidelines
for permanence and durability of the
Committee on Production Guidelines
for Book Longevity of the
Council on Library Resources.
10 9 8 7 6 5 4 3 2 1

To
Harold Kelly Martin, Jr.,
and
JoAn Watson Martin

CONTENTS

PREFACE

For years I have been interested in why ordinary Greco-Roman urbanites became Christians. What was it about early Christian language, symbols, and promises that drew them to align themselves with that fledgling religious movement? This study began by pursuing one small aspect of that question: early Christian use of slavery as a metaphor for salvation and leadership. How did Greek and Roman converts hear such language? Why did it draw rather than repulse them? Why would anyone want to be Christ's slave? As the resulting book indicates, I believe some interesting answers to these and other questions can be had by placing Christian language firmly in a sociohistorical context and by analyzing religious language with a view to its ideological functions.

My study of slavery and slave language in early Christianity began as a doctoral dissertation at Yale University under the direction of Wayne A. Meeks, whose name does not often appear in the footnotes of this book but whose influence is evident throughout. I gratefully acknowledge that influence and thank him for his careful, considerate guidance and consistently excellent advice. Many others, including teachers, colleagues, and friends, have made invaluable contributions, reading the manuscript (sometimes many times), saving me from errors, and offering suggestions. Though I cannot name everyone who has given encouragement and support, the following deserve explicit thanks: Abraham J. Malherbe, Bentley Layton, Susan R. Garrett, David Dawson, Elizabeth Meyer, Bruce Lawrence, Elizabeth A. Clark, Wilhelm Wuellner, and Dan Via. Many thanks are due as well to Charles Grench and Caroline Murphy of Yale University Press, and to Meighan Pritchard, my manuscript editor, for saving me from many errors. I would also like to thank Margaret Adam for compiling the index. The book is dedicated to my parents, my first and greatest teachers.

ABBREVIATIONS

AD	*Archaiologikon Deltion.* Athens.
AE	*L'Année épigraphique.*
Anderson	Anderson, J. G. C. "An Imperial Estate in Galatia." *Journal of Roman Studies* 27 (1937): 18–21.
ArchEph	*Ephemerides Archaiologikis.* Athens.
BCH	*Bulletin de correspondance hellénique.*
CIG	*Corpus inscriptionum graecarum.* Edited by A. Boeckh. 1825–77.
CIL	*Corpus inscriptionum latinarum.* 1863–.
Corinth	Meritt, B. D., ed. *Corinth: Results.* Vol. 8, pt. 1 (1931). J. H. Kent, ed. *The Inscriptions, 1926–1950.* Vol. 8, pt. 3 (1966). Princeton: American School of Classical Studies at Athens.
Demitsas	Demitsas, Margarites, ed. *Sylloge inscriptionum graecarum et latinarum Macedoniae.* Reprint of 1896 ed. 2 vols. Chicago: Ares, 1980.
Dessau	Dessau, Hermann, ed. *Inscriptiones latinae selectae.* 3 vols. Berlin: Weidmann, 1954–55.
Ditt. (or *SIG*)	Dittenberger, Wilhelm, ed. *Sylloge inscriptionum graecarum.* 4 vols. Leipzig: S. Hirzel, 1915–24.
IG	*Inscriptiones graecae.* 1873–.
IGR	Cagnat, R., et al., eds. *Inscriptiones graecae ad res romanas pertinentes.* 4 vols. Chicago: Ares, 1975.
IK (or *IGSK*)	*Inschriften griechischer Städte aus Kleinasien.*
Kern	Kern, Otto. *Die Inschriften von Magnesia am Maeander.* Berlin: W. Spemann, 1900.
Kos	Šašel Kos, Marietta, ed. *Inscriptiones latinae in Graecia rerperta. Additamenta ad CIL III.* Faenza: Frattelli Lega, 1979.
L.	Landvogt, Peter. *Epigraphische Untersuchung über den oikonomos: Ein Beitrag zum hellenistischen*

	Beamtenwesen. Strasbourg: M. Dumont Schauberg, 1908.
MAMA	Calder, W., et al., eds. *Monumenta Asiae Minoris antiquae*. Manchester: Manchester University Press; London: Green, 1928.
MittAth	*Mittheilungen des Deutschen Archäologischen Instituts in Athen*. Athens: K. Wilberg.
Raffeiner	Raffeiner, H. *Sklaven und Freigelassene: Eine soziologische Studie auf der Grundlage des griechischen Grabepigramms*. Innsbruck: Wagner, 1977.
Robert *EA*	Robert, Louis. *Études anatoliennes: Recherches sur les inscriptions grecques de l'Asie Mineure*. Paris: E. de Boccard, 1937.
Robert *H*	Robert, Louis. *Hellenica*.
SEG	Hondius, J. J. E., et al., eds. *Supplementum epigraphicum graecum*. 1923–.
Smyrna	*Die Inschriften von Smyrna* (vol. 23, pt. 1 of *IK*).
TAM	Kalinka, E., and R. Herberdey, eds. *Tituli Asiae Minoris*. Vienna: A. Hoelderi, 1901–.

INTRODUCTION

Slavery in the Roman Empire was, as it always is from our modern perspective, an oppressive and exploitative institution. During the early empire, from the time of Augustus to the end of the second century, millions of human beings must have lived in humiliation and destitution, serving the needs and whims, the pleasures and tempers, of other human beings. According to Roman law, a slave, though recognized in a sense as a human being (*persona*), was a thing (*res*). Owners had the right to bind, torture, or kill their slaves.[1] In literature of the time, one continually comes across the opinion that slave life is the worst imaginable. In short, modern sensibilities justifiably take offense at the ancient institution of slavery.

Many studies of Greco-Roman slavery written in the past few decades have rightly emphasized how complex ancient slavery was and, to the modern person, how confusing it can be. In addition to slaves' dual legal status, other apparent contradictions existed: for example, although slaves legally could own nothing, we know from legal as well as nonlegal sources that certain slaves actually controlled quite a bit of property and even had sometimes considerable sums at their apparently free disposal. Although slaves could not formally marry, thousands of tombstones survive in which slaves refer to their spouses using common marital terminology, and a variety of evidence indicates that at least a significant minority of slaves maintained family structures of their own (the percentage of all slaves that did so is completely unknown). Bits of historical evidence such as these have recently led many ancient historians to point out that, though the institution of slavery was severely oppressive, some slaves were able to manipulate it to become rather powerful persons with a certain degree of informal status in the society, compared, at least, to the majority of the people of the empire, who were, though free, poor and powerless. For this small but significant minority of slaves, slavery represented an avenue to influence and was therefore, remarkable as it usually sounds to modern ears, a means of social mobility.

As important as the subject of Roman slavery is, in this book I do not attempt a broad study of the institution of slavery as such. I offer no analysis of the overall significance of ancient slavery for economics or society. Nor do I intend to shed any great light on the narrower subject of the relation of early Christianity to slavery—to describe, for example, early Christian attitudes toward slavery, Paul's stance on the institution of slavery, or the position of slaves in the social structure of Christian house churches. Rather, my subject is the narrowly defined area of one particular function of slavery as a metaphor in early Christianity: how do we explain the positive, soteriological use of slavery as a symbol for the Christian's relationship to God or Christ? If the institution of slavery was as oppressive as it seems to have been, and if Greeks and Romans so feared slavery and despised slaves, how could slavery portray salvation positively for early Christians? Why, in other words, would any person of that society want to be called a slave of Christ? To address these questions, in this book I detail the complexity of slavery, and the ambiguity of slave status in Greco-Roman society, in order to analyze the religious and social—indeed, ideological—function of slavery as metaphor in early Christianity, specifically in the Pauline church at Corinth.

I have hoped that the shortcomings of a book with such a narrow focus—one function of one metaphor as seen primarily in one text—will be compensated by the offering of a full social and rhetorical placement of that metaphor. Religious language is inextricably intertwined with social structures, ideological constructs, and rhetorical strategies of the society at large. To analyze theological language from the point of view of theology alone is to distort its significance for any real social group, theologians included. The value of this book, therefore, will not be in its presentation of Roman slavery or its treatment of actual slavery and early Christianity, but in its microscopic analysis of the relationship of a piece of religious language to other forms of human society and discourse.

At first glance, the self-symbolization of Christians as slaves of God appears odd in a Greco-Roman context. Generally, biblical scholars have insisted that Christians were, for the most part, alone in this metaphorical use of slavery and that the normal inhabitant of Greco-Roman culture would have been offended at the idea. Yet, as some other scholars have pointed out, "slave of the god" is not such an impossible construction in Greco-Roman society. Though the phrase rarely refers to the religious participant, it is not by any means unknown. For example, characters in literature sometimes refer to themselves as slaves of a god or goddess. In

Sophocles' play *Oedipus the King*, Teiresias the seer says that he is not the slave (*doulos*) of Oedipus but of Apollo; therefore, he need not fear Oedipus's threats.[2] In a fragment from the comedian Philemon, a character admits that he has "one man" as his master (*kyrios*). But, he points out, thousands of people have the law as their master; others have tyrants; tyrants have fear. "They are slaves," he says, "of kings; the king [is slave] of the gods; the god [is slave] of necessity." Plato has Socrates call himself a fellow slave (*homodoulos*) with sacred swans, because they serve the same god.[3] To move to another time and place, it may be under the influence of Isis theology that Lucius Apuleius, in *The Golden Ass*, speaks of his relationship to the goddess as slavery (*servitum*) and claims that he realizes freedom by serving her (that is, like a slave: *servire*).[4] The terminology seems to cause no offense in this very Roman context.

We encounter other references to slavery to a god or goddess in inscriptions. A fascinating inscription survives from Dionysopolis in Asia Minor (modern Turkey) and probably comes from the second or third century C.E., a time when Asia Minor was quite romanized. The inscription was erected by a man who seems to have been a slave steward, or manager, of a free man's property. Only four letters of the man's name, "Neik," survive in the fragmentary Greek inscription. "Neik" first confesses to the god a few minor sins: although it is impossible to figure out exactly what happened, it seems he had for some reason lied about some pigeons, broken into a holy area, and stolen a sheep. Then Neik concentrates on his major offense: he had apparently promised freedom to one of the family slaves and had registered the slave with the temple as the promissory step toward the slave's manumission. His lord (*kyrios*), however, who seems initially not to have known about the agreement, later demanded the certificate of manumission in order to invalidate it. After Neik surrendered the certificate to his master he was pursued by the god, who insisted, through dreams, that his slave be turned over to him. Neik is in an unenviable position, caught between the demands of the god and the demands of his lord. The god insists on the manumission of the slave in opposition to the desires of the human owner. The god labels the slave as his own and in his capacity as the slave's new owner attempts to protect the slave from the former owner.[5] Here in firmly Greco-Roman Asia Minor a god lays claim to a man and attempts to protect him by designating him his slave.

In Macedonia, a woman named Strato dedicates a vineyard to the goddess Ma and, in the inscription, calls herself *doulē theas*, "slave of the goddess."[6] A Syrian named Loukios dedicates an altar to Atargatis, whom he calls his mistress (*kyria*); he calls himself her slave (*doulos autēs*).[7] These few examples indicate that metaphorical slavery to a god was not a completely unlikely construction in Greco-Roman society.

Generally, however, biblical scholars have emphasized its strangeness and have offered different explanations for why early Christians called themselves slaves of God and Christ. In the first half of the twentieth century an explanation offered by Adolf Deissmann was generally accepted. Deissmann linked the New Testament slave metaphors to Delphic manumission inscriptions.[8] As a slave who was to be manumitted was sold to the god (usually Apollo), so the Christian is sold to Christ. The ex-slave is actually free, and so, Deissmann said, the sale is fictitious. The ex-slave is nevertheless thought of as the slave of the god. Similarly, Paul and other Christians call themselves slaves of Christ and yet still claim to be, in some sense, free. Deissmann's thesis was initially influential, but in the last half of this century, it has generally been rejected.[9] Several scholars have pointed out, for example, that the actual Greek terms used in the Delphic manumission inscriptions are not those used by Paul, and, conversely, that Paul's terminology does not occur in the inscriptions.[10]

Most biblical scholars now explain the term *slave of Christ* by pointing to the Old Testament and Near Eastern political and religious language.[11] Paul's interpreters have turned to eastern concepts and the Old Testament because they believe, as noted above, that Paul's use of slavery to illustrate Christian life would be incomprehensible to the normal inhabitant of a Greco-Roman city. Hans Conzelmann represents the current consensus when he says that "the demand to become the *doulos*, 'slave,' of a god is radically non-Greek."[12] Having decided, therefore, that "slave of the god" is not understandable in a Greco-Roman context, these scholars look outside that context for the origin and, indeed, the meaning of the early Christian language about slavery to Christ.

I suggest that the consensus view among New Testament scholars overlooks several important factors that, taken into consideration, may significantly enrich our understanding of the use of slave terminology by early Christians—or that may at least complicate the picture. First, most early Christians, at least those represented by Paul's churches, lived in Greek and Roman cities, spoke Greek, and imbibed Greco-Roman culture, to a great extent, just like their non-Christian neighbors. Pauline Christianity grew up not in the Far East or in an ancient Babylonian empire but in the bustling, hellenized, romanized urban centers of the Mediterranean—places such as Ephesus, Laodicea, Corinth, Thessalonica, and Philippi. And Paul spoke not to ancient Israelites but to former pagans with such names as Crispus, Gaius, Julia, Stephanus. Did they cringe every time they heard Paul, their leader, refer to himself and to them as slaves of Christ? How could the designation symbolize salvation for that kind of Greco-Roman urbanite? Furthermore, it is problematic to assume too sharp a dichotomy between Jewish and Gentile (or "oriental" and Greek) symbol systems. The traditional division between the Jewish and Hellenistic worlds has been challenged by many scholars, who now doubt that we can point to any first-century Judaism that is not to some extent hellenized. Nor can we so easily point to any Hellenism of the first century that is not to some extent orientalized. Therefore, any explanation of early Christian language that assigns concepts to sharply differentiate Greek and Jewish worlds should be suspect.[13]

Another factor usually overlooked by the consensus explanation of metaphorical slavery has to do with what I call the genetic fallacy of historical explanation. Traditionally, explanations of the term *slave of Christ* point out the origins of the metaphor as if those origins provide its meaning in the early Christian context. That is, some scholars content themselves with saying that slavery metaphors come from Old Testament usage or from Near Eastern religious and political language. Such analyses give only a genetic explanation of the metaphor of slavery in early Christianity without explaining how the language actually worked for the people who used it. Historical guesses about the derivation of a term, however, do not give the meaning of the term. If one wishes to talk about the meaning of early Christian language, one must talk about that language in the context of the Greco-Roman city. Regardless of the origin of the language, one must explain how it worked among and for Greek-speaking Gentiles.[14]

The third factor to be kept in mind is the previously mentioned complexity of ancient slavery. In spite of the recent advances in our knowledge of Greco-Roman slavery provided by classicists and ancient historians— advances that often stress the ambiguity of ancient slave status—biblical scholars too often present a monolithic, oversimplified picture of *the* Greek or Roman concept of slavery.[15] Furthermore, many biblical scholars look only to the high literature of Greco-Roman culture (usually the philosophical writings) to find Greek and Roman concepts. It is not surprising that upper-class authors severely denigrate slaves—along with lower-class persons in general. We should not take such literature to represent the views of everyone in the society.[16] In the search for Greco-Roman parallels to Christian language, biblical scholars have generally cast their nets in too small an area. As I have already suggested, outside the more conservative, traditional worldview of Greco-Roman philosophy and upper-class literature slavery does occasionally represent the believer's relationship to the god. I focus on uses of language that may have occurred only outside the small circle of the intellectual and economic elite. This wider scope of vision will show that the metaphorical possibilities of slavery to the god were as complex as ancient slavery itself.

I should explain why I use the sources I do. In my analysis of Greco-Roman slavery I have used studies of Latin literature and inscriptions from the western part of the Roman Empire as well as similar materials from the eastern part. I defend these sources because it is commonly accepted by historians that in many respects Greek slavery and Roman slavery were quite different, especially if one is comparing Greek slavery of its classical period (fifth to fourth centuries B.C.E.) with Roman slavery of the early empire (first two centuries C.E.). Furthermore, there were other important cultural differences between east and west in the Roman Empire. I have felt justified in using some materials from both of these geographical and cultural areas for several reasons. For one thing, I take as my final focus the Pauline churches and, more specifically, the church at Corinth. In the first century, Corinth, though an ancient Greek city, was very romanized. It had been refounded by Julius Caesar in the previous century and settled by Roman freedmen, and most of its inscriptions were still in Latin until the time of Hadrian.[17] Therefore, although Corinth was in a Greek region, the people of Corinth must have been quite familiar with Roman ways. Indeed, the population of Corinth may even have been, to some extent, bilingual and bicultural during the time Christianity was establishing a foothold there. I believe Roman influence must also have been evident in other cities where Paul founded churches, such as Philippi (a Roman colony) and Ephesus (a center for Roman provincial government and the residence of the proconsul). Thus, even though many people in the countryside may have been relatively untouched by Roman ideas and practices, people in those cities, including all the earliest Christians, could scarcely have avoided such influence.

Next, I have avoided basing my account of Greco-Roman slavery on evidence from the West unless I have also pointed out evidence that the same or a very similar social situation also prevailed in the East, or at least in those parts of the East that are my concern. For example, in the first chapter I cite studies of slave families that use evidence only from Latin inscriptions from Rome, but I then point to evidence for slave families from Greek and Latin inscriptions in Asia Minor. Similarly, I use Roman laws and western evidence to illustrate the function of the patron-client structure, but I then also cite inscriptions and texts that show the same or very similar structures at work in cities of the East. The structures of slavery were not the same in all parts of the Roman Empire, but the particular aspects of Roman slavery highlighted in this study could also be found in certain eastern cities in the first century (though not necessarily in the countryside, where most actual production by slaves may have been taking place).

The discussion thus far may be summarized into two observations to be kept in mind throughout this book. The first is that the early Christians were urban people living in Greek and Roman cities. They were both hellenized and, to some extent, romanized. The second is that any explanation of slavery to Christ or God must recognize that the term represented salvation—not just obedience, humility, or humiliation—to those Christians. These observations suggest that any adequate analysis of this particular religious symbolism must be both soteriological and contextual. That is, the interpretation must explain both how the image could represent salvation and how it could have done so to Greco-Roman converts. Deissmann's analysis came closer than most to a contextual, soteriological interpretation of the slave metaphors. His thesis was in the end unconvincing to later scholars only because his interpretation was too dependent on one particular social context (Delphic manumissions) that was linguistically and socially too far removed from Paul's own discourse. In his attempt to be contextual, Deissmann chose the wrong context.

Other interpretations, however, have been, for the most part, either not contextual or not soteriological. The noncontextual explanations say that the "salvation" meaning of slavery to God comes from the Old Testament and from eastern religious and political concepts. This does not sufficiently explain how the image functioned to express salvation for Greco-Roman city dwellers. The nonsoteriological interpretations are contextual in that they use Greco-Roman meanings of slavery to interpret Christian language. They point out that slavery to God, for Greeks and Romans, would have implied unconditional obedience to God, humility, and absolute dependence. But they center only on what we might call moral-ethical connotations of metaphorical slavery. They do not explain the soteriological function of slavery to God, that is, how such slavery could positively represent salvation to early Christians.

When I say that an analysis of *slave of Christ* must be contextual, I mean to suggest that that context must be a social one. Too often biblical commentators limit themselves to a world of ideas. They look for particularly religious precursors to early Christian language rather than analyzing how the social institutions of Greco-Roman slavery might have informed the metaphorical appropriation of slave language. Here again, they are fishing in too small a pond—in this case, in the pond of ideas and, in particular, religious ideas—rather than in the broader area of full social reality. To explain language, to analyze how metaphors function within a society, we must look to all of a society and everyday experience within it. Limiting our interest to ideaistic, religious, or genetic explanations of the language will only distort an explanation of the function of language for any given social context.

In my analysis of the meaning of slavery as metaphor in early Christianity I attempt to avoid the problems listed above. To define the meaning of slavery as a metaphor one must examine the function of such language within a particular context, in this case the context of early Christian communities. To ask what the language meant is to ask how it was used; that use can be ascertained only by examining the full social context.[18] Furthermore, I assume that in order to explain what language means it is equally or more important to suggest how the language is heard as to guess what the author intended. Of course, the same language may be heard differently by different people even in the same historical situation. Therefore, the language will have a range of possible meanings, none of which can claim to be *the* meaning. But if we assume that the phrase *slave of Christ* meant anything at all in early Christian groups, we must suggest ways it could have functioned as a plausible linguistic structure for Greek and Roman urbanites of the first century. At any rate, these two aspects of my approach—attention to the probable responses of the hearers of the language and to the full social context of the language—should protect against the methodological problems I have mentioned.

In part, I am following the lead of Gerd Theissen. Theissen mentions the necessity for construing a "plausibility structure" or "plausibility basis" for early Christian language.[19] He means that we can explain what Christian language means only by imagining a way in which the language would be believable for inhabitants of a particular cultural system. We must guess what in a given society would allow persons to hear, for example, slavery to Christ as a plausible and compelling construction. Theissen suggests that "slave of Christ," "son of God," "freedperson of Christ," and "soldier of Christ" (see 2 Cor. 10:4–6) all reflect religious, symbolic appropriations of actual roles in society and the overtones of status and social mobility linked to those roles. In Paul's "position-Christology," of which slavery is one element, the status of the Christian is linked to the status of Christ. A person improves his or her status by loyalty to superiors. Theissen's observations are tantalizing but sketchy. I have expanded his analysis of Greco-Roman slavery, with attention to the significance of social status and social mobility.

Slavery is used metaphorically in various texts of early Christianity, including each of Paul's letters. But one passage, 1 Corinthians 9, is especially problematic. Here Paul insists on his freedom and authority as an apostle. He begins what looks like a defense of his apostleship ("This is my apologia to those who are accusing me" 9:3) by asserting his status as a free man (9:1). Only a few verses later, however, Paul portrays himself as a slave of Christ, as will be made clear below in an analysis of 9:16–18. In 9:19–23, Paul portrays himself as a slave of all. Surprisingly, Paul depicts himself as a slave even after having asserted his freedom, and slavery seems to have something to do with Paul's refusal to accept support from the Corinthian church. Slavery also seems to be related to Paul's avowed practice of changing himself to suit his audience and to his claim that he does it all for gain. How does any of this relate to Paul's own brand of leadership, his apostleship?

To address the different exegetical problems of 1 Corinthians 9, I focus on the function of slavery as the central metaphor in that text. In chapters 1 and 2, I examine the phrase *slave of Christ* in the context of Greco-Roman society. In 1 Cor. 9:16–18, Paul says that he receives no wage because he has been entrusted with an *oikonomia*, a stewardship. Paul here makes himself Christ's *oikonomos*, his slave steward or manager. But what is the significance of this self-portrayal? What does Paul have to gain by depicting himself as the managerial slave of Christ instead of as a free man *in* Christ?

In order to explicate this and other ways *slave of Christ* could have functioned for Paul and his hearers I offer an analysis of Greco-Roman slavery in chapter 1. Though various aspects of slave life are considered, I concentrate on middle-level, managerial slaves. By middle-level slaves I mean these who ran a business or worked as an agent or manager, those who occupied positions somewhere between top imperial slave bureaucrats and the slaves involved in common, manual labor and services. This aspect of slavery is often ignored by biblical commentators, yet it raises issues of status, social mobility, and the ambiguous meaning of slavery in the Roman Empire. Furthermore, middle-level slavery helps illustrate the role played by the slave as a representative for the master, a role that relates to Paul's apostleship.

The study of actual Greco-Roman slavery suggests ways slave language could represent the Christian's relationship to Christ. Slavery was a means of social mobility for some persons in the Roman Empire. Moreover, slavery to an important person bestowed on the slave a certain amount of prestige and power, a status-by-association. Once we recognize the significance of slavery to status and social mobility in the Greco-Roman world, we are better able to analyze Paul's rhetorical strategy in depicting himself as a slave of Christ in 1 Corinthians 9. We are also in a better position to understand the broader functions of slavery to Christ in representing salvation and authoritative leadership in early Christianity.

In chapters 3 and 4 I examine Paul's "slavery to all" in 1 Cor. 9:19–23. Scholars have debated several problems in these verses: Paul freely admits that he enslaves himself to everyone; he admits that he "becomes all things to all people"; he says he does it in order to gain; but he claims that his goal is the salvation of the people. These different elements of Paul's argument are usually approached as disparate, unrelated issues. In the first century, however, a rhetorical topos was current that combined them. In chapter 3, I outline that topos and examine its different elements: changeable behavior, the enslavement of a leader to the masses, the accusation that the leader seeks gain, and the claim that the enslaved leader actually works for the salvation of the people.[20] The topos usually described populist leaders who attempted to exercise their leadership outside the normal structures of patronal society. Their forms of leadership and their lifestyles conflicted with more traditional assumptions about the connection between high social status and leadership. Chapter 4 compares the role of this topos in Paul's rhetoric with its role in other rhetorical contexts. The comparison illuminates the different exegetical problems of 1 Cor. 9:19–23, the meaning of Paul's slavery within his rhetorical strategy of 1 Corinthians 9, and the meaning of chapter 9 within the overall argument of 1 Corinthians 8–10.[21]

Paul's complex use of slavery metaphors reflects the complexity of Greco-Roman slavery. By calling himself Christ's slave, Paul claims a certain kind of authority. At the same time Paul calls himself a slave of all, characterizing his self-support by means of manual labor as self-enslavement and social self-lowering. Some of Paul's Corinthian converts seem to have been unhappy about Paul's manual labor and about his use of metaphorical slavery to explain and defend it. That metaphors, like other aspects of language, are heard differently by different people in a society, suggests, however, that others at Corinth may have felt differently. The complexity of language mirrors the complexity of society. Conflicts over status, power, and value systems play themselves out in complex rhetorical struggles. By analyzing Paul's rhetoric and his use of slave language we will be better able to understand the conflict that arose between Paul and members of the Corinthian church he founded—a conflict he tried to settle, but perhaps exacerbated, by calling himself their slave.

1

ANCIENT

SLAVERY

AND

STATUS

In the early Roman Empire people could see slaves everywhere they looked. Slaves occupied all sorts of jobs, and they mingled rather freely with nonslaves, both freeborn people and freedpersons. Many slaves were, of course, in desperate positions, destitute, mistreated, and oppressed. But others seem to have lived relatively normal lives—normal, that is, compared with other people not in the highest class. Some modern scholars even seem determined to prove that slavery was a rather benevolent institution.[1] Of course, it was not. Nevertheless, in this chapter I will stress the opportunities available to some slaves in the early Roman Empire, as this aspect of Roman slavery is usually absent in modern biblical commentators' presuppositions about slavery. The term *slave* often conjures up for the modern reader images of permanently destitute agricultural and household workers, but there is no reason to believe that ancient persons understood the term in the same way. Furthermore, although social historians of Greece and Rome have increasingly emphasized the complexity and ambiguity of slavery in antiquity, biblical scholars regularly respond to New Testament slave images in predictable ways, with little attention to the wide possibilities for the function of such language in early Christian communities.

The daily lives of slaves, for the most part, are hidden from modern historians. Slaves generally did not write the books that have survived, and it is the surviving literature that provides most of the raw material for the social historian's research. But historians are not at a total loss. For one thing, Greco-Roman literature does offer glimpses of the lives, beliefs, and aspirations of the nonpropertied classes, including slaves. Second, by using nonliterary sources, such as inscriptions erected by the slaves and freedpersons themselves, we can obtain some idea of slave life in the early empire.[2] In this chapter I use a wide variety of materials—inscriptions, Greco-Roman novels, histories, satires, speeches, and handbooks on household management, agriculture, and dream interpretation—to paint a picture of slavery in the early Roman Empire. The purpose of massing disparate detail—from funerary inscriptions and lists of different jobs as found in slave inscriptions—is to enable the reader to appreciate better the intricate social web that defined the lives of at least some slaves in the early Roman Empire.

SLAVES AND FAMILY

One of the cruelties of slavery in ancient and modern times is its assault on basic family structure. Legally, slave marriages were not recognized, and it was the owner's prerogative to sell off members of a slave's immediate family.[3] These legal conventions were surely social facts as well. They should not blind us, however, to other evidence indicating that many slaves maintained the family structures common in the rest of society.

Years ago, R. H. Barrow, attempting to dispel the modern assumption that slaves had no families of their own, noted that "epitaphs suggest that an unbroken family life was securely counted on" by slaves.[4] Recent researchers have tried to test this hypothesis by more systematic analysis of inscriptions. Marlene Boudreau Flory collected slave inscriptions from *Corpus inscriptionum latinarum* 6 representing slaves from three large Roman households. The results of her research show that within the large Roman households many slaves maintained long-term, stable families.[5]

How and where these slave families actually lived remains open to speculation. Archeological research has yielded little information about slave living quarters. According to Flory, none has come from Rome itself.[6] Many slaves doubtless lived in the houses of their masters, sleeping wherever they could find available space. But there are indications that many others, especially those involved in businesses, lived apart from their owners in their own dwellings. One law, for example, speaks of slaves conducting business and making contracts in their own homes rather than in the homes of their masters.[7] An obvious possibility is that many slaves lived very much like most of the free population surrounding and mingling with them. Indeed, Beryl Rawson, in a study also based on the funerary inscriptions of *CIL* 6, showed that many families of the lower class in Rome combined persons of slave, freed, and freeborn status. Because of frequent manumissions and unions between slave, freed and sometimes even free persons, these groups, to a great extent, merged in daily life. This observation alone suggests that family life for these slaves could not have differed radically from family life of freed persons and the free urban poor. Furthermore, couples that included a slave and a freed partner often continued to live together in the same household, along with their children, and with expectations that the as-yet-unfree partner would eventually attain freed status. Therefore, though Flory's studies show that slaves most often married slaves within the same household (at least those of the Imperial household, which is what Flory was studying) even when they married outside the household they seem to have been able to maintain a family.[8]

The studies by Flory and Rawson are limited to inscriptions from Rome and mostly from the large imperial households of Rome. Slaves in other households and in other parts of the Roman Empire were usually in quite different situations. Therefore, we cannot uncritically project the results of Flory's and Rawson's studies onto the provinces. Nevertheless, other studies do provide at least minimal evidence that the existence of slave families was not at all limited to Rome. Richard P. Saller and Brent D. Shaw, for example, have published works specifically on the structure of families in other areas of the western part of the Roman Empire. Saller and Shaw analyzed thousands of Latin tombstones from the Roman West and found that when the commemorator of a tombstone (that is, the one who provided the inscription) could be ascertained it was usually someone from the nuclear family, that is, husband, wife, daughter, or son.[9] Saller and Shaw want to correct a certain received view that insists that the further back one goes before the modern and industrial ages the more extended the family becomes and that the dominance of the nuclear family structure is a relatively modern (and, according to some, degenerate) development. Therefore, although Saller and Shaw admit that their data proves only that immediate family members were more likely than anyone else to provide a funerary inscription for a deceased family member, they suggest that the evidence also testifies to "a sense of familial duty and feelings of affection." They thus offer a challenge to the view that extended family structures, "particularly the patriarchal family under *patria po-*

testas," was the predominant form of family structure in the Roman Empire.[10]

Some of the method and conclusions of Saller and Shaw's study are questionable. Contrary to the study's suggestions, inscriptions cannot be used, I believe, as reliable indicators of the quality of personal relationships. Inscriptions in the ancient world, as in our own time, usually follow customary formats with predictable expressions. We have no way of knowing whether the sentiments expressed on a tombstone are actually the sentiments of the provider or even whether the very presence of the inscription indicates anything more than a social and not necessarily affectionate relationship between the persons named in the inscription. Furthermore, although Saller and Shaw may have demonstrated the importance of the nuclear family in the ancient society, that does not necessarily imply the unimportance of the extended family structure. Nevertheless, the inscriptions prove at least the existence of slave families in the Roman Empire and imply that the nuclear family was more important for slaves than our literary sources suggest. One might expect that slaves would have had to depend on owners, fellow slaves, or other household members to provide funerary arrangements for themselves in the absence of normal family structures. But the evidence from these inscriptions suggests that slaves were just as likely as nonslaves to depend on nuclear family members rather than nonfamily acquaintances to provide funerary inscriptions for them.

For example, of the servile population of Noricum, the province between Italy and Germany, Saller and Shaw counted 119 expressed relationships between the provider and the recipient of funerary dedications. Of that number, 101 (85 percent) were nuclear family members. The percentages for the *familia Caesaris* at Rome and the *familia Caesaris* at Carthage are almost identical (82 percent and 85 percent, respectively). Of the civilian population at Noricum, 91 percent of those who provide funerary inscriptions are members of the deceased's nuclear family.[11] These figures indicate that in these western provinces, at least in terms of the conventions of funerary epitaphs, slave family structures did not differ substantially from the family structures and inscriptional conventions of the free populace. The data indicate that at least this kind of slave (those able because of money or position to immortalize themselves on stone) could hope for a family structure no less stable and secure than was experienced by most of the free populace.

Thus far I have cited studies of Latin and Western inscriptions. A study of slave and freedperson funerary inscriptions from Asia Minor, however, yields similar results for that area. Tables A and B in the appendix list 115 funerary inscriptions for slaves and 92 for freedpersons from Asia Minor.[12] Of the slave inscriptions (including 19 that I believe, for a variety of reasons, to be for slaves, though they do not say so explicitly), the provider can be determined for 103. In 70 cases, the epitaph is furnished by a slave for himself or herself and includes family members, or else family members provide the epitaph for a deceased slave. In other words, of the known providers of funeral epitaphs for slaves, 68 percent were family members.[13]

Of the 92 funeral epitaphs for freedpersons, the provider is known for 84. And, as with slaves, freedpersons were more likely to be commemorated by members of their own family than by anyone else.[14] Furthermore, when one compares the percentages for the slave inscriptions with those for the freedperson inscriptions, the figures are strikingly similar. Of those slaves and freedpersons who enjoy the status of an inscription, the slaves are as likely as the freedpersons to have a family. In other words, one's legal status as a slave, taken alone, may have had little to do with the ability to maintain a normal family structure, that is, a family structure resembling that of the surrounding society.

Table C in the appendix presents these same inscriptions in a different way. The inscriptions are divided into groups according to the relationships among the persons included in the inscription regardless of who provided the inscription. Of the 115 slave inscriptions, 30 give no indication of any familial relationship. This cannot be taken to signify that all of these slaves had no families, only that we can make no claims one way or another about family on the basis of the inscription as we have it.[15] In 74 inscriptions we encounter families. (This does not include cases of one parent plus children or a child providing for his or her parents.)[16]

The family category was further broken down into four categories: (A) those mentioning only husband and wife; (B) those mentioning husband, wife, and at least one child; (C) those giving evidence of extended families (including persons related by blood and marriage and dependent slaves or freedpersons); (D) slave inscriptions in which nonrelated persons are included along with the slave's family. This last category may include persons who are clients of slaves or socially dependent on them but for whom the precise relationship cannot be determined. For example, in *Tituli Asiae Minoris* (*TAM*) 2.1044, Chrysianos, a male slave, provides an inscription for himself, his wife, children, brothers, in-laws, and someone named

Artemon. Artemon could be a slave of the slave or perhaps a family member. But the position of his name in the inscription is last, usually a position, in inscriptions of this area (Olympus, second to third century c.e.?), occupied by nonfamilial dependents of the inscription provider. Also included in the D category are inscriptions that show a slave family sharing a tomb with a free family.[17] In these cases we can tell that the slave(s) is not dependent on the free family. But whether they share the tomb simply as equals or whether the free persons are somehow socially dependent on the slave is impossible to tell from the inscription (though the latter is clearly a possibility).

An examination of table C shows that among the slave inscriptions the family structure of husband, wife, and offspring is by far the most common, followed by some form of the extended family. When the inscriptions commemorating freedpersons are examined the results are similar. Of 92 funerary inscriptions for freedpersons, 54 show evidence for family (excluding man with children and woman with children). No family connection can be ascertained in 26 cases. When the familial inscriptions are broken down, the inscriptions of freedpersons do not agree as closely with those for slaves. For freedpersons, the structure most evidenced is that of husband and wife alone. Next is the "husband, wife, child" category, largest for slaves, smaller for freedpersons. I have no explanation for these figures other than speculations: perhaps freedpersons were more likely to have older children who provided funerary inscriptions for themselves and therefore did not need to be included in those of their parents;[18] or perhaps these freed couples have moved and left behind family connections. At any rate, in spite of these differences between the slave and the freed inscriptions, the figures suggest that those slaves represented by these inscriptions were no less likely than freedpersons to maintain nuclear families. We even have substantial evidence for slave extended families; as is the case with the freedperson inscriptions, 15 percent of the slave inscriptions show evidence of extended families.[19]

These studies of inscriptions must not be pressed too far. They do not prove that slaves enjoyed wonderfully secure and happy home lives within the context of the nuclear family. Nor do they prove that the majority of slaves were able to maintain even a minimal family structure.[20] Yet the evidence should dissuade us from assuming that a slave was automatically removed from the place and family of birth. It contradicts the idea that slaves, in the total absence of normal familial ties, gained their only family from the extended family structure of the owner's household. It also indicates a certain degree of social stability, and therefore power, for many slaves. At the very least, these studies illustrate the existence and importance of the immediate family for a significant minority of slaves both in the western and certain eastern portions of the Roman Empire.[21]

SLAVES AND MONEY

Under Roman law slaves could own nothing.[22] Many cases show, however, that in every sense but the legal one slaves controlled and possessed money and property independently. The legal device that allowed slaves to possess anything was the convention of the *peculium*. From Republican times it had been both customary and legally mandated that the head of the household owned all the family's property. Out of his property, however, he set apart a portion, called a peculium, for his sons or slaves. The slave had the revocable use of the peculium and thus might enjoy considerable economic or social independence. For example, slaves (or sons) could use the peculium to run a business or businesses. Therefore, though the master legally owned the money or property making up the peculium, the slave, in fact, seems to have had rather free rein with it.[23]

In the Greco-Roman world certain highly visible slaves, some of whom were downright famous, controlled substantial amounts of money. Greek and Roman authors were constantly carping about uppity slaves who were richer than honest, upstanding free men such as themselves. In the first century, the most obvious examples were the slaves of the emperor's household who held bureaucratic positions in the imperial administration. Pallas, Narcissus, and Callistus, all notorious slaves and later freedmen of Claudius, amassed huge amounts of wealth including lands, plantations, villas, and many slaves and freedpersons of their own. The often quoted epitaph of Musicus Scurranus shows that even less important figures in the imperial bureaucracy were well off. Musicus was a slave and finance officer of the Emperor Tiberius and worked in Gaul. On a trip to Rome he died, and his own slaves who were accompanying him on the trip set up an honorary funeral inscription for him there.[24] Among his entourage (surely only a part of the total number of his household slaves) were Venustus, buying agent; Decimianius, treasurer, Agathopus, physician; Epaphra and Anthus, in charge of silver; Primio, in charge of wardrobe; two chamberlains; four attendants; and Tiasus and Firmus, cooks. A woman's name, Secunda, ends the list. She is the only woman and the only one who does not list her responsibilities, though it is not difficult to imagine what they might have been.

Higher-placed imperial slaves are an obvious example of slaves with money. They were the most famous wealthy slaves in the first century.[25] But many slaves in households not connected with the imperial bureaucracy were able to put together quite a bit of capital. In literary sources one runs across this kind of slave regularly. In Athenaeus's *Deipnosophists*, the diners talk for pages about famous rich slaves of classical history. Most of the slaves discussed seem to be prostitutes, like Pythionike who, according to Theopompus, was a famous Athenian whore; they say she was honored with a fancy monument though she was the slave of a slave of a slave.[26] This is all exaggeration, of course, but we read of enough real cases to know that they existed and were famous.

We can only speculate as to where most slaves procured the money to buy their own freedom. In classical Greece, it seems to have been from the savings of the slave or from an association (*eranos*), which would advance the money to the slave. In the Roman period, it may have been provided in some cases by family members. At least some Christian churches provided funds for manumissions of Christian slaves.[27] We know this, however, only because church leaders tried to prohibit the practice; how long it continued or how common it was at any time is uncertain. On the basis of this church practice, we might guess that there were other organizations that loaned or granted money for manumissions, but the historical evidence is lacking. We must assume that most slaves who were manumitted for a price paid it themselves out of their own earnings.

The price of freedom for an educated or managerial slave could be quite high. A freedman doctor of Asisium in the West put up an inscription detailing his wealth, benefactions, and expenditures for various honors.[28] He paid 50,000 sesterces for his freedom, which cost him substantially more than any of the other honors: 2,000 to the government for his sevirate, 30,000 for statues in the temple of Heracles, 37,000 to the public for paving streets. Even so, he was still able to bequeath a fortune of 800,000 sesterces. As a slave doctor he had amassed a fortune by the standards of most of the society.

Slaves with money can be found in the East also. In Greek manumission inscriptions, the price for conditional freedom is commonly four hundred drachmae, according to a study by Keith Hopkins. This is equivalent to three and a half tons of wheat, or enough to provide a subsistence living for a peasant family for over three years.[29] The slaves who bought their freedom had to obtain this money somewhere. That they could earn such amounts, save it, and expend it in this way demonstrates some degree of monetary power, a greater degree than we might have thought possible under slavery.

Funerary inscriptions from Asia Minor offer some hint of slave money there. Though it did not cost much to erect an epitaph—even poor people could afford a simple one—some of those for slaves are elaborate.[30] The monument of Chryseros in Termessus, which he constructed for himself, his wife, and his deceased son, was an expensive structure, as the drawing of it in the published text shows.[31] Chryseros may have been not only a slave but also a shrewd businessman.

Besides purchasing funerary inscriptions, slaves also paid for dedicatory inscriptions. Sometimes the slaves, like free persons, mention that the inscription has been put up at their own expense.[32] But even when they do not say so, most of them probably still paid for the dedications themselves. The cost of many of these dedications would have seemed insignificant to the truly wealthy, but to the majority of the inhabitants of the empire, the expenditure would have looked impressive. In an inscription from about 90 c.e. Dokimos, a slave, brags that he paid twelve denarii for ten roof tiles for a sanctuary and the gilding for the coffered ceiling.[33] On an imperial estate in Galatia, the slave manager of the estate, Eutyches, boasts that he paid for a sanctuary complete with several statues.[34] He admits that he had the assistance of the local procurator, who probably supplied the land on which the sanctuary stood.

Another indication of the financial ability of slaves is the occurrence of their own dependents in the sources. I have already mentioned the imperial household and have drawn attention to Musicus Scurranus as an example of a slave from the provinces with many dependents (including slaves) of his own. Even lower-placed imperial slaves from the eastern part of the empire show evidence of having dependents. In a funerary inscription from Smyrna, Telesphoros Joulianos, a slave of Caesar, provides an inscription for himself, his wife (who seems to be a free or freed woman), her two sons (both free), another woman who has died (her relationship to the family is not specified, though she seems either free or freed), and the slave's own freedpersons and slaves.[35] Telesphoros functions as the patron not only of his immediate family, freedpersons, and slaves but also of a free or freed woman of no apparent relation.

We find slaves of private persons in similar situations. I mentioned

Chrysianos, the slave from Olympus in Asia Minor, who provides an epitaph for himself, his family, and another man named Artemon, who is probably not his slave but may still be dependent on him in other ways.[36] Also in Olympus, Helenous, a slave woman of a woman, provides a tomb for herself and family.[37] She then explicitly includes her own slave woman Melinne and Melinne's husband and child. In Xanthus, Stephanos, a slave, mentions a woman named Laina, whom he raised (*anathrepsai*). Laina was probably a slave foster child (*threptē*) bought and reared by Stephanos.[38] In Termessus, another Artemon, slave of Hermeos, provides a sarcophagus for his parents, himself, and a man, Erotikos, whom he raised.[39]

There are a few cases in which a slave seems to be the provider for unrelated, free dependents. In Olympus, Abaskontos, a slave *pragmateutēs* (agent or manager), provides an inscription for himself and his family. He also includes, however, Hermes, son of Papios, an "Olympene," and Hermes' wife and children.[40] Though it is not possible completely to sort out the entire list of persons and the relations between them, it is evident that this slave pragmateutes is providing for a considerable number of people, including a free citizen and his family. The position of the free man's name in the inscription suggests he is a dependent of the slave.[41] In one inscription from Cibyra (Phrygia, 145 C.E.), a slave of a high-status Roman constructs some kind of small building for his and his wife's burial place.[42] Another man, Artemon, not a slave, shares the inscription and provides for himself and his children. Artemon may be sharing the inscription on an equal basis, but the placement of his part of the inscription after that of Onesimus suggests that he may be Onesimus's dependent, or at least his social inferior.

Taken singly, these inscriptions offer little material for historical reconstruction. But taken together they indicate that quite a few slaves from both the western and eastern parts of the empire had more access to money and its power than we may have thought, influenced by our modern notion that slaves, by definition, are propertyless. Ancient Greek and Roman slaves erected their own funerary inscriptions, paid for religious dedication inscriptions, maintained their own families, and sometimes functioned as patrons for their own dependents. The most famous and visible of them even became wealthy. I do not mean to suggest that slaves were walking around the Roman Empire with complete freedom and great wealth. Doubtless most slaves possessed little or nothing. But many of them controlled quite a bit of property and money. Whether they did or not, and how much money they controlled, was probably closely connected to the kind of job they had.

In the Greco-Roman world, slaves could be found in almost any job that would be occupied by a free person. Roman and Greek literature portrays slaves in various occupations. In Greece they worked in shops as craftspersons, like those owned by Demosthenes' father who were employed making knives and beds. Slaves of Timarchus were shoemakers. Slave women were linen workers. Slaves worked as builders along with free workers on the Erechtheum in Athens. Their activities and wages were identical to those of free workers. In Athens of the fourth century B.C.E. much banking was carried on in the hands of slaves.[43] They were involved in book publishing, business, clerical occupations, entertainment, medicine, teaching, philosophy.[44] Many towns and cities in the East had public slaves who performed all kinds of jobs from temple maintenance to service as constables and keepers of the peace, such as those in Chariton's novel who resemble modern policemen.[45]

From the Roman West we have even greater specialization of slave jobs: slaves are barbers, mirror makers, goldsmiths, cooks, and architects.[46] In the West, more than in the East, it seems, male and female slaves were used as shopkeepers, though from the East we do have an inscription from the tombstone of a sixteen-year-old slave who kept a tavern near Philippi for his owners, whom he also calls his parents.[47] From Pompeii come receipts and business documents showing slave agents conducting business both for their owners and on their own behalf. Slave agents even lived in cities apart from their masters, conducting business for their owners.[48] The list goes on and on, including all kinds of craftspersons, fishermen, foremen, laborers, gladiators, personal servants, painters, and prostitutes.

Historians tend to assume that the great majority of slaves were lowly agricultural laborers and menial household servants, and for the most part this assumption may be correct. Many slaves, however, held bureaucratic, professional, or managerial jobs. It seems impossible, given our current knowledge of the lower strata of the ancient world, to ascertain how many slaves occupied what sorts of professions. A general idea is all we can hope for. Several studies of defined bodies of evidence address the topic of slave jobs; to these I now turn.

Susan Treggiari studied the jobs performed by slaves and freedpersons of different households of Rome by analyzing the inscriptions of familial columbaria at Rome.[49] For two families, the Statilii and the household of Livia, Treggiari lists the different jobs held by slaves and freedpersons who record their positions on their tombstones. Her lists show the remarkable differentiation, regarding status and activity, of the servile roles within the households. Because there are so many jobs, however, and the numbers become numbing, it may be helpful to divide the jobs into somewhat arbitrary categories. In table F in the Appendix, about 165 inscriptions listed by Treggiari have been organized into categories according to job type.

Treggiari notes that many members of the households do not record any job in the inscription. She supposes that most of the lowest-status slaves and freedpersons would be represented by this group. Furthermore, because her list includes only the *familiae urbanae*, agricultural workers, who may have been on the bottom end of the scale, make no appearance at all. She also notes that the very top of the slave social scale, the top administrative staff, "will have had separate private tombs" and are under-represented in her list of the jobs held by the slaves and freedpersons of Livia.[50] Therefore, her study of the household of Livia represents "a cross-section of the upper and middle grades" of the servile population of the imperial family.

Nevertheless, Treggiari's studies provide concrete evidence for several aspects of slave life. They portray slaves in many specialized, differentiated occupations. We see here the levels of slave hierarchy and the importance slaves themselves placed on their own positions within that hierarchy. Slaves of higher status are more likely than those of lower status to record their jobs. Treggiari's studies also emphasize the relative power and status of managerial slaves.[51]

The large households of imperial Italy, especially of Rome, present a special case within the Roman Empire. We have no comparable evidence from the Greek East for the same time, due partly to the differences of social structures (the huge imperial households like those in Rome are not found in the East) and partly to the epigraphic habits of the eastern population. People from different geographical areas did not record their deaths in the same ways. What evidence we do have reveals a similar wide diversity among slave jobs in the East.

Some studies have been done of inscriptions that are much earlier than the first century C.E. the primary historical period for this book. We

should not assume that slavery in Greece in the fourth to second centuries
B.C.E. was the same as slavery in the Roman East of the first century C.E.
Nevertheless, material from these earlier periods does confirm that slaves,
even in earlier Greece, occupied various jobs and professions.

Several stelae from Athens contain lists of names, many of which are
accompanied by designations of professions and residences. Scholars
throughout this century have taken these lists, which all derive from
around 330 B.C.E. to be related in some way to manumissions. These
scholars have for the most part assumed that the professions listed with
many of the names record those occupied by the freedpersons both before
and after their manumissions.[52] Table G in the Appendix categorizes the
professions listed. As the table shows, craftspersons predominate, but a
large number of merchants and dealers are also named, along with two
clerical workers and a doctor.

Only a few of the many manumission inscriptions at Delphi disclose
the freedperson's profession. They all fall within 198–140 B.C.E. and show
a preponderance of craftspersons: a leather worker, two fullers, two *tech-
nitai* (craftspersons of undefined type), two female flutists, two seamstresses, a smith, and a doctor. In addition are several household servants,
or perhaps persons of general slave status (*therapōn, paidiskē, paidion*). What
is notable here is the prevalence of various crafts and the absence of
managerial positions.[53]

Another document from Delphi (94 B.C.E.) thanks a Bithynian king and
queen for the gift of 30 slaves to the god and the city. It lists the various
jobs of the slaves: 18 to look after the sacred livestock; 4 involved in
productive crafts; 4 maintenance workers for the temple buildings; 2
craftspersons, according to Marcus Tod, "engaged probably in the man-
ufacture of the tiles and bricks required for the sanctuary;"[54] 1 cook; and 1
guard of the palaestra. Obviously, the jobs held by these slaves were
assigned according to the needs of the sanctuary.

Turning from manumissions to other sorts of inscriptions in the East
and from earlier to later evidence, we encounter an even greater diversity
of slave jobs.[55] There are cases of slaves in agricultural jobs, crafts, and
household servitude. But of those slaves and freedpersons who record
their jobs on tombstones, dedications, and honorary inscriptions, the
majority by far occupied administrative or managerial positions. In
Greece we find a slave who seems to have been a litter bearer. From first-
century Athens comes an inscription mentioning a man who may have
been an imperial slave and who calls himself an *aleiptēs* ("anointer"; proba-

bly a trainer for children or youths).[56] But two inscriptions mention slave
oikonomoi (stewards) and another a steward (*vilicus/oikonomos*) who collects
a 5 percent tax and who is probably a slave. Three inscriptions commemo-
rate *demosioi* (public slaves) from Athens and Sparta.[57]

From the general area of Macedonia come inscriptions for a public slave
in Larisa, Thessaly; a slave of a *comes* (like a pedagogue but of slightly
higher status), who may himself be a slave; and one oikonomos who seems
to be an imperial slave or freedman.[58] Several persons of uncertain status
may be slaves working as oikonomoi and *pragmateutai* (agents).[59] Also
from Macedonia are two cases of freedmen who give their professions.
Gaius Ioulios was an imperial freed *phrontistēs ho epi tōn klēronomiōn*. The
term *phrontistēs* is sometimes translated by the Latin *procurator;* this man
seems to have been the business manager and overseer of imperial property. The other freedman mentioning his profession is Aulos Kaprilos Timotheos, *sōmatenporos* (slave-dealer).[60]

Outside Greece and Macedonia, we do encounter a few slaves and
freedpersons in positions of agricultural labor and household service. We
also find mention of a gladiator, craftspersons, a weaver, public slaves, and
an *eirēnarchēs* (something like a policeman).[61] Most of the time, however,
when a slave or freedperson mentions an occupation, it is clerical, administrative, or managerial. Imperial slaves in Asia Minor occupied positions
as *arcarii* (treasurers) and *tabularii* (archivists, or secretaries), and there is
one imperial slave *kankellarius* (accountant) and one *tabellarius* (courier).[62]
Five inscriptions from Asia Minor record imperial slave stewards
(*oikonomoi, dispensator, prostatēs*).[63] There are also inscriptions from three
nonimperial slave stewards and eight pragmateutai.[64] Of the imperial
freedmen of Asia Minor we know of at least four procurators (including
those designated *epitropos,* a common Greek translation of *procurator,* and
one *epitropos a cubiculario*), two *adiutor procuratorum* (assistants to the procurators), *antepitropos* (vice procurator), and a few occupying clerical positions.[65] Among the nonimperial freedmen are three oikonomoi and two
pragmateutai.[66]

These studies illustrate the variety of jobs held by slaves.[67] Among the
inscriptions from Greece, Macedonia, and Asia Minor, however, the preponderance of managerial and administrative positions for slaves and
freedpersons is obvious. These slaves were probably more likely to set up
inscriptions than were slaves in lower-status jobs. Furthermore, slaves
were more likely to name their positions if those positions connoted some
degree of status and power.[68] Lower slaves, therefore, are certainly under-

represented in the inscriptional evidence, and most slaves probably held lowly, menial positions. Nevertheless, one cannot help but notice the majority of managerial slaves reflected in the inscriptions from the East. Slaves occupied many jobs, and slavery included recognized levels of hierarchy. More important, slaves higher up in the hierarchy—management slaves—held a fair amount of power and influence relative both to the other slaves and to the society at large.

MANAGERIAL SLAVES

Peter Garnsey suggests three categories for slaves in Roman society: those involved in production, those in "non-productive personal service within the households of the propertied," and those "active in the world of business and commerce as agents, or as managers of enterprises in which they themselves participated as bankers, shopkeepers, traders or craftsmen."[69] According to Garnsey, the slaves in this third category, compared to the larger number of slaves in the other categories, were of minor economic importance in terms of production. Nevertheless, they are important for the social historian because of their special position in the society. They were highly visible slaves whose informal social status was ambiguous and conflicted with their legal status. They were fairly independent of their owners' day-to-day control. They were frequently manumitted and were socially mobile.

Slaves in this third category served as inn managers, managers of mines, and even as a lessee of mines in Egypt. Business documents from Pompeii show slave business agents carrying out transactions for their owners and for themselves.[70] From the Greek East of the Roman Empire, however, most evidence for managerial slaves relates to those called oikonomoi or pragmateutai.

The term *oikonomos* was used to designate those slaves who worked as stewards of households or businesses; they were sometimes plantation managers or financial bursars. The most common Latin equivalents are *vilicus* (especially, but not only, when referring to a manager of a plantation or agricultural estate), *actor*, and *dispensator*. The Greek term did not always necessarily refer to a slave, or even to a steward: for example, in Athenaeus's *Deipnosophists*, the host of the banquet is called its oikonomos.[71] A careful study of the term, however, shows that for the early Roman imperial period it usually indicated a slave or freed manager.

Peter Landvogt's study of oikonomoi as reflected in inscriptions shows that the term had a variety of uses.[72] It could refer to a public official in a free state who functioned as an officer of the polis itself, of a political part of the state (e.g., a tribe, *phylē*) or of some other political body (e.g., council, the *boulē*). The term could also designate an official in the emperor's household in Roman imperial times or an agent of a private person.[73] In the earlier, Hellenistic period, the oikonomos could hold a rather high office in the royal administration. And in several free states of Asia Minor, the person holding the office of oikonomos was free and often a citizen (citizenship in such localities, of course, not necessarily being held by all free persons). Under the Ptolemies, the term designated a high government position. Landvogt claims, however, that by the early Roman period the situation had completely changed and that the oikonomoi were without exception taken from the slave population.[74]

Table I in the Appendix lists inscriptions mentioning oikonomoi, mostly from Greece, Macedonia, and Asia Minor. Landvogt's list has been included and supplemented, though I have left some areas out of consideration (such as Egypt, where the office, as well as slave status in general, presents a special case). In about half the inscriptions, the status of those holding the position of oikonomos cannot be determined. Many of these inscriptions record some decree of a city or council and include instructions to unnamed oikonomoi to carry out stipulations of the decree, such as the setting up of a statue or the disbursement of public funds. Here the oikonomoi may be public slaves. At any rate, they work as treasurers or scribes for the city government or council. In one inscription, the unnamed oikonomoi seem to be finance officers of the Serapis cult.[75] Several inscriptions also record the names of city oikonomoi. The names appear alone (without father or any other identifying designation), which could indicate slave status. Landvogt assumed that in such cases the oikonomoi were slave or freed.[76]

Several inscriptions mention oikonomoi who were probably free. Most of the time these persons occupied a city office that rotated among the citizens. For example, an inscription may refer to "those who are functioning at that time as oikonomoi" or "the one who is about to serve as oikonomos."[77] Otherwise, the oikonomos seems to be an officer for a council, tribe, or club.[78] There is only one case in which an oikonomos for a private person (as opposed to an organization) *may* have been freeborn, and he may very well be freed.[79]

As table I shows, however, in cases where status can be ascertained, the large majority of oikonomoi are slave or freed. In addition, nineteen inscriptions describe oikonomoi who are probably slaves.[80] Two in the list of oikonomoi are probably freed. In special cases, in certain cities of the East and at certain times, the office seems to have been held by free citizens and may have been a rotating honor. Yet my study of eastern inscriptions confirms Landvogt's claim that, for the Roman Empire as a whole and for the Roman imperial period, the oikonomoi were of servile status (slave or freed). Furthermore, in private life they were almost always of servile status and were mostly slaves.

Many slaves held positions as pragmateutai for their owners. The normal Latin equivalent is *actor;* the position was something like a business agent. As several scholars have noted, these slaves were employed by wealthy and powerful families to manage property and run their business activities. Therefore, such slaves were often quite influential persons within the local society.[81] The owner's power extended to them.

Table J lists pragmateutai from the Greek East.[82] Eight of them are certainly slaves; ten more are probably slaves, judging from the way their names appear in the inscriptions and other factors. One is certainly a freedman, and two are probably so. Thus, all these inscriptions have to do with persons from servile status (slave or freed) who worked as agents for private persons.

Like oikonomos, the term *pragmateutēs* did not always denote a slave. A puzzling phrase occurs in several inscriptions. A stele from Iulia Gordus in Asia Minor from 75–6 c.e. contains a decree passed by "the council and demos of Iulia Gordus and the Romans serving among us as pragmateutai."[83] This could refer simply to Romans carrying on business in these cities, but the terminology sounds rather more official, as if referring to an established association of Roman citizens who lived in these cities. It may even mean that there was an actual office of pragmateutes occupied by Romans within these local governments in the first century c.e. At any rate, these persons appear to have been free. But their situation is special and does not overturn the general impression that the term *pragmateutēs* usually indicates a slave or freedman agent or manager employed by a private family.

The inscriptions offer glimpses of the local importance, or perhaps self-importance, of these agents. One of them, P. Anteros, was honored by the *gerousia* (a local governing body).[84] Another freedman agent proudly provided the honorary statue, which had been voted by the council and demos (body of citizens), for the husband of his patroness.[85] Of course, by providing the honorary inscription, the freedman himself indirectly received honor. A slave pragmateutes in Olympus, Asia Minor, built a tomb for himself, his daughter, her children, and his own son. He also permitted, however, a free "Olympene" named Hermes and Hermes' wife and children to share the tomb.[86] Hermes was not the slave's owner but rather seems to have been his social dependent and inferior. The slave manager, therefore, was probably of higher social status than the free man.

Information about the owners mentioned in the inscriptions demonstrates that the slaves were aware that their influence derived from that of their owners. Often a slave mentioned the senatorial or consular rank of the owner or gave the master's title (for example, *primipilus*, the senior centurion of a legion).[87] One (probably) slave pragmateutes in 247–248 C.E. wrote on his family's tombstone that his master was "thrice asiarch." On another tombstone, Agathopous, a slave agent, neglected to give the names of his wife and children (he may not yet have had them), but he was careful to give the Roman name of his master.[88] In each of these cases, the slave noted status symbols of his owner and thereby basked in the reflected light.

Many managerial slaves probably worked on country estates.[89] Although little is known about these country slaves, some direct evidence does exist of the day-to-day activities of urban managerial slaves. A basket of wax tablets discovered at Pompeii in 1959 reveals one picture of slave agents at work. Because the tablets are business documents from the first century C.E. they provide direct evidence only for the Roman West; business in smaller provincial towns of the East was probably on a smaller scale. But the existence of such slave agents in the East may be taken to mean that the documents illustrate typical managerial slave activity for that area also.[90]

Five of the documents relate to a series of loans to a C. Novius Eunus, a dealer in foodstuffs. On 28, June 37 C.E., Novius borrowed ten thousand sesterces from an imperial freedman, Ti. Iulius Evenus Primianus.[91] The freedman's slave agent, Hesychus, handled the whole deal, making the loan to Novius, receiving grain as collateral, and agreeing to the interest charge of one percent per month. A few days later, on July 2, Hesychus rented out a facility in a warehouse in order to store the grain taken as security on the loan. He rented it from C. Novius Cypaerus through *that* man's slave agent Diognetus.[92] On that same day, July 2, Novius Eunus took out a second loan, this time for three thousand sesterces. But rather than borrowing from Hesychus's master, he borrowed directly from Hesychus himself. It seems that when Novius needed more money,

Hesychus decided to float the subsequent loan from his own funds in order to take advantage of the unexpected business opportunity.[93]

The next document in this series comes from August 29, 38 c.e., thirteen months later. Hesychus is still a slave, but not of Evenus. He calls himself "C. Caesaris Augusti Germanici servus, Evenianus," indicating that his former owner had ceded him to the imperial service. His activities in the imperial household seem to be the same as in the household of a private citizen, though possibly on a grander scale and with more prestige. Again from his own funds, he lends Novius 1,130 sesterces, which would have been the interest on the original loan. Probably Novius had paid off two-thirds of the original loan and was renewing the loan for the remaining third. A fifth document, dated September 15, 39, renews the balance of the small loan again.[94]

In these five transactions, Hesychus acts as an agent for his owner twice, once to make a loan and once to rent storage space. But in the other three documents, he conducts business on his own. A slave manager or agent in a position of responsibility could enhance his own social and financial position; these tablets show the process at work. By capitalizing on his master's position and business activities, Hesychus advanced his own position.

From the East we gain some idea of the activities of private slaves from the records of public slaves. Slaves owned by municipalities were used for many tasks, some of which were menial, such as collecting garbage, keeping the city clean, or building and maintaining roads. The more than one hundred public slaves who ran away from Cibrya in the first century c.e. may have been used for such labor. But slaves were often employed as state accountants and registrars: they collected fees, wrote receipts, and arranged for the erection of statues and inscriptions and the disbursement of funds.[95] The daily activities of clerical and managerial slaves in large families must certainly have been similar.

All of this varied historical information draws a picture—if somewhat sketchy—of a tiered slave structure. A slave hierarchy is not simply a modern reconstruction; inhabitants of the Roman Empire themselves recognized that there were different kinds of slaves. In fact, they seem to have recognized two basic divisions of slavery: menial slaves and those in positions of authority, "doing more of a free man's work."[96]

Discussing laws concerning insults and affronts, Ulpian notes that one can be sued for affronting another person's slave but that the rank of the slave is important: "I think that the praetor's investigation into the matter should take into account the standing of the slave; for it is highly relevant what sort of slave he is, whether he be honest, regular and responsible, a steward or only a common slave, a drudge or whatever (bonae frugi, ordinarius, dispensator, an vero vulgaris vel mediastinus an qualis-qualis)."[97] Part of what is at issue here is the value of the slave. An injury to a more expensive slave, as an educated manager would be, was a greater financial injury to the owner. But just as important was the social affront suffered by an owner when a slave representing him or her suffered insult. The slave, especially the slave agent or manager, was viewed as an extension of the owner's very person, as is made clear in the next paragraph of the legal text: "An affront to a slave sometimes affects the master also, sometimes not; for if the slave is posing as a freeman or if the person who beats him thinks that he belongs to someone else and would not have done it if he knew that the slave was mine, Mala writes that the striker cannot be sued as having affronted me."[98] Therefore, when the law differentiated managerial slaves from common slaves, part of the concern was economic, but part of it was the Roman sensibility to insult coupled with the societal common sense that persons of different rank deserved different treatment.[99] Managerial slaves constituted a different category and accordingly had to be treated differently.

These two basic levels of slaves are reflected in the dream handbook by Artemidorus, *Oneirocritica*, a valuable source of attitudes of the lower strata of Greco-Roman society.[100] As it is a practical handbook on the interpretation of dreams, its concerns remain close to the everyday concerns of ordinary people: health, financial state, business transactions, social relations. Furthermore, because it relates dreams of all persons—not just those of kings and the elite—it offers at least indirect access to desires and attitudes of the lower classes, including slaves of various levels.[101]

Artemidorus holds that dreams mean different things when dreamed by persons of different status. Often a dream that has one interpretation for a rich man will have an opposite interpretation for a poor man. Similarly, one dream will have opposite interpretations for a free man and a slave. For example, dreaming of crucifixion is good for a poor man; it means he will become wealthy and have honor. But it is bad for a rich man because it predicts that he will be "stripped bare." For slaves it means freedom.[102] Significantly, in accord with this interpretive rule, Artemidorus splits the slave population into two basic groups: common slaves and those "in a position of trust."[103] The oikonomos word-group is sometimes used to refer to someone to the second category, but the terminology is flexible. Such people may be designated as slaves "held in trust" (*en pistei*), or as those honored by their masters or having many possessions.[104] But conceptually the same class of slaves is meant, and often their dreams have different meanings from the dreams of lower slaves.

A few examples clarify the dichotomy. It is inauspicious for a managerial slave to dream that he is beheaded: "To a slave who enjoys the confidence of his master, it signifies that he will lose that confidence. For no one is beheaded without first being condemned and no one 'without a head' is trusted. For we say that a man who has lost his civic rights is 'without a head.' But to other slaves, the dream signifies freedom. For the head is master of the body, and when it is cut off, it signifies that the slave is separated from his master and will be free" (1.35, p. 35). The managerial slave's position is comparable to a civic right and qualitatively sets him apart from slaves of lower status. In a similar case, if a menial slave dreams he is dead or buried, he will be freed. But if a managerial slave dreams the same thing, he will be deprived of his "trusteeship" (*pistis;* 2.49, p. 126).

Sometimes Artemidorus treats common slaves and poor free persons the same: "If a man changes into a woman, it is auspicious for a poor man or a slave. For the former will have someone to look after him, as a woman does, and the latter will experience a less painful servitude. For a woman's work is lighter." Or in another case, "It is only auspicious for a house slave to dream that he is being carried by his master and for a man who is utterly poor to dream that he is being carried by a rich man. For they will receive many benefits from their carriers" (1.50, p. 41; 2.56, p. 129). In these cases slaves and poor free people occupy the same conceptual category; their dreams can therefore be interpreted in the same ways.

Significantly, in contrast with the category of most slaves and poor people is the category of rich people and managerial slaves. Artemidorus writes, "To be offered for sale is auspicious for those who wish to change their present way of life as, for example, slaves and poor men. But it is a sign of bad luck for the rich and for those in a position of trust" (4.15, p. 192). "Those in a position of trust" is usually Artemidorus's designation for slave managers.[105] This does not mean, of course, that he sees no difference between rich free men and slave managers. But it does highlight the special social position of such slaves and their relatively high status in Artemidorus's conceptual scheme.

Artemidorus's handbook is more a source for social concepts than for social "reality." In other words, it tells us less about actual slave activity than about how persons within the society conceptualized slave life. But the handbook demonstrates that people in Greco-Roman society recognized the ambiguity of slave status and thought of slaves as occupying two different levels in society. People acknowledged the special social position of managerial slaves and their power and influence relative to society as a whole.

Another factor highlighting the status ambiguity of middle-level slaves is the continuity of lifestyle between slave and freed status. For example, a slave might move from being a slave oikonomos to being a freed oikonomos, but the job, "boss" (owner/patron), location, family situation, and probably living conditions would remain much the same. The move from slave status to freed status, though important in legal terms and in the minds of the persons involved, probably made little external difference in the daily lives of these managerial workers.[106]

The lives of middle-level slaves were certainly ruled to some extent by the fact that they were slaves. But in their normal activities it would have been difficult to distinguish them from free or freed people, except perhaps in their roles as representatives for powerful people, and in these roles they would have appeared powerful, not weak.[107] Their independence, family life, financial abilities, and social power belied their legal status as dispensable. They were by no means at the bottom end of the social pecking order. Admittedly, they were dependent upon their owners, but many free and freed persons were in the same situation. Slaves could expect certain benefits from their owners and were expected to fulfill certain obligations to them, but again, many free and freed persons were in the same situation. In other words, slaves, especially managerial slaves, occupied positions within the prevailing patron-client structure of Greco-Roman society. The decisive factor for their daily existence was less their legal status as slaves than their positions as clients and patrons (for they were both) in that patronal structure.[108]

PATRON-CLIENT STRUCTURE

Throughout the Roman Empire, in Greek as well as Latin areas, the patronage system aligned people in society and provided channels for the exercise of influence.[109] Clients could expect favors, letters of recommendation, the pulling of strings, and even money handouts from social superiors to whom they attached themselves. Patrons usually expected in return honor and publicized deference, but they also could expect specific services and sometimes even financial help from their social inferiors and dependents. The system was one of interdependence, tying together higher and lower levels of the population and providing for those on the lower end the occasional opportunity to exercise power.

The benefits derived by clients from patrons varied. The most concrete was money. In Rome especially, but elsewhere as well, clients often received direct handouts from their patrons.[110] For example, in Philippi a man bequeathed land and the proceeds from it to his mother's freedmen.[111] But the financial benefits could be less direct. Eutyches, an imperial slave oikonomos on an estate in Galatia, set up this inscription in the second century: "Eutyches, imperial oikonomos of the Estates of Considiana, constructed the sanctuary with the statues, along with Fausteinus and Neikeronianus and Hermas, his children, with Claudius Valerianus, the most excellent procurator, providing." The procurator (*epitropos*) may be a freedman, judging by his name, and he probably provided the land for the shrine.[112] At any rate, here is an example of a well-placed imperial slave taking advantage of the patronage of a provincial procurator. Both of them receive honor by having their names on the inscription.

Often clients needed more subtle assistance, such as letters of recommendation. The letters of Pliny the Younger and Cicero provide many examples of such assistance. For example, when Pliny wanted to reward an Egyptian freedman who was an expert at douches, enemas, and massage and who had done him a good turn, he wrote a letter to the emperor requesting citizenship for the man.[113] Patrons were also expected to provide legal protection for their clients. This benefit was important for clients in a society in which rank and status were always expected to carry great weight in legal disputes. Protection at court was even more important for a slave businessman or agent, as he could not actually represent himself in the dispute. But even if he had been allowed to represent himself, his lower status would have practically decided the case against him in advance. A powerful patron provided, if not justice, at least legal success.[114]

The importance of patronal connections in court cases is demonstrated by the *commendatio*, which was actually a letter of recommendation admitted as evidence in court. The strength of the recommendation, however, derived not from any introduction of factual evidence or demonstration of the client's competence, but simply from the exercise of influence. As R. P. Saller says, the commendatio "was a testimonial whose efficacy derived from the author's friendship with the judge. The accuser or defendant became credible because he happened to be a friend of a friend, and so the favor really requested may sometimes have been nothing less than a favorable verdict."[115]

In this situation, the patron-client structure worked in various ways. One patron wrote a letter on behalf of his client, thus placing the client further in his debt. The patron requested the favor from the judge either because the judge was in his debt or because, perhaps, the patron was willing to place himself in the judge's debt. The language of these transactions was all in terms of friendship. The patron called his client "friend" because "client" could be socially offensive. But the friendship language merely masked the intricate play of debits, credits, and social hierarchy actually at work.[116]

Another informal benefit for clients is seen from the documents of the slave agent Hesychus, studied above. Hesychus's role as a dependent of and representative for his master put him in an opportune position to launch and further his own business career. Had his owner, who here functioned like a patron, been less wealthy and powerful, Hesychus would not have had the contacts and social weight he actually enjoyed.

I said above that the chief benefit for the patron from all these favors was honor.[117] In Rome, clients were expected to arrive at the patron's house early in the morning to greet him formally. A large entourage of clients, freedmen, and slaves tagging after a patron all over town advertised his or her status. As demonstrated in Chariton's novel, which takes place in Miletus and the eastern Mediterranean, this practice occurred in cities of the East as well as the West. When the wealthy Dionysios goes about town, the large number of "friends," freedmen, and slaves who accompany him is evidence enough of his high rank.[118]

Abundant inscriptions testify to the honor accorded patrons by their dependents. Freedpersons often paid for inscriptions and statues for their patrons, as did Aurelios Soterichos II in Termessus, Asia Minor.[119] But slaves who had money were also expected to participate in this rite of social etiquette. Just as free clients and freedpersons put up inscriptions to a god for the health and salvation of their patrons, so did slaves for their owners.[120] Sometimes slaves were expected to join other household members and dependents (including "friends" and other nonfamilial clients) in honoring someone of the household with a "gold crown," as in an inscription from Julia Gordus (Asia Minor) of 36–37 C.E.[121]

Honor aside, however, patrons received other, more concrete benefits from the patron-client relationship. Laws bound clients to certain duties toward their patrons. According to a law of Julian (second century C.E.), pantomimists and doctors were required to offer their services free of charge both to their patrons and to their patrons' friends (*Digest* 38.1.27). Patrons were sometimes named as heirs in their clients' wills. Likewise, owners received these benefits from their slaves. Pliny, for example, allowed his slaves to make wills as long as they left their money to persons within his household (*Ep* 8.16). As owners legally inherited from their slaves automatically, it is interesting to note the funerary inscription of the slave agent Dionysios in Lydia, Asia Minor. Often in funerary inscriptions of this area an amount of money is specified as a penalty should anyone try to bury an unauthorized body in the family's tomb. Dionysios names his (female) owner and her heirs as beneficiaries of the penalty payment of fifteen hundred denarii (*IGR* 4.1576). The arrangement is noteworthy because, from a strictly legal point of view, it was not necessary; Dionysios's owners would presumably have been the owners of his tomb and all money accruing to him anyway. But Dionysios's stipulation of them as the beneficiaries of the fine makes him look more like a client of his owners than like the slave that he formally was. Further, the stipulation shows how an owner or patron might benefit financially from social inferiors—even in the form of "gifts" from slaves.[122]

A freedperson could have a patronal relationship with someone other than the former owner. In the third century C.E. in Galatia, Eutychides, a freedman of the emperor Severus and his sons, honored an imperial procurator with an inscription. Though the procurator was not his former owner, Eutychides still calls him his "patron and benefactor." Surprisingly, even slaves could have patrons who were not their owners. I have already mentioned the inscription of the imperial steward Eutyches, who, although he was a slave of Caesar, benefited from a patronal relationship with the local procurator. Another example comes from Paulilia in Thrace. Aurelios Herodes calls himself "the slave of Posidonius," yet he sets up an honorary inscription for an imperial procurator named Aurelios Apollonios, whom he calls his patron.[123]

These examples show that slavery, especially higher- and middle-level slavery, was part of the wider social structure of patron-client obligations and benefits.[124] An individual's access to power and social progress depended more than anything else on her or his connections to someone higher up in the social pyramid. In this regard, slaves were in much the same situation as free people, except that in their owner they had a built-in patron. In order to understand the dynamics of Greco-Roman slavery, therefore, we must recognize that it functioned within the dynamics of Greco-Roman patronage.

Accompanying the actual give-and-take of patron-client activities was an all-pervasive patronal ideology. Common expectations about how relationships were supposed to work supported the patronage system. As I mentioned, patrons were expected to help their dependents. Favoritism for "friends" and clients was assumed. R. P. Saller, arguing that "patronal language and ideology permeated Roman society," explains the function of that ideology in official Rome: "The existence of a patronal, instead of a universalist, ideology in the realm of administration meant that Roman officials were not restrained by concepts of the impropriety of all favoritism, and they were relatively free to indulge in the natural human propensity to use their official positions to aid family and friends."[125] According to this ideology, certain behavior was expected of clients and social inferiors. As noted above, they were to honor and to publish the generosity of their patrons. Of course, by advertising the beneficence of their patrons, they also broadcast their own inferiority, which is precisely the reason some higher-class persons refused gifts from people they were unwilling to recognize as social superiors.[126] Naturally, clients were also supposed to stay within their place in the system. Most of all, they were expected to work for the interests of the patron. They learned, or at least the ideology told them, that by sacrificing their own interests in the short term and promoting the interests of the patron they could advance their own interests in the long run.

A variety of sources demonstrates this patronal ideology functioning within the slave system. The agricultural manuals offer clear examples of the ideology from the patron's perspective; these exist in both the East and the West and in both Greek and Roman times. Xenophon, in his fourth-century B.C.E. agricultural manual *Oeconomicus*, explains how a master wins the loyalty of the female slave overseer, who must supervise the household and the other slaves. First, of course, one must be benevolent to her: "We also taught her to be loyal to us by making her a partner in all our jobs and calling on her to share our troubles. Moreover, we trained her to be eager for the improvement of our estate, by making her familiar with it and by allowing her to share in our success" (9.11ff.). The male overseer can also be made loyal "by rewarding him, of course, whenever the gods bestow some good thing on us in abundance" (12.6ff.). Xenophon does not really believe that the slaves have any actual share in the master's property.

They are, after all, tools. But he is pragmatic enough to know that "slaves need the stimulus of good hopes."[127] Therefore, though the master knows better, he must convince the steward that the master's property is his property and that the master's success is his success.

The pseudo-Aristotelian *Oeconomicus*, largely derived from Xenophon, states even more explicitly than Xenophon that the two different kinds of slaves should have two different kinds of rewards. The author says that "every slave should have before his eyes a definite goal or term of his labour." But managerial slaves, "those in positions of trust," are different from the laborers. He says, "A share of honour should be given to those who are doing more of a freeman's work" (1.5.2,6). And though no one will take the same care of another's property as of one's own, the master can instill in the slave manager a desire for the success of the venture by honoring the slave a bit and by being a good example of management himself (1.6.3–4).

Latin gentleman farmers later took up these themes from their Greek predecessors. Varro, writing in the first century B.C.E., realized that the management of one's slaves, especially one's managerial slaves, required care. He is remarkably candid about the ideological use of benevolent patriarchalism:

> The foremen are to be made more zealous by rewards and care must be taken that they have a bit of property of their own (*peculium*), and mates from among their fellow-slaves to bear them children; for by this means they are made more steady and more attached to the place. . . . The good will of the foremen should be won by treating them with some degree of consideration; and those of the hands who excel the others should also be consulted as to the work to be done. When this is done they are less inclined to think that they are looked down upon, and rather think that they are held in some esteem by the master. They are made to take more interest in their work by being treated more liberally in respect either of food, or of more clothing, or of exemption from work, or of permission to graze some cattle of their own on the farm, or other things of this kind; so that, if some unusually heavy task is imposed, or punishment inflicted on them in some way, their loyalty and kindly feeling to the master may be restored by the consolation derived from such measures (*On Agriculture* 1.17.5).

Columella, writing in the first century c.e., also realizes the importance of psychological manipulation of one's slaves and dependents. Unlike many owners, Columella insists that the slave manager should not be allowed to pursue business interests of his own, because he exists solely for the advancement of the owner's interests.[128] But if the master is wise, he will convince the slaves that the master's interests are their interests. One way to do this is to include them in his own deliberations, or at least to appear to do so. Columella notes, "I observe that they are more willing to set about a piece of work on which they think that their opinions have been asked and their advice followed" (1.8.15).

In Columella's writing, the patronal ideology perpetuates itself further down the social scale. More than his predecessors, Columella realizes that the slave manager must also be taught to be a kind father figure. He should be an example for the other slaves, as the master is his example. He should be quick to confer honors on good slaves and must be able to delegate authority.[129] Even the slave manager's wife must be careful to gain the loyalty of the slaves under her. When they are ill, she should herself take care of them, "for attention of this kind is a source of kindly feeling and also of obedience. Moreover, those who have recovered their health, after careful attention has been given them when they were ill, are eager to give more faithful service than before" (12.1.6). Columella realizes that slave managers are themselves in patronal roles. Their actions therefore are also to be informed by prevailing patronal ideology, which links inseparably the progress of the client to the progress of the patron, or that of the slave to that of the owner.

These writers seem manipulative and perhaps even cynical in their careful calculations of kindnesses, but it is important to recognize the success of their ideology. Their social inferiors generally seemed to share the assumption that a client's well-being was completely wrapped up in the well-being and benevolence of the patron. Slaves and freedmen put in charge of their patron's wealth were proud when they were able to increase it, as their tombstones show.[130] One freedman goldsmith states that he made good profits from his handiwork and that the lion's share went to the patron. His tombstone boasts that "he did nothing which did not meet with his patron's approval."[131] The very names of slaves and freedpersons and the epithets they accepted for themselves demonstrate their acceptance of patronal ideology: many slaves were named Philodespotos, "master-lover," and one freedman is complimented as being a master-loving man in spite of the fact that this very term occurs in literary sources as an insult similar to "slavish."[132] Several slaves honored a deceased fellow slave by saying he was a real lord-lover (*philokyrios*). They bear, probably without shame, names that bespeak servitude, for example, Hope-bearer, Pilot, Gain, Well-wed, and Changeable. Another man, an oikonomos from first-century Nicaea, is honored on his tombstone for his "good life and work-loving slavery."[133] These details suggest that at least many slaves seem to have accepted their positions in the patronal structure of society.

The obligations and benefits of patronage provided the actual and ideological framework within which many slaves, especially those in higher positions, worked. It is no wonder, therefore, that so little evidence exists of revolutionary sentiment and activity among slaves. As John D'Arms has pointed out, the patron-client structure tended to diffuse conflict among the different strata of society. He claims that "from the emperor on down, patron-client ties had an integrating effect promoting cohesion vertically between groups of differing rank and status, and inhibiting class-consciousness and horizontal group action."[134] It was both belief and social reality that subservience to a powerful patron was the surest route to power for oneself.

D'Arms's recognition that the patronal structure and its supporting ideology had an antirevolutionary function is not a modern conception; ancient authors also realized that the careful use of patronal structure mitigated antihierarchical sentiment. I have already mentioned the agricultural writers who advocated the use of benevolent patriarchalism to cement slave loyalty. The same motif occurs in more explicitly political contexts. In Dio's *History*, the speech of Maecenas to Caesar advocates monarchy; to this end, Maecenas says that the good leader should take personal responsibility for the rearing and education of future senators and knights. The king should be a strict taskmaster, censuring their mistakes but also instructing them in right living. He, like a good patron, is their provider. Dio realizes the usefulness of this pairing of kindness and strictness for dissolving revolutionary sentiment: "Have no fear . . . that anyone who has been reared and educated as I propose will ever venture upon a rebellion."[135]

The strength of the patron-client structure and its accompanying patronal ideology solidified the hierarchical and authoritarian social forms of the empire. The structure discouraged class consciousness and solidarity from developing among the lower classes along horizontal lines, but it did allow some upward movement for those few persons who could make use of the vertical lines connecting clients with patrons. Any move up, however, required firm connections with powerful and important patrons or, if one were a slave, with a powerful and important owner.[136]

Middle-level, managerial slaves occupied visible positions in cities throughout the Roman Empire for the duration of its domination. Because of their positions and their connections with powerful patrons they had opportunities for social advancement unavailable to most of the free poor.[137] Aristotle presents an argument relevant to this point: he says that a slave is a sharer of the life (*koinōnos zōēs*) of the owner.[138] A free but lowly laborer, however, is further from the employer. Whereas the slave derives virtue from the master, the free laborer can expect no such benefit. Even through the eyes of the upper-class Aristotle, one can see the possibilities open to some slaves and closed to patronless free persons. (The term *patron* is anachronistic for Aristotle's time, but its use in this case is functionally justifiable, as Aristotle's analysis itself shows.)

If the above was true in Aristotle's day of common slaves, it was even more so in Roman times of managerial slaves: being connected to someone in power, even if only as a slave, was the next best thing to being in power oneself. And in a society that knew little social mobility, these slaves, who could often expect eventual freedom, enjoyed more of that limited commodity than most people.

They did move up. One of the most famous examples is Marcus Antonius Pallas.[139] Initially a slave of Antonia—daughter of Mark Antony and Octavia—and later of Claudius, Pallas was a rich man relatively early in his career, owning an estate in Egypt. He amassed enormous wealth, gained his freedom, and became head of the imperial *fiscus* (treasury). Pallas was, even in his own day, an especially notorious example of the social-climbing slave. But he is only one example of first-century slaves who rose to positions of influence, which disgusted the upper classes and probably delighted the lower classes—at least those other slaves who could hope to emulate his example.

Imperial slaves such as Pallas enjoyed a higher status and greater degree of social mobility than other slaves. For example, Narcissus and Epaphroditus, freedmen of Claudius and Nero, respectively, enjoyed great fame or notoriety, depending on one's perspective. Narcissus received the *quaestoria insignia* from the Senate in 48 C.E. Epaphroditus rose rapidly from low to very high (freedman) status. Free men such as Juvenal had ready examples of highly placed imperial freedmen in Crispinus, Licinius, and others. These few examples must suffice here, but P. R. C. Weaver's several studies on the slaves and freedpersons of the imperial household have well documented and illustrated their social mobility.[140]

Of course, most slaves, not being in managerial positions, could not hope for any future even remotely as bright as those of the high imperial slaves. But the difference between Pallas and managerial slaves in nonimperial households was one of degree, not kind. And though first-century Rome seems to have offered the greatest opportunities for slave social advancement, the phenomenon can be found in other times and places as well. Even classical Greece, whose slave system differed in many ways from Rome's, knew examples of slave social mobility. A slave named Pasion managed the largest banking business in fourth-century B.C.E. Athens. He was eventually freed and honored with Athenian citizenship, but this was quite rare for classical Athens.[141] Pasion himself had a slave named Phormio, who was later freed, granted citizenship, and who ran a shipping business. Plutarch mentions Evangelus, the slave business manager of Pericles, who seems to have run all of Pericles' business.[142] We can imagine his relatively high position in society based on the position of his master.

In the Roman period, of the many nonimperial slaves who later attained high station, one of the most famous is Epictetus, the moral philosopher, born about 55 C.E. His master was Epaphroditus, the freedman and administrative secretary of Nero. Epictetus, while a slave of Epaphroditus, had studied under Musonius Rufus. He became a widely respected teacher in his own right. Much less famous but probably much wealthier was Zosimus, an *accensus* (aid) for M. Aurelius Cotta Maximus, consul in 20 C.E. He provides an inscription advertising in verse the many benefits he received from his patron; by doing so, he celebrates his own rise to wealth and position.[143]

People in the East also knew of upwardly mobile slaves. About a monument from around 120 C.E. that stood in the Corinthian agora, the editor of the corpus of inscriptions states, "Those who had charge of its erection were the most outstanding members of the Association, Titus Flavius Antio[chus], freedman of the Emperor, and Tiberius Claudius Primigenius." Primigenius was probably the son of a freedman. Corinth had many leading citizens who had risen from slave status.[144] Another Corinthian inscription illustrates the rise of a nonimperial freedman; it dates from the Augustan era and records the family of Quintus Cornelius Secundus. The names of the family members are all Roman except one, that of the son-in-law, who is called "Quintus Maecius Cleogenes, freedman of Quintus (Maecius)." It appears that the daughter married her maternal grandfather's freedman. The grandfather mentioned here, Quintus Maecius, may well have been the author of epigrams that have survived in the Greek Anthology.[145] So in Corinth a slave could hope to rise high enough to marry the master's granddaughter, even within an important family.

Slavery in the Roman Empire functioned as a conduit for social mobility for several reasons. For one thing, usually when a slave of a Roman citizen was manumitted, he or she was also granted Roman citizenship. Therefore, in the first century, a Roman slave was better situated than a free foreigner for becoming a Roman citizen.[146] There were less formal ways slavery served as access to higher status. The agent Hesychus is one example of a slave who improved his financial and social standing simply by capitalizing on his own proximity to his master's business. Moreover, slaves often could hope for the tangible benefits of education paid for by their masters. In both the East and West and in Greek and Roman times, slaves were trained in everything from handcrafts to philosophy. After manumission, the ex-slave might go on to become a famous cook, writer, scholar, grammarian, or philosopher.[147]

For a select few, therefore, slavery could bring access to financial resources, citizenship, education, and the patronage of higher status persons. Recognizing the importance of all these factors, modern historians have made it a commonplace that slavery functioned in the Roman empire as "a compulsory initiation into a higher culture," as J. L. Myers stated many years ago.[148] As surprising as it may sound to modern ears, slavery was arguably the most important channel through which outsiders entered the mainstream of Roman power structures. The mere fact that so many inscriptions from the Roman Empire were erected by freedpersons testifies to the function of slavery in social mobility. Freedpersons were not ashamed, it seems, of their freed status; it demonstrated their own progress.

Many of the interpretations contained in Artemidorus's dream handbook have to do with social mobility, testifying to its importance in the minds of urbanites of the Roman Empire. A large number of these interpretations concern the social mobility of slaves. Predictably, slave dreams are often related to manumission, such as this one: "If a slave dreams that he has no teeth, it signifies his freedom. For his not paying his dues to his master is symbolized by the fact that he does not provide his teeth with nourishment; his not receiving nourishment from anyone is symbolized by the fact that he is not nourished by his teeth. In either case, he will be free."[149] As is almost always the case in Greco-Roman society, Artemidorus here refers to manumission not as some ontological state of freedom or even a political concept of *eleutheria* (liberty). Philosophers were the ones who talked about manumission in those abstract ways. Artemidorus, rather, is talking about the more mundane Roman values of prestige and honor. Manumission was coveted not so much because it brought independence and self-rule—it seldom did—but because it was a step up in society. Thus in several interpretations the significance of manumission for informal social status (as distinct from formal legal status) is stressed. Artemidorus gives one case history as follows: "A man dreamt that he had three penises. He was a slave at the time and was set free. He then had three names instead of one, since he acquired an additional two names from the man who set him free" (5.91, p. 242). The slave at manumission derives power and status directly from the master, as is here represented by the sexual symbolism. His three names, also derived from the master, are the conventional Roman insignia of citizenship—and, therefore, of a certain degree of respectability.

Sometimes honor is specifically predicted for slaves. Artemidorus notes that it is auspicious for slaves to dream they are struck by lightning, "since those who are struck by a thunderbolt no longer have masters and no longer toil. Bright garments similar to those worn by the manumitted are placed upon them, and as if they had been honored by Zeus, men associate with them just as they associate with freedmen who have been honored by their masters" (2.9, p. 89). Clearly, the social prestige is almost or equally as desirable as the manumission itself.

Slaves dreamed about even more glorious honors, and Artemidorus's interpretations offered no discouragement: "To be sacrificed [in a dream] and to have one's throat cut on the altar of a god or publicly either in the national assembly or in the marketplace is a good sign for all men, especially for slaves. For they will possess a glorious and renowned freedom" (2.51, p. 127). A slave who heard this might well imagine himself headed for respectability, even publicity, akin to that of Pallas or Narcissus.

We would have expected the importance of dreams signifying freedom. Rather more surprising are the many interpretations that predict a slave's upward mobility while remaining a slave. Artemidorus's two main categories of slaves are regular slaves and managerial slaves. The household, however, may be broken down into a more differentiated hierarchy. While discussing the meanings in dreams of different household articles that the master uses, Artemidorus lists different kinds of slaves in what seems an order of ascending status: servers (*therapontes*), underlings or helpers (*hypēretai*), stewards (*oikonomoi*), and financial managers (*hoi kata ton oikon tamias*). Concubines and emancipated female slaves are in another category of objects—just below wives (1.74, p. 55).

Various dreams predict a move up within this household hierarchy. As mentioned earlier, if a slave dreams he is changed into a woman, it means he will move into a less troublesome slavery. The Greek (*aponōteron*) suggests that his labor will be less manual or laborious (1.50, p. 41). In another instance, Artemidorus claims that he knew of a slave who dreamed he "stroked his master's penis." The dream proved to be auspicious: the slave was made the pedagogue of the master's children, which represented for him a promotion in the slave hierarchy (1.78, p. 60). Several dreams predict that the slave will be promoted to a managerial position over the owner's household, business, or both. For example, dreaming of frogs is a good sign for slaves who work with people, a fact Artemidorus proves by a case known to him: "I know of a household slave who dreamt that he struck some frogs with his fist. The man became overseer of his master's house and took charge of the other servants in the house. For the pond represented the house; the frogs, the servants in the house, the punch, his command over them."[150] Similarly, it is good luck for a slave to dream he is flying in his owner's house. "For he will surpass many in the house" (2.68, p. 133). In another case, Artemidorus knows of a slave who dreamed that his master agreeably "prostituted his own wife to him." Consequently, the slave became the manager of all the master's property and household. The dream had signified that the master would not be jealous of his slave, which translated into upward mobility for the slave (4.61, p. 211).

These examples show that lower-status persons realized that slavery could result in social integration and mobility. Another passage shows that they realized the social advantages of being a member of an important and powerful household as opposed to a less powerful household. Artemidorus writes, "For slaves, dreaming that one is flying up into the heavens always signifies that they will pass into more distinguished homes and frequently even that they will pass into the court of a king" (2.68, p. 132). Historians realize that a slave's power and status were dependent on those of the owner. The well-placed slave of an important woman or man was an important person. It mattered less that one was a slave than whose slave one was. Artemidorus's handbook indicates that this fact did not escape his customers' notice.

THE UPWARDLY MOBILE SLAVE IN POPULAR CULTURE

The actual cases of slaves who rose from lowly origins to enviable positions in society and the common realization that slavery could function as a route to higher ground all fed the popular theme of the "slave who made good." Within popular Greco-Roman culture and its ways of viewing the world, one finds a recurring motif of the upwardly mobile slave, the poor person who moves through slavery finally to attain a position of power, wealth, and influence. The theme surfaces in a variety of literary sources, from romances to satires to histories, and seems to have enjoyed wide currency in the first century C.E.

The Greco-Roman romances or novels that have survived pose both problems and opportunities for the historian.[151] Although they are clearly fanciful stories and not history, they provide fascinating glimpses into the society and popular views of the Hellenistic and Roman worlds. Often they reflect simply the biases and assumptions of the upper class: disdain of laborers, presuppositions about natural nobility (that upper-class persons are virtuous because of a superior nature), and typical caricatures of slaves and lower-class persons. Even with their rather higher-class prejudices, however, they provide bits of social history.

The plots of the romances are generally predictable. Usually, two lovers of noble rank are separated before they can consummate their love. Often one or both are kidnapped by pirates and sold into slavery. They go through all sorts of perils as they journey almost endlessly around the Mediterranean, experiencing war, shipwreck, danger, and so on. Though many people try to seduce one or both of them, the couple is usually able (or at least the woman is) to remain faithful. And finally, through perseverance, luck, or the interference of a god or goddess, they triumph over all adversities and are reunited and live happily ever after.

This plot structure appropriates and abets the popular theme of the successful slave. In most cases, the hero or heroine is of noble stock and becomes a slave as a tragic twist of fate or divine anger. The slavery functions as an obstacle to be overcome by the character's inherent and unconquerable nobility. Such a use of the slave motif could hardly have been encouraging to someone of truly low origins, as the novels emphasize that only by being born noble could the character have ever overcome the temporary circumstances of servitude. Yet the plot shows that slavery can be perceived as a means to a greater end. Furthermore, the entire plot structure may mitigate the pain of low status and encourage hope for self-betterment. When Callirhoe, the Syracusan noblewoman of Chariton's romance who becomes a slave, realizes that her child will be born in slavery, she lifts her spirits by recalling the great men who began as slaves: "What of all we hear of children of gods and kings born in slavery later regaining the honor of the fathers, Zeuthus and Amphion and Cyrus?"[152] Callirhoe recognizes the motif of the successful slave and identifies her child's fate with that of famous slaves who made good.

This same narrative structure is the backdrop and presupposition for a large section of Petronius's *Satyricon*, a Latin novel set in the West. The long scene comprising Trimalchio's banquet spoofs the ex-slave and nouveau riche businessman Trimalchio and his gauche freed friends. As a prelude to the banquet, the reader is told about a scene painted on the wall of the entryway of Trimalchio's house (*Satyricon* 29). It depicts a slave market with the names of the characters painted in. Trimalchio is in the midst of the slave market holding the staff of Mercury and being led by Minerva toward Rome. The mural then represents Trimalchio learning to be an accountant and finally being made a steward. Tongue in cheek, as if to suggest that the change in circumstances was too quick to effect a change in character, the narrator concludes that at that point in Trimalchio's career the wall space was about to give out, so the next scene jumps ahead to portray Mercury whirling Trimalchio about by the chin and depositing him in a high official throne. Here on the wall of a fictitious freedman's house is the visual representation of the successful slave theme, which becomes the springboard for Petronius's satire in the following scene.

Later in the supper, after Trimalchio is quite drunk, he proudly tells his story himself. He admits unabashedly his servile origins. In his eyes, his low beginnings only emphasize the virtues, sound sense (*corcillum*), and business acumen ("Buy well and sell well!") by which he rose to wealth. He came from Asia as a slave boy. For fourteen years he was his master's sexual pet and entertained his mistress as well. He gained power in the household—by the will of the gods, naturally. He pursued business, overcame hardships, inherited his owner's wealth, and became a powerful and immensely wealthy man in his own right: a first century rags-to-riches success story and all thanks to a well-connected and well-used slavery. Or, as Trimalchio says, "Who was a frog is now a king!" (Qui fuit rana, nunc est rex, 77). The statement is a fitting end for a scene begun with a wall painting of Trimalchio on the slave block.

Of course, the entire scene is fictitious and satirical and is meant to look ridiculous. But the satire worked well because the basic plot, the successful slave theme, was familiar to first-century readers.[153] Petronius is laughing at the expense of lower-class aspirations and self-descriptions. In fact, two different attitudes toward the slave's rise can be seen in section 57, where the main characters, who are upper class, laugh at a self-made freedman. The freedman admits his servile past and then recounts, like Trimalchio, his own rise through slave ranks to high status. "Who ever had to ask me twice? I was a slave for forty years, and nobody knew whether I was a slave or free. I was a boy with long curls when I came to this place; they had not built a town hall then. But I tried to please my master, a fine dignified gentleman whose finger-nail was worth more than your whole body. And there were people in the house who put out a foot to trip me up here and there. But still—God bless my master!—I struggled through. These are real victories: for being born free is as easy as saying, 'Come here'" (57). Perhaps he protests too much; certainly the narrator thinks so. But though Petronius may view the freedman's story as bombastic and embarrassing, many freedpersons probably did not hesitate to use this popular plot as a way of characterizing their past. In fact, we have some direct evidence that they did, as when Statius traces Claudius Etruscus's ascent through slavery to high status, or when the freedman Publilius Satur (first century c.e., Capua) illustrates on his tombstone his sale by a Greek slave dealer to the Roman who eventually became his patron.[154]

In the *Satyricon*, one sees what could be done with the myth of the upwardly mobile slave when used by an opponent of such mobility. Such opponents were legion. Juvenal and Martial, to name only two, were caustic critics of upwardly mobile slaves. Juvenal facetiously calls them "the knights of Asia, of Bithynia and Cappadocia too, and gentry that were imported bare-footed from New Gaul" (*Satire* 7.13–16). Like Petronius, he portrays characters who defend their servile origins by pointing out that it was through slavery they arrived where they did, as respectable clients of respectable patrons (1.99–109). Martial also never tired of bemoaning the vicissitudes of fate, especially when that fate had raised those of low origins to high positions. Two epigrams, for instance, attack Zoilus, a one-time slave who had risen to the very high social position of *eques* (often translated as "knight"). Martial says that his equestrian ring would be better suited around his ankles, where he was more accustomed to wearing rings (*Epigrams* 3.29; 11.37).

Antipathy toward upwardly mobile slaves was not limited to the fertile imaginations of satirists of the Roman imperial period. Athenaeus in the third century c.e. provides the following quotation from Anaxandrides of the fourth century b.c.e.: "Slaves, my good sir, have no citizenship anywhere, yet Fortune shifts their bodies in all kinds of ways. Today there are many men who are not free, but tomorrow they will be registered at Sunium, and on the day after, they have full admittance to the marketplace. A divinity guides each man's [each *slave's*] helm" (6.263). Being registered at Sunium, an Attic deme, would have been seen as a first step toward citizenship and full integration into public life in Athens. In the Greek world, citizenship did not normally follow manumission. The speaker in the quotation, however, is reflecting not social fact but his own fear of lower-class social mobility. This version of the traditional "slave today, citizen tomorrow" axiom was just one in a long line of recurring upper-class reactions against social climbing.

Most of the occurrences of the theme of the upwardly mobile slave are from upper-class authors hostile to such mobility. These authors use the theme to bemoan the status chaos they perceive around them and to try to solidify the rigidly hierarchical structure of Greco-Roman society. Thus their presentations of the successful slave are always negative. But the same theme was used by other authors in quite positive ways. Some texts depict good characters using slavery as a means of upward social mobility for good ends. These slave heroes are rare in surviving literature, but they are there.

In romances, the hero or heroine who goes through slavery is usually by birth a person of high status. But one text that has been called a romance, though it is by no means a typical representative of the genre, is the *Aesop-romance*.[155] Its hero, Aesop, is an ugly, black, physically handicapped slave of truly low origins. He belongs to a relatively powerful master, but he gains fame in spite of the master's opposition, rather than because of the master's patronage, as is normal in the popular version of the theme (for example, the story told by the freedmen at Trimalchio's banquet). At any rate, Aesop consistently uses his innate intelligence to get the better of his master and mistress. His true nature shines through the externality of his humble position and ugly features. He eventually becomes a respected wise man and political counselor, though even after his success he faces continual opposition from the fickle populace. He gives good, though unpopular, advice, and in the end he dies a heroic martyr's death for the sake of truth and honor. Whatever the original social context of the *Aesop-romance*, it looks as if it functioned to challenge rigid social structures and upper-class prejudices and to provoke hope among those frustrated with low-status positions, especially slaves. In any case, Aesop is a positive role model of the upwardly mobile slave.

In the first century, Cyrus represented another positive portrait of the successful slave. As noted above, Callirhoe, the heroine of Chariton's novel, compares her fate to that of Cyrus, who, according to popular tradition, overcame his servile origins to become the Persian emperor. This tradition about Cyrus surfaces in several texts. Dio Chrysostom knows the tradition and puts it into the mouth of an educated slave who is arguing that true freedom is an inner reality, related to a virtuous nature, and has nothing to do with external condition or social status. In Dio's oration, the slave claims that he could free himself. His opponent answers that, of course, the slave could raise money and pay his master for himself. The slave then responds, "That is not the method I mean, but the one by which Cyrus freed not only himself but also all the Persians, great host that they were, without paying down money to anyone or being set free by any master. Or do you not know that Cyrus was the [lampbearer] of Astyages and that when he got the power and decided that the time was ripe for action, he became both free and king of all Asia?"[156] The tradition to which Dio refers has puzzled some modern scholars who are more familiar with the accounts of Cyrus in Xenophon and Herodotus. But the portrayal of Cyrus as rising from slave status must have been common at the time, as implied by Callirhoe's statement above. The history of Justin also contains the tradition.[157] Perhaps the best representation of Cyrus as the successful slave, however, comes from the history by Nicolaus of Damascus.

Persons familiar with Xenophon's *Cyropaedia* may find the portrait of Cyrus in the fragments by Nicolaus of Damascus surprising. Nicolaus lived during the Augustan era and was at one time a friend and counselor of Herod the Great.[158] As part of his "Universal History," Nicolaus relates Cyrus's rise to power. Contrary to the accounts of Xenophon and Herodotus, Cyrus was not, according to Nicolaus, of noble lineage. He was a Persian whose father, driven by poverty, had become a robber. His mother herded goats. To avoid starvation, Cyrus, while still a young man, enslaves himself to an imperial slave of Astyages, the king of Media.

Cyrus's master, the overseer of "those who sweep outside the palace," is impressed by Cyrus's diligence. He rewards Cyrus and commends him to the man in charge of the "inside" sweepers.[159] This new master takes Cyrus into the inside, but he is cruel and often beats Cyrus. Cyrus turns to another overseer who is impressed with him and who promotes him to a position among the royal lampbearers. Cyrus continues to display his virtue. He works night and day; he exhibits "much prudence and manliness" (66.6); and he eventually works his way up, through several rewards, promotions, and a few lucky breaks, to become the head cupbearer to the king of the Median empire. Despite his lowly origins and slave status, Cyrus eventually mounts a rebellion and wrests the empire from Astyages, his master.

Nicolaus's fictitious narrative repeatedly points to Cyrus's virtues as the reason for his rise to power. Cyrus is diligent; in spite of his servile status he displays nobility, virtue, prudence, courage, high-mindedness, justice, and truth.[160] Of course, fate also has had a hand in Cyrus's rise (66.12). The gods have chosen him, and so he succeeds in liberating both himself and the people who are unjustly oppressed by the Medes.[161] For the most part, the story teaches the common moral-philosophical doctrine that true nobility (nobility according to nature) and hard work can overcome the merely external circumstances of birth and status. It should be noted, however, that slavery functions in the plot as the means for Cyrus's rise to power. Because he becomes the trusted slave of a powerful man, he is able to appropriate that man's power and eventually becomes powerful in his own right.

These popular presentations of Cyrus are important in that they provide one instance of the mixture of eastern and western concepts and ideologies in the first century. The historical Cyrus was clearly from the East, and his actual history represents social and ideological factors not of the Greco-Roman world but of the eastern, Babylonian-Persian world. Therefore, if the traditions about Cyrus were historically accurate—that he began his life as a slave and worked his way up through slavery to become emperor—his life would be evidence only for a certain eastern understanding of the function of slavery and only for an earlier eastern form of slavery itself. Actually, however, these traditions about Cyrus are probably not historically accurate, and the importance of the accounts for this study is precisely that they circulate in the West, in the Greek and Roman ideological worlds. As the preceding analysis demonstrated, the picture of Cyrus as the upwardly mobile slave, though perhaps having its source in an earlier eastern form of slavery, had, by the first century, made its way into Greek and Roman texts and traditions. The accounts of Cyrus's slavery occur in the writings of Nicolaus of Damascus, who was from Syria but who wrote in Greek, spent much of his life in Rome, and demonstrated his own romanization by writing a biography of Augustus; in the speeches of the Greco-Roman Dio Chrysostom; and in the history of Justin Marcus Junianus, who wrote his account of Cyrus in Latin in the third century C.E., probably using earlier Greek sources.[162] Even in the West, therefore, Cyrus could be used as a readily accepted example of the upwardly mobile slave.

I have noted both actual cases and fictional accounts of upwardly mobile slaves in the Roman Empire in order to illustrate ancient conceptions of slavery that included the idea that slavery could be a means to higher status and power. This is further portrayed by a few texts which suggest that people of low status would even consider voluntarily submitting to slavery in order to reap benefits in the future from the slave-master relation.

The freedman at Trimalchio's banquet who brags about his rise from slavery claims that he was really a king's son. He voluntarily became a slave for what it would later bring. He says he "preferred being a Roman citizen to going on paying taxes as a provincial."[163] It may seem that Petronius is exaggerating his fiction in order to make the character look more ridiculous, but the exaggeration must have had some basis in fact and, more significantly, in popular imagination.[164] Indeed, a statement by Cassiodorus in the early sixth century is evidence of actual voluntary enslavement for social advancement. Cassiodorous tells us about a slave market in southern Italy: "There stand ready boys and girls, with the attractions which belong to their respective sexes and ages, whom not captivity but freedom sets a price upon. These are with good reason sold by their parents, since they themselves gain by their very servitude. For one cannot doubt that they are benefited even as slaves by being transferred from the toil of the fields to the service of cities (*urbana servitia*)."[165] The parents may have sold the children simply for the money, but Cassiodorus thinks that the main reason was the possibility that the children would be better able to improve their lot by means of urban slavery than rural poverty.

Finally, we recall that in Nicolaus's narrative Cyrus voluntarily enslaves himself in order to improve his situation. Whereas in some accounts Cyrus becomes a slave because of fate or the accidents of history, in

Nicolaus's account he chooses slavery within a powerful household over freedom and independence as a patronless poor man. These examples show how slavery could be viewed in a Greco-Roman context as a means of social mobility to the extent that even voluntary self-enslavement was conceivable among some portion of the population.[166]

SOCIAL STRUCTURE AND SOCIAL IDEOLOGY

The institution of slavery itself was never really questioned.[167] Slaves may have resented their bondage, but given the chance they acquired slaves themselves. When freed, they simply moved up a notch in the system, becoming themselves masters and mistresses and pulling their dependents along with them. Almost no one, slaves included, thought to organize society any other way.[168]

Individual slaves could seldom be fixed permanently and unambiguously in the structure. They were constantly becoming free, important people to be reckoned with—or at least that seemed true in the eyes of many persons. Even while still slaves, many of them had money, power, and influence that belied their legal status. To the more conservative-minded citizen, the neat categories of social status and position always seemed about to crumble under the strain of ambiguity. What did it matter being free if an upstart freedperson from Syria commanded more respect than you did? Or what great honor was citizenship as a Roman freedperson if you still had to bow and scrape before someone else's slave business agent, who could give or withhold an important loan?

In spite of the ambiguous social position and the upward social mobility of some slaves, few people in the Roman Empire actually experienced real social mobility. Generally, the society was a firm, static pyramid of legally mandated statuses, a rigid hierarchy.[169] But in such a rigid society (which may be even more rigid ideologically), tension often develops when someone's legal status is not consistent with informal status indicators such as education, wealth, job, or access to patronal power. Where does one place a slave on a status scale if that slave is wealthy or educated or powerful? Or, to pose the problem differently, how does one fix the status of an educated free man who has lost his source of income and must depend on a wealthy patron, who may be from a less prestigious family, to pay his bills? Some sociologists studying status have called this situation "status inconsistency"; the concept proves to be useful in any analysis of status and social mobility in the Roman Empire, including an analysis of the social mobility of slaves.[170] People in Roman society were often bothered by the anomalies related to status they saw around them. To an aspiring but not yet wealthy free person of that society, for example, a rich slave was not only an anomaly but may have been perceived as a threat.

The satires of Juvenal were driven to a great extent by Juvenal's rather "middle-class" resentments of upwardly mobile non-Romans, including slaves.[171] Juvenal was highly educated and free but always in need of money. He felt he did not receive the respect his formal status deserved and therefore deeply resented many slaves and freedpersons, who enjoyed more respect than their status merited.[172] Petronius's satire is also mainly driven by the same tensions of status inconsistency, as are many of the writings of Martial and Horace.[173] On the other side, slaves also bemoaned status inconsistency. Athenaeus quotes a slave's words from a fourth-century B.C.E. author, Epicrates: "What is more hateful than to be summoned with Slave, Slave! to where they are drinking; to serve, moreover, some beardless stripling or fetch him the chamber-pot, and to see [food] lying spilt before us . . . which, though left over, no slave may touch, as the women tell us" (6.262d). Here the slave resents having to serve younger men and taking orders from women. He resents that his legal status takes precedence over other categories of self-description: age, education, masculinity, and so on.

This slave presents a view of status and slavery as seen from below. Generally, people of the upper class were wary of social mobility; they consequently despised slaves and nursed a consistently negative view of slavery and social mobility. For example, Seneca found it ludicrous that a free man would hustle himself off to gardens owned by someone else's slave in order to pay the slave an obligatory social call (*On Benefits* 28.5–6). The "Apocolocyntosis of the Divine Claudius" was probably not actually written by Seneca, but doubtless he, like most of his class in the first century, would have agreed with its complaint about slaves who moved up in the world. The satire castigates Claudius for granting citizenship to so many foreigners (ex-slaves). It characterizes Claudius's era as one big Saturnalia—a heyday for slaves (see sections 3 and 12). Pliny, for his part, spends a good two letters complaining about the honors given Pallas, Claudius's freedman. The problem is not just Pallas's dishonorable character (in Pliny's estimation). Pliny is angry because this slave—which is what Pliny calls him though he was actually freed—was honored at all. "And yet," he says, "people of good family could be found who were fired by ambition for distinctions which they saw granted to freedmen and promised to slaves" (*Ep.* 8.6.16; cf. 7.29). For Pliny, Seneca, Juvenal, Martial, and others, the upward mobility of slaves was perceived as a threat. These men were willing to tolerate such mobility as long as it remained within certain bounds. They even promoted it as long as they were able to maintain strict control over it. Pliny, for example, promoted the careers of his own and others' freedmen.[174] But generally, the reaction toward slavery and social mobility in literary sources is one of ridicule and opposition. It is important to realize, however, that the ancient person's attitude toward slavery and social mobility depended on his or her position in society. Therefore, although Petronius's fictional freedman could speak of slavery as something one might enter voluntarily, Seneca says that "no kind of slavery is more dishonorable than that which is entered into voluntarily."[175]

A similar split between the attitudes of the upper and lower classes can be seen in their respective views toward manual labor. As the next chapter will analyze Paul's manual labor and its significance for his status in the early church, this is a convenient point to examine the views of the ancients toward manual labor. The views of the upper class on this subject do not represent those of the general populace. It is common knowledge, for example, that Greco-Roman literary sources view manual labor as despicable and beneath the dignity of any gentleman or lady. Plato's antibanausic rhetoric provides some of the clearest examples of this attitude. Most activities of craftspersons and artisans are considered "slavish, servant-like, illiberal." Weaving, for example, is called servile. In a famous passage in the *Republic*, Socrates rants that manual labor degrades a person in body and mind and renders the person unfit for philosophy and therefore unfit for politics as well.[176]

Plato's views were shared by most upper-class educated persons in his day as well as in the Roman era. Aristotle, in his *Politics*, names activities that are *thētikon* (suitable for hired laborers) and *doulikon* (suitable for slaves). Here the terms are synonymous and carry clearly negative connotations. Indeed, for Aristotle the definition of *eleutheros*, "free man," is related to manual labor, or rather the avoidance of it. An eleutheros is a free-born gentleman, nonlaboring, living a life of leisure and certainly not living for another's benefit, as does a hired laborer or slave. That is why, Aristotle says, it is a mark of the nobleman, the beautiful man (*kalos* means both), to have long hair. The long hair shows that he does not engage in manual labor, as it would get in the way if he did. The very definition of *to kalon* specifies the absence of any craftlike skill (*banausos technē*).[177]

Manifestations of this upper-class attitude are everywhere. It was de rigueur among all Greek and Latin literati to share Plato's and Aristotle's aristocratic views toward work.[178] It is extremely rare to find an author who does not despise manual labor and manual laborers. Dio Chrysostom may seem moderate (compared, for example, with Cicero) when he advocates granting citizenship in Tarsus to linen workers. But Dio was an exception, and one must realize that he would never have realistically considered such activity for someone of his station. Dio was certainly more benevolent in his views than Plato and likewise has a more kindly view of slaves than some other aristocrats, as evidenced by his discourses on freedom and slavery.[179] But he would no more have practiced a manual craft than become a slave. For an upper-class person, the two were equally humiliating and despicable.

The upper-class attitude was certainly adopted by some persons not in that class. As Ste. Croix writes, "Since in a class society many of the values of the governing class are often accepted far down the social scale, we must expect to find disparagement of craftsmen, and therefore even of artists, existing in the ancient world not only among the propertied few. In particular, anyone who aspired to enter the propertied class would tend to accept its scale of values even more completely as he progressed towards joining it."[180] Despite this observation, there are several reasons to believe that lower-class persons, the actual workers themselves, generally held quite different views toward manual labor.

The funerary inscriptions of craftspersons prove that they viewed their work proudly. A woodcutter from Phrygia in the fifth century B.C.E. says, "By God, I never saw a better woodcutter than myself!"[181] The term *technē*, which often has a negative connotation when linked in literature to crafts, is a positive term in *IG* 2².10051, from the fourth century B.C.E. Alison Burford has shown that inscriptions provide a different view of manual labor from that reflected in upper-class sources. She admits that ascertaining workers' attitudes from inscriptions is a difficult business, "but," she concludes, "it seems legitimate to argue that they all shared to some extent a positive attitude towards their profession."[182] Workers proudly state their occupations on their inscriptions, which they would not have done had they shared the views of the upper class toward their work.

Once again, Artemidorus's dream handbook provides a point of view not encountered in most Greco-Roman literature. Handcrafts and workers' occupations frequently make appearances in the book, and the aristocratic disdain of such activity is noticeably absent. For example, in dreams, one's craft corresponds to one's mother, "since it nourishes," or to one's wife, "since it is in the highest degree one's own."[183] Therefore, if a person dreams that his or her mother is ill, it means the person's business will be weak and disorganized. On the other hand, if a man dreams he has sex with his wife and she yields willingly, it forebodes well for his labor. "For the wife represents either the craft or occupation of the dreamer, from which he derives pleasure, or whatever he controls and governs, as he does his wife" (1.78, p. 58). Though this reveals a chauvinistic attitude about women, it conversely shows a surprisingly positive attitude about work. Crafts and manual labor in general are not at all despised in the handbook. Craftspersons are assumed to take pride and even joy in their work. Their concerns are not about the shame or dishonor of their jobs. If they are worried, it is that they may be unemployed or not able to find *enough* work.[184] But the mere fact that a laborer is subordinate to an employer presents no stigma to the laborer. Indeed, it is auspicious for an artisan to dream that he has more than two ears. "For there will be many employers whom he will obey" (1.24, p. 28). Craftspersons and artisans dreamed of success in their work, not escape from it.

The radical difference in attitudes between the upper and lower levels of the population regarding manual labor, therefore, provides an appropriate parallel for differing class attitudes toward slavery and language associated with it. Slave terminology almost always carries negative connotations in Greco-Roman literature. Slaves are despised, and terms such as *doulos* and *servus* connote abuse or degradation. Other related terms derived from the institution of slavery are likewise devoid of positive meanings. The same terminology, however, seems to carry different meanings in other contexts. I mentioned above that the term *philodespotos*, so negative in the literature, occurs often in inscriptions as a name for slaves and freedpersons.[185] In fact, a rather highly placed public slave of Sparta around 100 C.E. named Philodespotes was honored more than once by inscriptions set up in his town.[186] The names of other slaves and freedpersons reflect the same phenomenon. Terms scorned among the authors of Greco-Roman literature are worn without embarrassment by persons lower down in the social scale. Even such words like *verna* (homebred slave) and *doulos* (slave) occur in inscriptions as proper names. One freedman has the nickname *Doulion*. No shame at all seems to be attached to the name, no hint of humility, no stigma. In one inscription from Athens, it looks as if some litter bearers erected a funeral epitaph for a colleague. They call him an "honorable slave."[187] The phrase would have been an oxymoron for upper-class authors, but not for these fellow slaves.

Furthermore, many slaves seem to have had no reticence about calling themselves slaves in their inscriptions. The terms for slave (*doulos, oiketēs, sōma, servus,* etc.) and those for freedman (primarily *apeleutheros, exeleutheros,* and *libertus*) and their feminine equivalents occur so often in inscriptions that one might think there were legal requirements that slaves and freedpersons state their status when erecting an inscription. Why else, one might ask, would they voluntarily call attention to their servile status? But as far as I can determine, no such law existed, and a comparative study of the inscriptions suggests that the practice was not legally mandated. In some cases, slaves and freedpersons do not state their status explicitly, though other information on the inscription indicates that they were slaves or freed.[188] Therefore, when others of the same area do call themselves "Slave of Gaius" or "Freedwoman of Artemis," we should assume that in most cases they willingly used the terms to identify themselves. In a few cases, where more than one inscription concerns the same man, only one text gives his status.[189] These cases suggest that the person involved was presumably not required to call himself a slave or freedman; he offered the information without compunction. As there is thus no reason to believe that slaves or freedpersons were required to call themselves such, we must assume that they (or their families) volunteered the information. They must have had none of the qualms about such a self-description that one would expect based on the literary sources. The terms did not mean the same thing to these people as they did to upper-class authors.

Why, then, did slaves and freedpersons record their status in inscriptions? For one thing, their title as "slave of so and so" served in their society the way a last name and title do in ours: it identified them. We might suppose that they would not have wanted their status remembered if it was so low. But that supposition only suggests that we are misinformed about the common ways people conceptually placed a slave in that society. Moreover, slaves may have called themselves such because of other, intangible factors—sentiment, for example. A freedman of an important family in Rome calls his wife, who is a slave of the same family, his *conserva,* his "fellow slave," though he is no longer a slave himself.[190] The term obviously was not so humbling in his circles.

Most important, slaves and freedpersons may have willingly given their status in order to emphasize their connection with someone higher up in the patronage structure of the society. Marlene Boudreau Flory, on the basis of slave and freedperson tombstones in Rome, believes that occupational titles were placed on epitaphs "for their prestige value."[191] Proudly calling oneself a groom would have provoked snickers or scorn from member of the upper class. Lower-class people obviously had different reactions entirely; we may feel sure they never snickered when they read it on a neighbor's tombstone. In the same way, naming oneself the slave of an important person was a way of claiming status for oneself. Flory has shown that slaves in Rome are careful to stress on their tombstones their connections to important persons. She observes, "Slaves who belonged to or freedmen who had been manumitted by Romans of superior legal condition to their own evidently regarded the legal position of their owner or patron a status symbol worthy of commemoration on their tombstone."[192] She notes that one freedman is proud to mention the occupation of his patroness "as part of his own title." Another man stresses his wife's connection to an important member of the owning family.[193] Flory's study concentrates on the West, but as we have seen, the same phenomenon obtained in the East. Slaves and freedpersons did not hesitate to call themselves such. They used the term as a title and as an opportunity to link themselves to more powerful people. They seemed to feel no shame in their slavery as long as they could enjoy this status-by-association.[194]

CONCLUSION

The complexity and ambiguity of slavery in Greco-Roman society, especially in the early Roman Empire, means that, for some people—who, though a minority, were highly visible—slavery was a means of upward social mobility and was recognized as such throughout the society. Upper-class people bemoaned the fact; people originating from or caught in low-status positions celebrated it. Slavery did not mean the same thing to different people in the society: Seneca insists that voluntary slavery is the most despicable form of life (*Ep. Mor.* 47.17); by contrast, people with fewer options embraced it. A gentleman, for his part, would confidently espouse the truism, "Men desire above all things to be free and say that freedom is the greatest of blessings, while slavery is the most shameful and wretched of states." But an actual ex-slave could advertise his accomplishments on his tombstone and declare, "Servitus mihi nunquam invida fuisti" (Slavery was never unkind to me).[195] The terminology of slavery meant different things for different people because the social institution of slavery functioned differently for different people.

The positive meaning of slavery, however, depended on certain factors. The lowest levels of slavery, and that may have been where most slaves served, knew few possibilities for improvement. Middle-level managerial slaves, educated slaves, and those trained in skills could nurse hopes more confidently. Furthermore, the wealth, position, and disposition of the owner were directly relevant for ascertaining a slave's own position in society and for predicting his or her future. The slave of a shoemaker likely had little status, but the slave of a local power broker or of a respected aristocrat could in turn hold considerable power and respect. A slave of Caesar was even higher, potentially holding power and enjoying an informal status rivaling important free provincials.

The social realities and myths of slavery in the early empire present several different ways of assessing the meaning of slave metaphors in early Christianity. We should expect the verbal connotations of phrases such as "slave of Christ" to have been no less complex than the social meanings of Greco-Roman slavery.

2

SLAVE

OF CHRIST

AND

1 CORINTHIANS 9

Many of the ways Paul uses slavery as a metaphor are readily grasped by modern readers and so will receive only brief attention here. For example, sometimes slavery operates as a negative symbol for the pre- or non-Christian state. In Rom. 8:12–17, 21–23, for example, slavery characterizes that from which Christians have been delivered. In place of the "spirit of slavery" they have received a "spirit of sonship" (8:15); salvation is the deliverance from slavery (8:21). This use of metaphorical slavery figures prominently in Galatians also (4:1–9, 24–25; 5:1).

Another use of slavery in Paul's writings is as a metaphor for unconditional obedience, which again is not at all surprising, as that is part of our common understanding of slavery. In this regard, Paul can talk about slavery to sin, or the metaphor can be turned to positive use as a way of thinking about unconditional obedience to God, Christ, or righteousness (Romans 6). The "slavery to sin" theme is not unlike the way slavery so often functions in the moral philosophers' writings: to depict the sacrifice of the autonomous will to the unconditional and domineering control of passions, desires, circumstances, or whatever controls the weak person. On the other hand, Paul's positive application of slavery to one's relationship to God (Romans 6) is not generally found in the moral philosophers.

Similarly, ministry to God or to other Christians is also portrayed as slavery. Slavery can operate as a metaphor in this way because a slave's activities were also supposedly pursued with a view to the interests of the owner and with no prospect of self-interest. In fact, slavery was commonly defined as living for the benefit or profit of another. As the previous chapter argued, this assumption was part of the patronal ideology of Greco-Roman society. Even when an owner realized that it was to his or her own advantage to convince the slave that the owner's prosperity also meant the slave's prosperity, this ideological maneuver was carried out with the underlying assumption that slaves existed for the interests of their owners. Therefore, when Paul pictures himself or other Christians as enslaved, especially when they are enslaved to one another, he sometimes means that self-interest has been sacrificed to the interests of the others (as, for example, in Gal. 5:13). Later, I will examine in depth this use of metaphorical slavery as it relates to 1 Cor. 9:19–23, in which Paul says he enslaves himself to all.

As this brief survey has suggested, modern people tend automatically to think of slavery as a negative condition of life from which one needs to be delivered, a state of unconditional obedience, and the surrender of self-interest to the interests of the other. But two other metaphorical uses of slavery in Paul's writings are not so readily understood. One is the use of "slave of Christ" as an authoritative title for leaders. The second is the use of slavery to Christ to symbolize Christian salvation based on upward mobility and power by association.

SLAVE OF CHRIST AS A DESIGNATION OF LEADERSHIP

In the salutations of two of Paul's letters—Rom. 1:1 and Phil. 1:1—and in Gal. 1:10, Paul styles himself a slave of Christ, using the term as a leadership title. Paul and Timothy identify themselves as "slaves of Christ Jesus" (Phil. 1:1) in counterpoint to the identification of the recipients as "the holy ones . . . with the overseers and servants." The placement of "slave of Christ" in apposition to *klētos apostolos* ("a called apostle") in Rom. 1:1 also shows that it is a title of leadership. In Gal. 1:10, Paul defends his apostleship and its independence from human control. At the beginning of the letter he had announced himself as "Paul, apostle not from human beings nor through any human being but through Jesus Christ and God the Father." In verse 10, he again sets up humanity and divinity in opposing terms: "If I were still pleasing (*areskein*) human beings I would not be a slave of Christ." The term *areskein* often occurs in contexts of slavery, the slave's purpose being to please the master.[1] Furthermore, the term "slave of Christ" serves here, as "apostle" did in 1:1, to identify Paul and to emphasize his independence from purely human authority channels.]

Later in this chapter I will return to the precise function of the Pauline use of "slave of Christ" as a title of leadership. For now, I only wish to point out that Paul did not invent this use of the phrase. Other New Testament texts reveal that "slave of Christ" crops up in early Christianity apart from Paul and surely was used before Paul as a title for leaders of the early Christian movement. Although a thorough investigation of the non-Pauline occurrences of slave imagery in the New Testament is beyond the scope of this book, a brief look at some of those uses will help illuminate Paul's own use of the metaphor.

The synoptic gospels contain several parables in which a large household ruled by the master and staffed by slaves illustrates the kingdom of God, the world, or the church. For example, in Matt. 21:33–41, *doulos* is used of the financial agents of the householder who rents out his vineyard to tenant farmers. It is certain that the slaves are to be taken as prophets who represent God. They bear the master's authority and carry on his work. To affront them is to affront the owner (cf. Matt. 22:1–14). In Matt. 24:45–51, the parable of the faithful and unfaithful managerial slaves, the master places a slave in charge of the household during his absence. The slave is supposed to disburse necessities to the other members of the household, that is, to the other slaves. The good slave manager is the one who does just that; the bad slave manager abuses his authority, though it is only a derived authority, and takes advantage of his position to oppress his fellow slaves. One can only guess about the original form of this parable and how it might have been interpreted during Jesus' own lifetime. If Jesus actually told it, it may have been heard as an indictment of religious and/or political leaders. Incorporated into the church's document, however, it took on meanings more directly related to the everyday life of the Christian community and probably functioned in early Christianity, therefore, as a warning to church leaders to exercise well their derived authority.

The possibility of such a church context for interpretation is even clearer in the case of the parable of the unforgiving slave in Matt. 18:23–35. The implicit analogy of this parable is that the church is like a large, imperial household in which slaves conduct business, borrow money from the king, lend one another money, and so forth. All the slaves, high and

low, must recognize the derivative nature of their positions in the household.

Luke uses slave language to characterize leadership within the church
even more clearly than Matthew. Sometimes doulos and similar words
represent simply Christians, as in Luke 17:7–10. Sometimes the terminology recalls Old Testament usage, designating as slaves of God those
who prophesy or proclaim God's message (Luke 2:29; Acts 2:18; 4:29). In
the Lucan version of the faithful slave manager, however, the managerial
slaves clearly represent church leaders (Luke 12:41–46). Luke sets up the
parable by having Peter ask if Jesus had told the previous parable, the one
about slaves needing to stay awake for the coming of the master, for the
benefit of everybody or for them specifically, presumably meaning the
disciples. Jesus responds with the parable about the faithful and wise slave
oikonomos. In this parable the term *doulos* is reserved for the managerial
slave. The other slaves of the household are represented by the words
therapeia, paidas, and *paidiskas (therapeia = therapontes).*[2] By the time this
parable assumes its place in Luke's gospel, "slaves of the lord" (*douloi
kyriou*) is understood to refer to church leaders. They are oikonomoi, and
their activities include representing the master and caring for the underslaves of the household. The parable stresses the derivative nature of their
authority. The master rewards the faithful performance (note *pistos,* 12:42)
of the managerial slave with, one might say, upward mobility, the slave
being placed in charge of the owner's entire estate (12:44).

When we come to Acts, we find that for this author Paul exemplifies
the faithful church leader who serves as a slave of Christ. In Acts 16:17,
the woman at Philippi possessed by the "Pythic spirit" proclaims that Paul
and Barnabas are "slaves of the most high God," and as such they announce the "way of salvation." The term *slave,* therefore, here as so often,
denotes the representative role of the apostles as God's agents. In his
speech to the Ephesian church leaders in Acts 20, Paul himself characterizes his ministry as slavery to the Lord (Acts 20:19). For the author of
Acts, Paul is the model slave leader. He does not abuse his authority or
take advantage of the other Christians; rather, he is humble and especially
helps the weak (20:19, 34–35).

The Gospel of John provides an interesting commentary on the early
Christian use of *slave* to designate its leaders. For the most part, John
avoids using the *doul-* word group to refer to the disciples (see, however,
John 13:16 and 15:20). *Slave* always carries negative connotations in John;

it is not used, as in other early Christian texts, in the neutral or positive sense of *representative* or *agent*. Yet one passage indicates that John is not unfamiliar with the early Christian designation of its leaders as slaves. In John 15:14–15, Jesus says that he will no longer call the disciples slaves (*douloi*). They are now friends (*philoi*). Slaves do not know what their lord does, but Jesus is now telling his disciples what he is doing, thus raising them in status from douloi to philoi. This may be John's rejection or reinterpretation of traditional Christian terminology that portrayed Christians, and especially leaders within the movement, as slaves of Christ. In any case, this text shows the occurrence of the designation within Johannine Christianity.

In contrast to the Gospel of John, the Apocalypse uses slave language extensively to refer to Christians, especially Christian leaders and prophets. The recipients of the prophecy are called God's slaves, as is John himself (Rev. 1:1; 2:20; 19:5; 22:6). Prophets, both ancient and those contemporary with John, are especially worthy of the title (10:7; 11:18; 19:2). The designation of prophets as slaves of God is built, of course, on the Jewish tradition that called its prophets, and Moses in particular, slaves of God (see 15:3). Even the angelic messengers are simply the fellow slaves of the prophets and other Christians (19:10; 22:9). The Apocalypse amply illustrates how Christian leaders were called slaves of Christ within a branch of early Christianity independent of Pauline Christianity.

This brief survey would not be complete without mentioning the formulaic occurrence of the title *doulos* in the salutations of three of the catholic or general epistles. "James, slave of God and the Lord Jesus Christ . . ." (James 1:1); "Simon Peter, slave and apostle of Jesus Christ . . ." (2 Pet. 1:1); "Jude, slave of Jesus Christ, brother of James . . ." (Jude 1). The very way the word *doulos* occurs in these texts reveals its function as a recognized title of legitimacy. Before we too quickly overtheologize the term as a moral attempt at humility, we should remember how common the term had become in early Christian circles and how dominantly it was used for leaders. Christians had used the term for so long as a title for their leaders that any connotations of humility, if there ever were any, would have worn off long ago. A title borne for so long by leaders must have come to acquire leadership status.

One of the things that indicates that "slave of Christ/God" was not a self-humbling depiction is the frequency of its use in pseudepigraphical texts of the New Testament. I have already mentioned the letters of James, Jude, and 2 Peter. Paul is also made to announce himself as the "slave of

God and apostle of Jesus Christ" in Titus 1:1. It is not likely that a word heard as shameful or humiliating would be so freely used by pseudepigraphical authors to label those late, great figures in whose names they wrote (even if they do sometimes portray Paul as lowly in the sense that he is "the foremost of sinners" [1 Tim. 1:15]). Moreover, various Christian writers refer to others as douloi of God or Christ. "Paul" calls Epaphras a "slave of Christ" (Col. 4:12); Timothy is a "slave of the Lord (2 Tim. 2:24). One should probably read Titus 1:7, which speaks of the overseers as oikonomoi of God, as portraying local church leaders to be slave managers within the church, as we have seen to be the case in Luke 12:41–46 above. The very fact that so many early Christian authors use "slave of Christ/God" for those very figures they wish to hold up as authoritative proves that the term was not heard as self-effacing. It was a title of authority and power by association. Slaves of Christ are those who represent Christ; they are active in the world as Christ's agents and wield his authority. Furthermore, it is expected that they will be rewarded with higher status, more authority, and more power.

Depicting leaders as slaves of Christ is nowhere defined or defended, which indicates that the language was an assumed and common element of the symbolic world of early Christianity. Within that context, the title *slave of Christ* carried authority by recalling the founding leader. Modern readers have interpreted the term as self-effacing, understanding it in a context of a Christian morality of humility, only because they have reacted to the word *doulos* as it would be heard by moderns or by upper-class Greeks and Romans. As the previous chapter showed, however, in most of Greco-Roman society, calling oneself a slave of someone was not necessarily to make a shameful or humble statement. But in order to realize that the metaphor did function as a positive depiction of leaders, one must imagine how it could have worked this way in Paul's social context.

In the first place, as scholars have endlessly explained, the doulos image had a long pre-Christian history in the Greek Old Testament. The Jewish Scriptures were, of course, the authoritative texts for the early Christian movement. Early Christians, therefore, thought of their own leaders and prophets as slaves of God on analogy with the great prophetic figures of their adopted traditions: Moses (Josh. 14:7 [Alexandrinus]), Joshua (Josh. 24:30; Judg. 2:8), the prophets (Amos 3:7; Jer. 7:25; 2 Esd. 9:11; Dan. 9:6 [Theodotion]).[3] What may be surprising—it is at least noteworthy—is that, by calling its leaders slaves of Christ, this rather insignificant religious movement raised its own contemporary leaders to the high status of the great leaders of old. In a context informed by the Septuagint, calling oneself a slave of Christ put one in company with Moses. One could not make a stronger claim to authority.

Scholars have also correctly pointed out that there was something eastern about calling people slaves of the god.[4] Traditionally minded Greeks and Romans thought about such large eastern empires as Persia and Babylonia when they encountered people who gladly identified themselves as slaves of a great king. Chariton, for example, seems self-consciously upper-class and Hellene when he characterizes such willing slavery as barbaric.[5] In his novel, such a structure exists only in the large kingdoms on the eastern edge of the Roman world. Probably, therefore, early Greco-Roman converts to Christianity and their neighbors felt an eastern influence in this new religious group and in its language about slavery to its god. The use of this language does indeed testify to the eastern origins and backgrounds of the early Christian movement.

But one need not be content with talking about the origins and backgrounds of the slave metaphor. The structure of Greco-Roman slavery outlined in the preceding chapter provides a more than adequate context for the positive function of doulos as a designation for leaders. The large households of the parables, for example, recall those eastern societies and courts with large staffs of slaves in varying positions of responsibility. But Roman imperial society as well furnishes a context for such social structures. Those reflected in the parables would have been equally recognized by hearers in Palestine, Asia Minor, Greece, and Italy.

As explained above, in the patronal society of the Greco-Roman city, slaves of lower-class persons held little power or prestige, but the slave agent of an upper-class person was to be reckoned with.[6] He could keep free citizens waiting on his convenience. Upper-class persons doubtless resented his position; lower-class persons probably coveted it. And if the slave agent of the local power broker enjoyed such importance, a slave agent of Caesar enjoyed even more. He could keep local power brokers themselves waiting.

In such a patronal society, as long as the hearer understood that *Christ* signified the god-founder of the movement, the phrase *slave of Christ* would have carried, to all but the upper levels of the society, meanings not of humility but of authority and power. The power of the slave, of course, was inextricably linked to that of the owner. Therefore, the perceived status and authority of the leader as slave depends on the perceived status and power of Christ. To despise Christ is to despise the slave representative, but conversely, and this would be the position of early Christians, to accept and respect the power of Christ as a god is to assign a great amount of authority to his slave agent, the Christian leader.

What did it mean, then, that the term *slave of Christ* was such a prevalent designation of leadership in early Christianity? What would it have meant for a Greco-Roman group to use *doulos* as a common title for its leaders? This question has several answers. For one thing, this kind of language testifies to a certain marginality of early Christian groups when viewed from some perspectives, such as the more conservative, Hellene perspective, or that of upper-class persons. The "slave of God" language reflects the eastern origins of and influence on early Christian groups; this very easternness would have made these groups look marginal to some segments of the population. Furthermore, easternness aside, it is not hard to see that upper-class persons, those already in positions of power, would probably have found such language repulsive, or at least disagreeable. They had little to gain and much to lose by becoming anyone's slave. For some people, the fact that Christians unabashedly called their leaders slaves of Christ would have been sufficient testimony to the Christians' servile natures and deservedly low social position—and to the marginal position of their group.

Admittedly, marginality may work either for or against a social group, or it may do both at the same time. It may keep some people from joining, but it may solidify even more firmly the group itself. For instance, many of the parables use the social structure of the king or householder with his slaves and servants. The slaves are representatives of the patron and dependent on him. They derive their identity from their place in the patronal structure and possess power and position because of that structure. This early Christian appropriation of patronal society as the scaffolding for its own symbolic representation is simply an adoption into symbolic form of a dominant social structure. Yet the manner in which the Christian group uses this structure reveals a certain sectarian mentality. The people within the household deal with one another as fellow slaves in that household. They are contrasted with outsiders, who appear in the parables as tenant farmers, potential wedding guests, and so on. The outsiders are not slaves within the household; nor are they of lower status than the insider slaves. They are simply outside. But outsiders do not share in the power by association held by the slaves of the king or patron.

By construing the church as a large household staffed by slaves at various levels of authority, early Christians reinforced their own sense of the difference between themselves and the rest of society.

That early Christians named their leaders slaves of their god also says something about the nature of authority in early Christian groups. The groups recognized their leaders as representatives of the founder. This way of construing authority may seem to relativize the authority of leaders: they are mere representatives, deriving their authority from a source outside themselves. But actually, conceptualizing leaders as slave representatives tends to strengthen the authority of the leaders; although they speak as mere mouthpieces of the founder, that very fact precludes challenges to what they say. "I'm merely obeying orders," in spite of its self-effacing claim, may mask a not-too-subtle exercise of power. Understood in this way, slave-agent status reinforces rather than weakens the authority of the leader, as can be seen clearly in the frequent use of the *doulos* title in pseudepigraphical literature of the New Testament. One does not, in the end, relativize the authority of Peter, James, Jude, or Paul by thinking of them as slave agents of Christ. Rather, one ties what they say more firmly to the unquestioned authority of the founder whom they represent.

When Norman Petersen says that "Paul self-consciously minimizes his social superiority as a father by viewing himself as a father who is in enslavement with his children," he oversimplifies the actual social realities of slavery within the Greco-Roman patronal structure.[7] By depicting himself as a fellow slave, the leader need not be making a self-effacing or egalitarian statement. The leader definitely places himself and the others in a common situation, but he does not, by that characterization alone, put himself on an equal footing with his readers. Hierarchies prevail within the household. Calling oneself a slave of Christ may have been used in certain contexts to humble oneself, but it just as likely functioned in other contexts to make one's authoritative statements that much more unassailable.

The common function of *doulos* to imply representative authority shows how firmly early Christian groups were tied to the patronal structure of society. As I have already argued, to conceive of one's leader as the slave agent of the founder, thus making oneself a fellow slave and, structurally speaking, an underslave, makes the entire group a household. The use of this language dates back in the early Christian movement as far as research can go—to the earliest remembrances of the parables of Jesus—and it seems to have functioned in all available strands of earliest Christianity (the general epistles, the Synoptics, Revelation, Paul, and even the Gospel of John). The Christian movement was thus apparently willing to view itself along the lines of patronal structure from its very beginnings. This does not mean that there were not more egalitarian voices or metaphors in early Christianity. Much early Christian language reveals such tendencies. But the early Christian use of household language is one bit of evidence that there was no egalitarian stage of early Christianity followed by a hierarchical stage, at least so far as symbolic language is concerned. In other words, if I may use symbolic language about Christians and their leaders to imagine how they thought about the structure of their groups, there was no early egalitarian movement followed by an institutionalized structure fashioned on the pattern of the patronal household. Rather, it is much more likely that egalitarian and patronal symbol systems were two different ways of thinking about the structure of the movement from the beginning. Furthermore, the use of the slave-leader motif was not antipatriarchal, though it may initially appear so to us. On the contrary, the conception of the leader as the slave of Christ actually reinforced the structuring and symbolizing of Christian groups on the model of the patriarchal household.

This brief survey of the use of *slave of Christ/God* in early Christianity as a title of leadership provides a necessary context for Paul's use of the metaphor. The title is used in this way in the salutations of two of his letters (Rom. 1:1; Phil. 1:1); Galatians also furnishes an interesting example of the authoritative use of *slave of Christ*. Initially, the function of the slave metaphor in Galatians is puzzling. In this letter Paul is clearly concerned to emphasize his authority as an apostle. Furthermore, in his argument against submitting to circumcision, Paul portrays the Christian life as freedom and the non-Christian life—either as a pagan or a non-Christian Jew—as slavery (Gal. 2:4; 4:3–9; 31; 5:1; cf. 3:13). It seems curious, therefore, that Paul begins the letter with the assertion that he is a slave of Christ (1:10). The letter also concludes with a reference to that slavery when Paul says that he is independent of the criticisms of his opponents because he bears on his body the "marks" of Christ (6:17). Paul's reference to *stigmata* has been variously interpreted. But certain points argue that the reference here would be understood as the tattoo—or, somewhat less likely, a brand—sometimes placed on slaves. For one thing, "tattooed" or "branded" was a common way of referring to slaves. And the purpose for which Paul brings up the marks is to preclude judgments on his actions by outsiders. The only one who legitimately judges a slave is that slave's master. This rhetorical move also occurs in Gal. 1:10 and Rom. 14:4, both of which explicitly use the metaphor of slavery to assert that the believer is answerable only to Christ.[8]

Therefore, in Galatians, a letter in which Paul usually portrays the Christian life as freedom and sonship in opposition to slavery, he nevertheless asserts, seemingly with no irony, his own slavery to Christ. This is only an apparent paradox, however, as *slavery* does not mean the same thing when used in these different ways. In one case, the aspects of slavery that provide the meaning are labor, drudgery, the unconditional obedience to a merciless master. In the other case, however, the aspect of slavery that provides the meaning is the role of slave agents as indisputable, authoritative representatives of the powerful owner. Paul himself may not have reflected that he was using slavery in such different metaphorical ways. He may not have intended to use metaphorical slavery in two opposite ways: one positive and one negative. But his intentions did not then and do not now limit the effects of his language. The social reality of slavery was so multifaceted and ambiguous that one could appropriate its terminology for different metaphorical uses without self-conscious reflection, and that is apparently what he did in Galatians.

Given the social historical sketch of slavery in the preceding chapter and the various ways Paul uses slavery as a metaphor, we can now see the different possibilities for the function of *slave of Christ* as a title. In some contexts it could carry meanings of humility; at other times it implied power. Furthermore, even in one context the term could be taken differently by different hearers. The evaluative ambiguity of the terminology (is it shameful or honorable? powerful or powerless?) corresponded to the social ambiguity of Greco-Roman slavery.

"SLAVE OF CHRIST" AS SOTERIOLOGY

I have already noted that not only Christian leaders but all Christians were called slaves of God or Christ (see Luke 12:41–46; Rev. 1:1; 7:3; 19:5; Matt. 6:24 and par.). Understandably, what calling the Christian the slave of Christ in these contexts often means is that the Christian owes Christ the unconditional obedience and unquestioning loyalty of a slave. The Christian is as absolutely dependent on God as the slave is dependent on the mercy and goodwill of a good master. Most modern readers are content to limit the meaning of metaphorical slavery in biblical texts to the above, which I call the moral-ethical function. This is the interpretation given, for example, by F. S. Malan in a study of Romans 6.[9]

Malan recognizes that Paul's language in Romans 6 about being either a slave of sin or a slave of God and righteousness is informed by the actual structures of slavery in Paul's society. He writes, "The submission of 'yourselves' to be someone's slave, refers to the custom prevalent in Paul's day that a free man could sell himself into slavery to obtain money to pay his debts. The point of comparison is the obedience which a slave owes his master."[10] Malan emphasizes not the money the slave gains from the self-sale or any of the other benefits the slave might expect to accrue from the slave relationship. Rather, he emphasizes the unconditional obedience expected of the slave. For Malan, the slave imagery functions quite simply: "The point of comparison in the imagery of masters and slaves is the obedience which slaves owe their masters."[11] Malan must admit that Paul also compares the return one receives from slavery to sin with those one receives from slavery to God (Rom. 6:20–23). But this contrast of different slaveries—the good slavery versus the bad slavery—is not really interesting to Malan; it is merely a rhetorical device to persuade Paul's hearers to moral behavior. As Malan states, "The reference to the futility and disgrace of the old way of life as opposed to the glory, significance and immortality of the new way of life, aims at persuading the believers to abandon sin and to dedicate themselves to do what is right."[12]

I do not dispute the claim that Paul wishes to urge his hearers to behave morally. But Malan's concentration on this one strategy as *the* emphasis and goal of the passage turns it into a moralizing discourse on human responsibility. It ignores that, for Paul, righteousness (*dikaiosynē*) is a sphere in which one lives, complete with obligations and benefits, loyalties and rewards. In Romans 6, Paul is not simply making a moralizing point—presumably Paul has no reason to believe the Romans are acting immorally. Rather, he realizes, rightly, that his statements about the law could lead to charges of libertinism (Rom. 6:1, 15). He avoids libertinism not by reintroducing the law—or any law—but by setting up an either/or situation: one must live either in the sphere of sin or in the sphere of God. As each sphere entails its own obligations and returns, Paul can contrast the two by comparing them to slavery to two different masters, a good one and a bad one. But in order for this strategy to work, Paul must presuppose that in early Christianity the image of slavery functioned to depict not just moral obligation but also salvation.

The moral-ethical interpretation of slavery to God, as exemplified by Malan's article, disregards the soteriological aspect of the image, an aspect that is clearly reflected in the sources (see Rom. 6:20–23; 1 Thess. 1:9; 1 Cor. 6:20; 7:23). Paul can so readily use the image of slavery to God or Christ as a symbol for salvation because this language had already been used in this way in the Old Testament and in non-Pauline, early Christianity.[13] The Psalms say that the Lord "purchases the lives of his slaves" (Ps. 34:22 LXX). The psalmist expects salvation from God *because* he is God's slave (Ps. 143:12; 123:2 LXX).[14] Therefore, when Paul talks about Christian salvation in terms of being bought in the market, he need not explain this surprising image. To his hearers it was not surprising or disturbing; it was already a recognized way to talk about Christian salvation.

Once we have placed slavery in its full Greco-Roman context, we can see its possibilities for use as a salvific image. An obvious way it symbolizes salvation is by recalling the benefits a slave might expect from a good master as opposed to a bad one. In Rom. 6:20–23, Paul can speak of slavery to God as the positive counterpart to slavery to sin by contrasting the returns or benefits of slavery to one master, sin, with those of slavery to a better master, God. *Telos* (end, reward, payment), *karpos* (fruit, returns), and *ta opsōnia* (wages) all have economic meanings that inform their theological use in Romans 6. In other words, one need not decide whether telos means "spiritual reward" or "payment rendered." For Paul's readers it meant both at the same time, drawing a theological meaning from sentiments that might initially appear crassly materialist.

Similarly, in 1 Thess. 1:9, Paul characterizes the conversion of the Thessalonians as turning from idol worship to become slaves of the "living and true God." The functional element of this contrast is the difference between being a slave of a good or more powerful master as opposed to a bad or less powerful master (cf. Gal. 4:8–9). From a living master one can expect life. The promise of deliverance follows in verse 10: "We await Jesus . . . who delivers us from the coming wrath." Slavery is able to mean these things for early Christians because the relative benefits of slavery to different masters were readily recognized. Conversion, therefore, could be represented as the prudent choice to enter into the more profitable relationship.

Other possibilities for soteriological uses of slavery sprang from the status implications of certain forms of slave life. As discussed in chapter 1, slaves of high-status persons could enjoy a certain derivative status them-

selves. Slave agents especially, but also slaves in other household positions, possessed this power by association. Moreover, slavery functioned—and was perceived to function—as a mode of social mobility. The
career ladder from low slave position to high slave position to freed client
status and even to citizenship and perhaps wealth was made possible by
the role slavery played in the patron-client structure of society. Slavery to
Christ would for that reason have been an appealing image for people
caught in low-status or dead-end positions. To understand how slavery to
Christ could mean salvation in the symbolic universe of early Christians,
we must recognize that the prospect for increased status attached to such
slave imagery could even be formulated in soteriological terms: to raise
one's status by becoming the slave of a good and powerful master was to be
saved from a harsher or less honorable fate.

To take a particular case, the slave language in 1 Corinthians 7 makes
sense only if one presupposes the status implications of slave structures
and the use of status as a way of conceiving Christian salvation. In 1 Cor.
6:20 and 7:23, Paul reminds the Corinthians that they were "bought for a
price." I say "reminds" because it is obvious from the way Paul suddenly
injects the image into his discourse, without introduction or explanation,
that his readers must have already been familiar with this kind of language
to portray one's becoming a Christian. Most scholars have agreed that
Deissmann's explanation of *buy* (*agorazein*) to mean redemption *from* slavery by way of sacral manumission must be rejected. *Priasthai*, not
agorazein, is the word most commonly used in those contexts.[15] *Agorazein*
refers not to the sale of a slave to a god by which the slave is actually freed,
but to the ordinary sale of a slave by one owner to another owner. Therefore, when Christ buys a person, the salvific element of the metaphor is
not in the movement from slavery to freedom but in the movement from a
lower level of slavery (as the slave of just anybody or the slave of sin) to a
higher level of slavery (as the slave of Christ).

In order to understand Paul's rhetoric in 1 Cor. 7:22–23, which depends on the status-improvement meaning of slavery to Christ, one must
recognize that salvation is here depicted as upward mobility within slavery. Paul has just said that Christians who are slaves should not let their
condition bother them.[16] "For the slave who has been called in the Lord is
a freedman to the Lord, likewise the free man who has been called is a
slave of Christ. You were bought for a price; do not become slaves of
human beings" (7:22–23). Paul is not simply mitigating the pain of slavery
by claiming that in Christ all people are in basically the same situation, as

if, because in Christ all are slave and yet all are free, the external, worldly status of each individual is unimportant. According to such an interpretation, the differences of status between Christians are annulled in the eschatological leveling of everyone to paradoxical freedom within slavery to Christ. This interpretation of 1 Cor. 7:22–23, however, takes *apeleutheros* to be not *freedman* but *free man*. Hans Conzelmann, in his commentary on 1 Corinthians, explains Paul's rhetoric along these lines. "The statement that the slave who is called in the Lord is the Lord's freedman does not really fit. If he were a freedman, then without detriment to any obligations of clientage and piety he would in fact be free. The meaning is rather that if he is in the Lord, if he belongs to him, then he is free in the eschatological sense, free from sin. He is *apeleutheros*, 'a freedman,' not in relation to the Lord, but in relation to his erstwhile status as a slave. Both statements belong together: the free man is really free as a slave of Christ. In this servitude lies the common factor: the freedom of the slave and of the civilly free man."[17]

Conzelmann's interpretation, however, does not adequately recognize the complexity of Greco-Roman slavery and the social meanings of Paul's terms. Had Paul wished to emphasize the eschatological freedom of the person in Christ, he would have used the word *eleutheros*, not *apeleutheros*. The second had definite social significance in that it stressed the relationship of the freedperson with the patron. Freedpersons identified themselves on their tombstones by giving their names and "*apeleutheros* of [patron's name]". *Freedman* or *freedwoman* in this context did not simply proclaim the individual's freedom; it placed that person more specifically in society as an ex-slave and now client of this particular patron. It provided social identity in terms of both legal status (slave, freed, or free) and connections to persons higher up in the patronal structure (slave of Julia; freedperson of Gaius). By calling the slave a "freedman of Christ" rather than a "free man *in* Christ," Paul stresses precisely what Conzelmann denies: that the status of the person is the issue, not eschatological freedom. Of course, as Conzelmann notes, Paul is not concerned here with the "obligations of clientage." He is rather playing on the benefits of clientage to Christ over clientage to a human patron.

The slave, according to Paul, should not be concerned about his or her current state of slavery. In reality he or she is not the slave of just anyone but the freedperson of Christ. This is status improvement in two ways. First, a freedperson has higher status than a slave, and Paul has raised the slave to the status of freedperson. More important, however, Paul puts the slave in an even higher status position than the freedperson of a human patron: he makes the slave the freedperson of the Lord. The slave's real status is not defined by current legal status, but neither is it defined as simply an improved individual condition: freedom. The slave's real status is determined by his or her placement in a different household entirely: the household of Christ. The slave is a freedperson of the Lord and shares in the benefits, status, and obligations that relationship brings.

Up to this point I have explained Paul's rhetoric by recalling the status-improvement aspects of slavery to an important master. That is, I have insisted that slavery is functioning here as a positive metaphor for Christian salvation by upward mobility. But within this same passage, slavery functions in a quite different way—indeed, in an opposite way—to define one person's status as relatively lower than someone else's. This becomes clear when we realize that Paul's rhetorical strategy does not simply re-define the status of Christian slaves; he also redefines the status of free Christians. As Paul makes the slave the freedperson of the Lord, so he makes the free man the slave of Christ. Paul is building on common Christian language that portrays all Christians as slaves of Christ. But Paul does not say here that all Christians are slaves of Christ. He specifically singles out the free man as the slave. Because he has just designated slaves as freedpersons of Christ, he is introducing not a leveling of all Christians to one condition but an actual reversal of normal status. In order for this reversal to take place, *slavery* must carry different valuations within the scope of a few verses. Having described Christian salvation as slavery to Christ, Paul then turns around and establishes a difference between meta-phorical slaves of Christ and metaphorical freedpersons of Christ in order to stress the lower status (relatively speaking, that is) of the slaves of Christ (higher-status Christians).

Paul's rhetoric here is misrepresented if the issue is taken to be one of individual state rather than status of persons in relation to other persons.[18] Some biblical commentators, for example, represent the issue as one of eschatological freedom, building on some philosophical concept about the ontological or political freedom of individuals. For example, Kenneth Russell, writing about 1 Cor. 7:22, says, "In both sides of the balanced sentence the point is made that it is not the social rank which tells the truth about the Christian. The man who belongs to the slave class is actually, like all Christians, a slave of the Lord. All, regardless of their social class, have been freed and all have, as a result, been reduced to slavery."[19]

Paul's language, however, clearly reflects the Greco-Roman preoccupation with status and the place of persons within the patronal pyramid of society. In that social context, Paul's statement actually exalts the slave over the free person rather than leveling them to the same position. This strategy seems subtle to moderns only because we do not appreciate the importance of status for early Christians and because we do not comprehend the clear status significances of Paul's use of the words *slave*, *freedperson*, and *freeman*. To Paul's contemporaries, his language was not subtle at all. He took the highest-status person, the free man, and placed him in the lowest-status position of the household. Then he took the lowest-status person, the slave, and gave him a status above his fellow Christian, though still without making him an eleutheros, a free man. Paul thereby keeps both persons within the household of Christ, yet within the hierarchy of that household, he reverses their normal status positions. Freedom is not the issue here; status is.

Usually, and understandably, these verses are interpreted to propose the theological paradox that all Christians are simultaneously free and still slaves of Christ; by putting the situation in these terms, it is thought, Paul is simply destroying normal social distinctions by introducing eschatological or theological categories. Kenneth Russell again illustrates this view: "Paul, in facing the question of social distinctions, has gone beyond the surface to the heart of the matter. He has shown that the social divisions of the world cannot divide the members of Christ. He has consoled the slave by offering him freedom before God but reminded him as well that he is a slave of Christ."[20] The passage is actually more complicated. Paul does not here destroy the divisions between persons of different statuses. He first redefines the arena for status by taking it out of normal discourse and placing it within the symbolic universe of the household of Christ. Then he reverses the status of those within that household, giving higher status within the household to those who held lower status outside the household.

Paul can make this rhetorical move because he draws on commonly accepted language that portrays Christian salvation as passing from some worldly household into the household of Christ through the purchase enacted by Christ; thus Paul's next statement that Christians were bought for a price like slaves in the market (7:23). Because they are now slaves of Christ, they should not willingly become slaves of any human being. To do so would be to pass from high-slave status in a highly placed household to a position in a lesser household.[21]

It is important that Paul redefines the statuses of Christians by speaking of their relative statuses within the same household. Some may object at this point that, after showing that *slave of Christ* should be taken as a high-status indicator in early Christianity, I have now taken it to be a low-status designation within Paul's argument of 1 Cor. 7:22–23. But I have not taken *slave of Christ* as being low status in this passage. I have only taken it as representing *lower* status in relation to *freedperson of Christ*. Each of these terms is given some value only in relation to other terms. A slave of Christ has high status in relation to a slave of anyone else or even in relation to a poor, patronless, free person. Furthermore, the slave of Christ has high status only if the hearer of the language attributes to Christ himself high status and power. The valuations of the terminology are completely relative to other terms.

In Roman society, slaves occupied positions not simply as slaves, but as slaves within particular households, which we might imagine as different ladders. Different households (ladders) themselves had different statuses. Therefore, a move up for a slave could consist of either a move up within the same household or a move from slavery in a less important household to slavery in a more important household. But the move from slave to freed status was always a move up as long as the slave was not transferred to a radically less important household. This is why slaves even of powerful people still desired manumission—not because they were simply moving from bad slavery to good freedom but because they were taking a step up their particular ladder. A slave of Caesar on manumission did not, of course, become a freedperson of someone else but a freedperson of Caesar. He moved vertically within the same household. As I argued above, slaves did not seem to desire manumission simply because it brought individual liberty or because slavery was perceived unambiguously as an evil but because manumission was a step higher on the slave's particular social ladder. It is likely, however, that many slaves of Caesar would rather have remained slaves of Caesar than become freedpersons of some nobody. In Roman society, the move from slavery to freed status took place within a particular household, and the status of the household was just as important, if not more so, as the legal status of the dependent (whether slave or freed) in determining that person's overall status in society.

In other words, "slave of Christ" in 1 Cor. 7:22–23 is not a low status indicator. It is simply a *lower* status indicator than "freedperson of Christ" used in the same context. For Christians it would still be a higher status indicator than "slave of anybody else." Yet Paul's rhetoric is complex, because he has used commonly salvific language (Christians as slaves of

Christ) and turned it to a surprising use by making Christian slaves freed-persons of Christ and free Christians slaves of Christ. His language mixes different, indeed conflicting, valuations of the terms. The subtlety of Paul's argument, however, does not spring simply from the subtlety of his genius or from some theological paradox of freedom in slavery but from the complexity of language reflecting the complexity of society.

In these verses, Paul capitalizes on the ambiguity already present in the phrase *slave of Christ*. The term could be understood as a positive metaphor for salvation as social mobility and power by association. It could also be heard as carrying only relative positive value, bestowing lower status than *freedperson of Christ*, but status nonetheless. Further, it could be understood negatively as implying humiliation, unconditional obedience, or lack of independence. Those people who were themselves in lower-status positions could likely appropriate the positive meanings of the term more readily than people in higher-status positions. Higher-class persons probably were not in the least attracted to the idea of being a slave of anyone, Caesar or Christ included. Appropriately, therefore, Paul picks out precisely the high-status Christian (not even the freedperson, but the free man) and makes him the slave of Christ, while the slave is elevated to a higher position as freedperson of Christ. Paul thereby redefines the hierarchy of status in the church by employing the existing soteriological motif of the Christian as slave of Christ and the readily recognized status implications of the master-slave and patron-client social structure.

THE ROLE OF CHAPTER 9 IN 1 CORINTHIANS 8–10

Now that we have seen how *slave of Christ* functioned in early Christianity as a designation of leadership and as a soteriological image, we can turn to 1 Cor. 9:16–18 and consider how Paul uses this concept to characterize his own apostleship. Though Paul does not explicitly call himself Christ's slave here, he uses terminology that would have been recognized as depicting him as Christ's slave oikonomos—as a slave representative of Christ.[22] But recognizing that Paul is here picturing himself as Christ's slave leaves us many problems.

At the beginning of the chapter, Paul seems intent on depicting himself as a free man. For this reason, several scholars have assumed that Paul's goal is a defense of his freedom and independence.[23] This assumption initially seems well-founded in light of the many parallels between Paul's Corinthian correspondence and moral philosophy of the early empire.[24]

Much of 1 Corinthians reflects a debate between Paul and his Corinthian opponents concerning freedom and its proper use. For example, many scholars agree that Paul is echoing Corinthian slogans in chapters 6 and 10, when he says repeatedly, for example, that "all things are permitted." It seems that at least some of the Corinthian Christians were familiar with traditional moral philosophical, and in particular Cynic and Stoic, conceptions of the wise man (*sophos*).[25] The sophos was the only truly free person, the only true king. Therefore, everything was permitted for the wise man because his will was perfectly attuned to reality and the good. According to some interpreters, then, chapter 9 is simply a straightforward defense by Paul of his right to be included among the free, the wise, and the apostles.

Paul's defense, however, is not so straightforward. Indeed, the beginning of chapter 9 ("Am I not a free man?") and the first words of 9:19 ("For it is precisely as a free man . . .") form an inclusion showing that Paul's freedom is at issue throughout 9:1–18. But most of that section deals with Paul's financial support. The primary issue in 1 Corinthians 9, therefore, is not simply Paul's freedom or apostleship but the connection of that freedom to his means of self-support by manual labor.

Debates among Greco-Roman philosophers and rhetoricians concerned the proper ways of supporting a free person's professional activities. Ronald Hock has delineated four major means of support for the philosopher: charging fees, becoming the resident philosopher of a household, begging, and performing manual labor.[26] Neither Paul nor the Corinthians seem to have ever considered the option of begging in the Cynic style. But perhaps some people at Corinth expected Paul either to accept payment for his services or to become a household philosopher, so to speak, to his house churches. The first option, accepting fees, would have been a natural possibility. Matt. 10:10 bears witness to an old practice of support for evangelists.[27] Paul knew of such traditions and approved of the practice in general (1 Cor. 9:14). As for the second option, the Corinthians may have naturally expected Paul to be supported as their household philosopher. After all, he did stay in the homes of his converts (Rom. 16:23; Philemon 22).

For most philosophers, however, manual labor was out of the question, as they considered it demeaning and below the dignity of a member of the intelligentsia. Plato's statement that "the practice of mechanical art repels the man whose soul is free" was the accepted view. Any free citizen, such as Paul, who claimed a position of leadership would work as a craftsperson only in the direst circumstance.[28] Yet, unlike most apostles, Paul worked for his living and refused to allow the Corinthian church to support him. For some Corinthians, probably those of higher status, Paul's pursuit of his trade would imply not only his humble station but also an inability on their part to support their apostle. If to the eyes of respected society Paul's manual labor made him appear servile, it is only natural that his converts, or at least those who shared upper-class attitudes, would want their leader to assume a more comfortable and reputable position and cease the unnecessary practice of his craft.

With this as the background of 1 Corinthians 9, many scholars assume that Paul is insisting that he is free in spite of his self-support by manual labor. According to this interpretation, Paul refused support in order to maintain his independence and freedom from the control of the Corinthian church. Unfortunately for Paul, so the theory goes, he could only maintain that freedom paradoxically by practicing what was considered a slavish trade.[29] In chapter 9, therefore, Paul defends himself by insisting that his manual labor is necessary for maintaining his freedom.

This interpretation runs into insurmountable problems, however, upon closer examination of the language Paul uses in his "defense" in 9:16–18. If he were simply trying to defend himself against accusations that he is not free—in other words, if he were addressing criticisms that had already been stated by actual persons at Corinth—one would expect him to use their own philosophical texts against them by saying that he rejects the usual arrangement (support from his churches) because his very freedom allows him to reject the privileges of freedom.[30] He would say that he is so free that he can exercise his freedom by willingly forgoing the benefits of freedom. This mode of argument had strong precedents in rhetorical and moral philosophical contexts. Isocrates, for example, in *Nicocles*, has the king point out that he possesses power to do whatever he pleases (note his use of the term *exousia*—authority, freedom), but he proves himself a good king by exercising self-control. For the good of his subjects he does not exercise all of his rights.[31] Other ideal figures, Heracles especially, provided models of those truly free individuals who, though in superior positions, voluntarily gave up freedoms in order to benefit humankind. Epictetus presents Heracles as one who meets and overcomes hardships in true Cynic fashion. Although Heracles is ruler of all land and sea, he voluntarily fulfills his servile tasks and endures sufferings.[32] Dio Chrysostom also speaks of Heracles as one who knew "that everything belonged to him exclusively." Nevertheless, Heracles voluntarily suffered and performed servile tasks, willingly cleaning out the stables of Augeas. Heracles is the misunderstood hero, the one who is slave and king at the same time.[33]

As these texts indicate, there were legitimate arguments within the moral philosophical sphere of discourse to defend the abrogation of one's own freedom. Yet Paul does not use such stock arguments. He proceeds in none of the expected moral philosophical directions. Rather than depicting a free surrender of his freedom, Paul takes the surprising tack of stressing his slavery, as will be seen from an analysis of 1 Cor. 9:16.

PAUL AS SLAVE OF CHRIST IN 1 COR. 9:16–18

As mentioned above, Paul's language in 1 Corinthians is informed by Cynic and Stoic terminology and discussions of freedom. Yet, although Paul begins 1 Corinthians 9 by asserting his freedom, he then admits that he works under compulsion and unwillingly. In 9:16, Paul straightforwardly says that he has no boast in his preaching because he does it out of necessity (*anagkē*). Although the translation of verse 17 is still debated by scholars, the most likely interpretation, and that accepted by most scholars, takes the first part of the verse as hypothetical and the second as realistic: "If I *were* to do this willingly (which I do not) I would have a wage (*misthos*). But if I do this unwillingly I am entrusted with a stewardship."[34] In other words, Paul has just said in verse 16 that he preaches under compulsion, or unwillingly. In Philo's *Every Good Man Is Free*, acting unwillingly (*akōn*) is interchangeable with acting under compulsion (60–61; note: *anagkazesthai*). By stating that he is compelled to preach and that he therefore does not do it willingly, Paul explains why he does not receive a wage from the Corinthians. When Paul asks, in verse 18, "What then is my pay?" he does so having already rejected the possibility that he is entitled (that is, as Christ's slave agent) to receive pay in the normal sense, thus opening up the possibility that he may receive pay in an abnormal sense. The whole subject of Paul's wage in these verses will be pursued below, but for the moment, it will suffice to note that Paul here says he is not able to accept pay because he is Christ's slave agent.

By denying that his ministry should be understood along the lines of wage labor, Paul is able to introduce an alternative way of conceiving his work: he builds on his prior claim to work under compulsion and suggests that he is not a wage laborer who expects and receives a wage from his churches but someone who works unwillingly as an oikonomos. He receives no wage from the Corinthians because he has instead received the trust of a stewardship from Christ.

Paul's argument that he preaches under compulsion and unwillingly would never have been made by first-century moral philosophers. Indeed, a comparison of Paul's unwillingness with philosophical discussions of voluntary and involuntary action reveals that Paul rejects a moral philosophical defense of his apostleship in 1 Cor. 9:16–18 and instead portrays himself in those verses as a slave of Christ.

The theme of voluntary and involuntary action pervades much moral philosophical discourse. The Stoic wise man (the Stoics seldom spoke of wise women) is the only one who is free, rich, a king. One of the proofs of this freedom is his refusal to do anything against his will. His will, it is said, is so attuned to the direction of cosmic fate, or, according to Epictetus, to the divine will, that he can never be forced to go against it. He cannot be compelled. People who can be compelled are either weak and cannot resist the bad and hold to the good, or they are foolish and have not adequately learned what the true good is. At any rate, it had become a truism that the true wise man, the "true Cynic" as Epictetus understands him, does nothing unwillingly (Epictetus 3.22.40–44).

The terms used in this discussion vary somewhat. To talk about the freedom of the wise man, the sophos, as only voluntary action, the philosophers speak of "the power of self-action" (exousia autopragias), or "the ability to act as we wish" (to exeinai hōs boulometha diexagein), which is Epictetus's definition of freedom.[35] When referring to involuntary action, the philosophers speak of "being compelled" (anakazesthai) or "prevented" (kōluesthai), "acting unwilling" (akōn poiein), or possessing a will that is "hinderable and constrainable" (kōluton ē anagkaston).[36] Clearly, Paul's vocabulary in 1 Cor. 9:16–18 fits this context.

What are we to make of Paul's ready admission that he acts as an apostle only under compulsion? In a context of Cynic and Stoic debate, such an admission looks like a rhetorical mistake. It is possible, of course, that Paul has in mind here not the moral philosopher's use of compulsion, willingly, and unwillingly, but the use made of these terms in, for example, Aristotle's ethics. According to Aristotle, "An act is compulsory when its origin is from outside, the person compelled contributing nothing to it."[37] A deed done involuntarily and under compulsion receives no reward or payment. In this case, Paul would be using these terms to set up something like a legal fiction or metaphor. He does not receive reward, just as he would not receive blame, because his actions are committed under compulsion.

Lucian is aware of the possibilities for this kind of defense. In one essay, he derides intellectuals who accept salaried positions in households (*On Salaried Posts in Great Houses*). Later, when he takes a salaried post in the imperial administration, he writes an "Apology" for his actions. In the course of his apology, he notes that he could claim he was compelled by circumstances to take such a job. He could say, for example, that poverty or something else forced him to take the post against his will. He rejects this defense, however, as shameful (*Apology* 8). Therefore, as Lucian's remarks show, the suggestion that Paul is using compulsion in a rhetorical move informed by Aristotelian legal-ethical theory scarcely relieves us of our problem. Paul is still admitting actions committed under compulsion in a context heavily informed by moral philosophical assumptions about the nature of freedom. One of those assumptions, as Lucian knows, is that a truly free person cannot be compelled.

Thus far, our suggestions about the background for Paul's use of the theme of compulsion have centered on philosophical discussions, and in particular on the moral philosophers and Aristotelian legal theory. The most natural suggestion, however, is that Paul uses these terms in a more ordinary, everyday sense. As the essays of the moral philosophers themselves show, in much popular conversation freedom was defined as "doing what one wants." In two orations by Dio Chrysostom, for example, apparent and real slavery are discussed (Discourses 14 and 15). Dio assumes that most people understand slaves as those who must obey someone; slaves act involuntarily and under compulsion. The slave exists for the benefit of the master and is under the master's power. Put simply—and this is the point Dio wishes both to defend and to attack—whoever has power to do as he or she wishes is free; whoever does not is a slave (14.8–13; see also 15.19).

Dio attacks this definition by pointing out that free people commonly obey others and submit to the wills and advice of different persons, such as physicians, army generals, or captains of ships. In such situations, only fools would do whatever they wished. But eventually Dio agrees that the truly free act as they wish, because they are wise enough to will only the good and beneficial. Even a slave, therefore, may be truly free if the will is completely, but autonomously, attuned to the circumstances (14.18). The point of the discourses is to show that what people normally call freedom and slavery have no relation to real freedom and slavery; true freedom is a matter of the will, regardless of one's social circumstances. As Epictetus writes, one is in prison wherever one is unwillingly (*akōn*). Socrates was not really in prison because he was there willingly (*hekōn*). Just after this comment, Epictetus calls the one who cannot accomplish this freedom of the will a slave (1.12.23–24: *andrapodon*).

The connection between compulsion, slavery, and the will emerges clearly in Philo's essay *Every Good Man Is Free*. Philo argues that slavery is not being bought, obeying another, or performing servile tasks or manual labor. Rather, for Philo, slavery consists in being compelled, which means acting involuntarily ("If he is compelled, it is clear that he does something unwillingly").[38] The good person, however, will always do the good voluntarily. "Whence," Philo concludes, "it is clear that he does nothing unwillingly and is never compelled, whereas if he were a slave he would be compelled, and therefore the good man will be a free man."[39] Philo wishes to correct popular conceptions of slavery and maintains that one's external condition of servitude does not necessarily mean one is truly a slave. Philo later, nevertheless, reveals his own upper-class bias when he lets slip the opinion that slaves are those who do "necessary servile labors." True free men, like Heracles, will disdain to act in accordance with the wishes of their inferiors even if in a condition of slavery.[40] Philo is not nearly as consistent as Dio or Epictetus. He seeks to believe that freedom is an inner reality and unrelated to external circumstances, but he cannot quite imagine his good man, who is necessarily free, in any realistic condition of slavery. It is clear, at any rate, that in both popular understandings and moral philosophy, slavery was linked with compulsion and involuntary behavior. Words appearing in such contexts include ones used by Paul: *anagkē*, *akōn*, *hekōn*.[41]

The suggestion that Paul's language here refers to slavery is supported by his contrast in these verses between working for pay (*misthos*) and being entrusted with a stewardship (*oikonomia*). The term *oikonomia* does not in itself necessarily indicate slave status; it is a flexible term used in a wide variety of contexts.[42] The primary meaning of the word has to do with the management of a household and, by extension, the management of businesses, cities, states, and governments. Nevertheless, in the early Roman imperial period the word *oikonomos* almost always points to someone of servile status.[43] Although anyone could have an oikonomia, usually only slaves and freedpersons were oikonomoi. Paul's specific words, "to be entrusted with an oikonomia," are those used by Artemidorus in his dream handbook to refer to managerial slaves.[44] Therefore, saying that one is entrusted with an oikonomia is usually equivalent to saying that one is an oikonomos. Paul's contemporaries would have realized that most oikonomoi were slaves or began their careers as slaves.

One last linguistic indication that Paul is here describing himself as Christ's slave agent lies in his opposition of "being entrusted with an oikonomia" to "having a wage" (*misthos*). The term *misthos* occurs in a variety of contexts. It is usually translated in the New Testament as *reward*, but that translation may reflect the tendency to theologize words in the Bible.[45] That is, the everyday meanings of Greek words are often passed over in an attempt to give a word a more religious meaning. The ordinary, common translation is *pay*. The payment could be the financial remuneration for public services in a Greek city, such as that received by Athenians for jury duty or the payment of those who held public office. Mercenary soldiers are those who fight for pay. *Misthos* is the word used for a physician's fee. The word does occasionally also function like our less concrete term *reward*.[46]

Though *misthos* usually means *wage*, Ste. Croix has shown that simply receiving a misthos did not make someone what we would call a wage laborer or hired labor.[47] An architect or someone of significantly higher status than a hired laborer might receive a misthos; in this case the word would likely translate as *salary*. Thus Philostratus defends the practice of charging a fee (misthos) for lectures, a practice for which Sophists were known (*Lives of the Sophists* 494, 482). Receiving a misthos did not in itself make these lecturers wage laborers (*misthōtoi*), which would have been considered an insult in higher circles. Later in this chapter I will return to the specific significance of Paul's implication here that he does not work for pay. At this point it will suffice to note that *pay* is the ordinary meaning of the word *misthos* and that Paul says that, were he to serve as an apostle willingly, he would receive pay.

When *misthon echein* is understood as "receiving a wage," it becomes clear why Paul counterposes this phrase with "being entrusted with an oikonomia." By portraying himself as Christ's slave agent, Paul implies that he would not receive a wage. It is true that slaves were usually paid by their masters for their work. This was probably even more often true for managerial slaves than for common laborers, but *misthon echein* is not a normal way of referring to this financial arrangement.[48] By claiming that he does not work for a wage but has been entrusted, against his will, with an oikonomia, Paul clearly indicates to people of that society that he characterizes himself as Christ's slave agent.

Throughout this enquiry, Paul's rhetoric has begun to look more and more surprising when seen from the point of view of the moral philosophers. These philosophers stressed the freedom of the individual. When persons found themselves in undesirable situations, they were simply to conform their will to the situation. Even suffering, according to Cynics and Stoics alike, could be voluntarily endured.[49] But these philosophers never spoke of the wise man as unwillingly doing the undesirable thing. Paradoxically, the slave was not a slave if she or he willingly endured slavery. On a more mundane level, the philosophical preaching delineates the popular conceptions they were attacking. Popularly speaking, slaves acted unwillingly, free people willingly.

Paul is appropriating the ordinary, popular use of the terms *hekōn*, *akōn*, and *anagkē* to imply that he is Christ's slave. By doing this in a context already informed by moral philosophical discourse, he seems either to ignore the moral philosophical use of the terms or deliberately to fly in the face of it. Either way, it is clear that Paul's claim to act unwillingly and under compulsion would have been heard as an admission of slavery. To people familiar with the moral philosophical discourse, Paul is committing a philosophical faux pas. To those unfamiliar with that discourse, his statements simply indicate that he accepts for himself the designation "slave."

In other words, Paul's language would have been heard in at least two different ways. To people with some education, familiar with moral philosophical discourse, Paul's self-description would sound shocking. To their ears Paul is admitting, in the worst way, that he is not, after all, a free man, a wise man, a true philosopher. He knows not philosophical freedom but rather servility and weakness. Persons untrained in philosophical terminology would hear Paul's language as simple signals that he is a slave. As the preceding chapter has shown, however, calling someone a slave— among the lower strata of the population—would not necessarily have been so humiliating. Such people would hear Paul's claim that he is a slave without the negative evaluation that accompanies such terminology in philosophical discourse. These untrained hearers, therefore, could conceivably grant to Paul's self-description a positive valuation, if he is a slave not of some lowly, unimportant person but of a person of power and high status. Paul's slavery in 1 Cor. 9:16–18, therefore, could sound positive to lower-class persons, because it portrays him in a high status-by-association form of slavery, as a slave of Christ.

CHAPTER 9 AS A FICTITIOUS DEFENSE

My analysis thus far has shown that Paul is defending himself poorly in 1 Corinthians 9, if indeed the goal of the chapter is an outright defense of his freedom. There are other reasons, however, besides the inadequacy of the defense itself, to doubt that 1 Corinthians 9 represents a real defense on Paul's part. One such reason is the place of chapter 9 within the argument that stretches from 8:1 to 11:1. When read within Paul's overall argument, chapter 9 functions as a digression that advocates a certain kind of behavior rather than as a real defense of Paul's freedom.

Indeed, in 1 Cor. 9:3, Paul calls his account of himself his apologia, his "defense to those who are finding fault" with him. Taking this verse as their cue, many scholars, as shown above, have proposed that chapter 9 represents an actual defense against people who were challenging Paul's right to be called an apostle. Reading the chapter in this way, however, made it difficult to see how chapter 9 fit with the issue of eating meat offered to idols, which is the subject of both chapters 8 and 10. Therefore, scholars often conjectured that chapter 9 comes where it does due to later editing, or at least that it is an ungraceful and ill-conceived digression by Paul.[50] Indeed, when chapter 9 is taken out of its context, it seems like a straightforward defense of Paul's apostleship and freedom.

Yet the integrity of 1 Corinthians 8–10 has been demonstrated repeatedly. H. F. von Soden and Hans Conzelmann, for example, showed the theological connections binding together 1 Corinthians 8 and 10.[51] From a formal point of view, Wilhelm Wuellner has shown that chapter 9 is a perfectly good example of a digression that follows appropriate rhetorical form.[52] By means of the digression and following common rhetorical practice, Paul presents himself as an example to support his advice contained in chapters 8 and 10.

In its context, therefore, chapter 9 functions primarily as an example for behavior rather than simply as a defense of Paul's apostleship. True, Paul calls the section his apologia. Chapter 9 is thus a digression, in the form of a defense, that advocates some particular behavior. Why does Paul set up his illustrative digression as an apologia (9:3)? Possibly there were genuine opponents in Corinth ("those who would examine me," 9:3) who had already complained about Paul's laboring to supporting himself. On the other hand, Paul may be debating with merely hypothetical adversaries, perhaps for the purpose of delineating a point of view to which his own example will serve as corrective and counterpoint.

The second possibility appears to be the more likely. Nothing indicates clearly that Paul, as early as the writing of 1 Corinthians, had actually heard criticism against himself for refusing support from the Corinthians. Such explicit criticism seems to have arisen only later, as shown by Paul's very different approach to the problem in 2 Cor. 10–13. In 2 Cor. 11:7–11 Paul's tone is clearly defensive; in 12:13 it is even sarcastic, implying that Paul knows that some people have taken his rejection of support as an affront. But none of this overt defensiveness surfaces when Paul brings up the subject of his self-support in 1 Corinthians. Indeed, a comparison of the hardship lists of 1 Cor. 4:11–13 and 2 Cor. 11:23–29 suggests that there has been a shift in the argument between the writing of the two lists. In the first is a reference to manual labor (1 Cor. 3:12), which is noticeably absent in the later list. ("Toil" in 2 Cor. 11:27 could conceivably imply manual labor but not nearly as explicitly as the terminology of 1 Cor. 4:12). Probably manual labor has been left off the second list because Paul's self-support by manual labor has itself become an explicit bone of contention only by the time Paul wrote 2 Cor. 10–13.

More important, even if one takes 1 Corinthians 9 as a defense, the chapter functions primarily as an example for the behavior advocated in chapters 8 and 10 (giving up one's privileges for someone else's sake). But if some Corinthians were already criticizing Paul for refusing their support, he would be foolish to use the very bone of contention as the prime focus for the behavior he is advocating. In other words, if Paul had already been explicitly criticized for giving up his privilege of support, it would not make sense of him to use that action as an analogy for behavior he is urging on his very critics.

For these reasons, it is more likely that Paul himself introduces the subject of his refusal of support.[53] He does so, of course, knowing that his refusal (and its consequence, self-support by manual labor) will be frowned upon by some people at Corinth—precisely those who dislike the idea of giving up their own perquisites (eating meat) for the sake of other Christians. Because he realizes that his behavior will be initially unacceptable to that group of Corinthians, he puts the chapter in terms of a defense. He defends himself proleptically against accusations he knows are a real possibility. But he does so because the two subjects (giving up the right to eat meat and giving up the right to church support) are analogous: both require behavior that high-status persons would disdain. This does not necessitate, however, the supposition of overt criticism by the time of the writing of 1 Corinthians 9. Rather, in that chapter Paul mounts a fictitious, rhetorical defense of himself for refusing to live like the other apostles and for rejecting support from the church.

The purpose of chapter 9, as noted above, is to advocate some particular behavior. One might take Paul's point to be that Christians in general are to give way to the needs of others. According to such a reading, Paul would be saying that, just as he gives up his right to financial support, so Corinthian Christians should give up their right to eat meat offered to idols so that they will avoid offending other Christians. Chapter 9 would thus be advocating a general ethic of giving up one's own self-interest for the good of the other.[54]

Yet this interpretation does not adequately consider the status-specific nature of Paul's language in chapter 9. Paul specifically states his defense in terms of his move from freedom to slavery by depicting himself first as a slave of Christ (9:16–18) and then as a slave of all (9:19–23). Furthermore, Paul chooses his practice of self-support as the specific example of the kind of behavior he is advocating. This manual labor, which represented a clear move down the social scale for Paul, caused some confusion in the minds of at least some of his converts, because, according to the opinions of some people of that time, manual labor was incongruous with leadership. Paul's status as a manual laborer was inconsistent, in the eyes of some, with his status as an apostle. By using his role as laborer to advocate behaviors discussed in chapters 8 and 10, he raises questions about the conventional social hierarchy.

Paul's goal in chapter 9 is not to make a general ethical statement—that Christians should give in to the interests of others. Rather, he uses status-specific language and concentrates on status images in chapter 9 precisely because his goal is to change the behavior of a particular group in Corinth, those who are themselves taking their own high positions too seriously. Throughout chapter 9, Paul constructs his argument in terms that were loaded for the higher-status Christians at Corinth, because it is that group he is addressing. They were unwilling to change their lifestyles in order to please less important Christians. They did not want to give up their perquisites, such as their philosophical freedoms and their social activities, which included eating meat; they wanted to remain leaders of the church at Corinth but from a secure position of social superiority. Paul's choice of imagery emphasizes that he, their first leader, is a high-status person who has taken on low status. He challenges the other leading Christians to do the same.[55]

Let us return to the idea of 1 Corinthians 9 as a defense. In this defense, Paul posits opponents who imply that self-support by low-status activity is inconsistent with leadership. Paul's posited opponents share a higher-class, moral philosophical view by which the sophos is authoritative, free, kingly, and rich (cf. 4:8), and by which manual labor is despised. Paul himself introduces this view in order to demonstrate, by his own practice, that normal status indicators are overturned in Christian forms of leadership. Chapter 9, therefore, is both a defense and an example. Paul defends his leadership as legitimate despite his low-status activities. This defense in turn functions as a pertinent example, because the larger issue throughout the preceding and subsequent discussions (1 Corinthians 8 and 10) is precisely one of status: advocating that those of high status be willing to give up their perquisites in the interests of those of low status.

PAUL'S SLAVERY TO CHRIST IN THE ARGUMENT OF 1 CORINTHIANS 9

As seen earlier in the chapter, Paul begins by claiming his status as a free man but ends by admitting his servile status. His description of his role as a slave is full of ambiguities and complexities. He is not an average slave; he has been "entrusted with a managerial position," an oikonomia, and his master is not just anyone but Christ. The ambiguities and complexities permit Paul's self-designation as a slave oikonomos of Christ to function rhetorically in a complex but effective manner in the letter. Indeed, Paul's self-portrayal as a slave can mean several different things in the Corinthian context.

For one thing, Paul contrasts "being entrusted with an oikonomia" with "receiving a wage." The word for *wage* used here, *misthos*, could itself be ambiguous; it was not a value-neutral term. It could be taken simply as *reward*, but it could also imply that those who received a misthos, that is, the other apostles who accepted support, were wage laborers (*misthōtoi*). To people with higher-status sensibilities, this was an unflattering image. In spite of the occasional positive use of the term, in many contexts the word retains a negative connotation given it by those people who never had to work for a wage and who usually despised the people who did. In the *Iliad*, for example, one of the hardships Apollo is said to have endured was working like a laborer at a fixed wage, suffering low status indeed for a god. Generally, from an upper-class point of view, it is the low-status person who works for a misthos.[56] This attitude allowed some writers to portray philosophers who taught for fees as wage laborers, selling their services like hired help. The tradition goes back to Socrates, who said that he was a free man (*eleutheros*) because he would accept neither gifts nor a wage (*dōra, misthos*). According to Epictetus, philosophers who do not stand up to those in power are only parasites; they hire themselves out for pay.[57]

Lucian made great use of this kind of language in his essay *On Salaried Posts in Great Houses*. He speaks of philosophers who attach themselves to households and allow themselves to be supported by one patron. According to Lucian, this practice is "done of necessity by those who are in it for the pay" (§ 1; my translation). He sneers at "this sort of wage-earning" and calls their patrons "paymasters" (*misthodotai*; §§ 3 and 4; see also 6). It is perfectly all right, of course, for athletic instructors, the "mob," and all lowly people (*tapeinoi*) to have paymasters; they are used to such treatment. But this kind of thing is not suitable for educated people. When higher-class people submit to such a wage contract, they have given up their freedom (*eleutheria*, § 4). They have become servile because they are always having to worry about their wages. The picture of an educated man standing in line with the rest of the household help, stretching out his hand to receive his pay, evokes from Lucian an accusation of "shameful wage-labor."[58]

Later, when Lucian defends himself for accepting a salary, he argues that there is a great difference between being paid by a private patron for filling a servile position and being paid by the emperor. All wage earnings, he cries, should not be lumped together. Lucian says that no one, not even the emperor is completely wage-free (*amisthos*); therefore, all people, from the small to the great, are wage earners (*Apology* 11, 13). His argument follows a common rhetorical practice: The speaker takes a word or concept that has normally objectionable overtones and stretches it to show a wider application than it has in normal discourse. One thus argues that the popular opinion about the matter is too simplistic and even false. The speaker redefines the word or concept, robbing it of its negative meanings, and either neutralizes it or gives it a different, positive meaning.[59] The rhetorical strategy demands, however, that the speaker's audience normally understand the term or concept in the way rejected by the speaker.

In his *Apology*, Lucian uses precisely this rhetorical strategy. He argues that in one sense (not the normal sense) all people of all statuses receive a misthos. Therefore, there is nothing shameful about receiving a wage. The argument obviously presupposes the audience's opinion that there is indeed something objectionable about people—at least those of Lucian's class—receiving a misthos. This need not be the opinion of everyone in society. But at least for Lucian's audience, those educated persons of higher status, working for a wage carried a certain stigma.

Because higher-class readers of Lucian's essays would have recognized that working for a wage was less than honorable, at least among their circles, we should expect that upper-class hearers of Paul's language in 9:17 would have had a similar reaction. In this verse, Paul contrasts his own apostleship as an oikonomos with those who receive pay for their preaching. He himself probably intends no disparagement of those who receive a misthos for their preaching. To some of Paul's readers, depicting leaders as wage earners likely carried no negative stigma. But we are concerned with how Paul's language was heard as well as how he intended it; we may imagine that Paul's higher-status readers were dismayed to hear their other leaders (their "superapostles" or Christian "household philosophers"?) described as wage laborers. This is, after all, Paul's terminology and likely not their own. The implication that the other preachers worked for wages must have raised the eyebrows of precisely those people who objected to Paul's method of self-support by manual labor, whether or not Paul intended such a reaction.

Paul's language throws into question the assumptions of those who expect their leaders not to work. He depicts his own activity as slavery, and his choice of words implies that accepting funds from the churches constitutes wage labor. His rhetoric overturns the clear categories of his contemporary readers, who assume that leaders are free, exercise authority, and do not work, whereas lower-status persons do work. Paul's language forces his readers who share upper-class views to think of leadership in confusing ways that stress the ambiguity—not the "givenness"—of normal status indicators.

Second, by portraying himself as Christ's slave oikonomos, Paul uses a category of honor that functions in early Christianity as a recognized designation of leadership to support his own unique manner of leadership, that is, as a leader who supports himself by manual labor instead of by the church. Obviously, some Christians at Corinth find Paul's manual labor shameful or humiliating, as 2 Corinthians 10–13 indicates. Yet by the fact that they are within the Christian community, they share its language and are familiar with the different elements of its symbolic universe. Paul therefore appropriates a shared image, the Christian leader as a slave of Christ, to explain how he can be a Christian leader and yet refuse financial support from the Corinthians. His practice is construed as part of his role as a slave of Christ, which in early Christianity was a recognized title of authority and leadership.

But Paul's apostleship as Christ's slave oikonomos claims authority only in a paradoxical manner. Paul's use of *slave of Christ* shows the derivative nature of his authority: it is not the straightforward, unambiguous authority of a rich, free patron, but it is authority nonetheless. In fact, for leaders whose lifestyles or formal status indicators are ambiguous or low, the derivative form of authority may be more effective in that it precludes any questioning of their authority by other, more regular criteria such as wealth, education, or legal status. In such a situation, the leader as representative is a firmer authority. True, the leader-as-slave form of authority represents authority as entering through the back door, as it were, but that very approach may make it more secure—and therefore more powerful.

Although I have approached 1 Corinthians 9 as a fictitious defense rather than as a response to already stated criticisms, I do think there were some people at Corinth who found Paul's self-support offensive (see, for example, 2 Cor. 11:7; 12:13). In fact, I believe that Paul's self-description in 1 Corinthians 9 likely catalyzed a shift from hushed to open opposition to his means of support. Certainly 2 Corinthians 10–13 suggests that Paul's depiction of himself as servile and weak was only too convincing with some Corinthians. At any rate, I have claimed that Paul—in 1 Corinthians 9—is not answering actual, stated charges. On the other hand, because Paul sets up his arguments in 1 Corinthians 9 as an apologia (9:3), we should reconstruct opponents even if they are, at this point, only fictitious, set up by Paul for his own rhetorical purposes.

According to this reconstruction, in 1 Cor. 9:1–18, Paul sets a rhetorical trap for these opponents. He admits to working under compulsion: he serves involuntarily, like a slave, and for that reason deserves no wage. His more educated opponents nod vigorously. "Ah, so you are a slave after all, as we have implied?" "Yes," answers Paul, "a slave of *Christ*. In fact, Christ's slave *steward*." Immediately Paul has defused their criticism and accusation. Those familiar with the philosophical use of the language— probably those of higher status with greater access to education—understand the language in that context, by which Paul's statement sounds like an admission that he is servile, not free, and not, therefore, an apostle. But because these same people are Christians, they share the common Christian vocabulary that talks of its leaders as representative slaves of Christ. Paul knows of the moral philosophical use of this language, but he wrests their language away from them, gives it its ordinary usage as depicting everyday slavery (rather than "philosophical" slavery), and then forces the language into the Christian vernacular shared by all the Corinthian Christians, not just those enlightened by moral philosophical debates. Once Paul defines himself as a slave in this sense, no one within the Christian community can criticize his self-characterization. Furthermore, within the common Christian discourse, Paul's slavery to Christ has a positive connotation—as a high-status designation—especially for lower-class people. Only in upper-class circles, in philosophical discourse, does such a title imply degradation.

It is important to see, therefore, that up through 9:18, according to one form of discourse, at least, Paul has made no move toward humility or self-lowering, even though he has defined himself as a slave of Christ. He has, however, redefined the categories for leadership and authority. Instead of thinking about leaders in the normal ways—as patrons, wealthy, kings, those who are free and do as they will—Paul moves the debate into the common discourse of early Christianity, which talks of its leaders as slaves of Christ. Again, this is not to make Christian leaders less powerful or authoritative but to insist that the discussion be carried on in the context of Christian discourse rather than in that of the upper class or of moral philosophers. Far from giving up his authority, Paul seeks in 9:1–18 to establish it beyond question. His rhetorical strategy of 9:16–18 does shift the discourse away from that of the opponents: he defuses what could have been a higher-status, more educated criticism of his self-description by forcing the discussion outside the specialized higher-status uses of the language and into a discourse that includes uneducated, lower-status Christians. Paul forces any potential interlocutors to play on his turf.

Finally, by introducing ambiguity into the prevailing symbols of leadership, Paul opens up opportunities for a different model of leadership: the leader as enslaved. He does this first by portraying the leader as the slave oikonomos of Christ in 9:16–18. This theme serves as an introduction to Paul's self-enslavement to all, which occurs in 9:19–23. I said above that up through 9:18 Paul has not lowered himself. This is because Paul's self-description as a slave of Christ does not mitigate his authority but confirms it. This statement needs to be qualified. In verse 18, Paul strangely says that his wage or reward is that he is able by preaching "free of charge" to present the gospel in a way in which he does not make use of his right in the gospel. In other words, the reward Paul receives for preaching as a slave of Christ is the opportunity to give up his authority, his power. Note, Paul's slavery to Christ does not mean that he has given up power; it provides the *opportunity* to give up power. According to his argument, because he is a slave of Christ Paul does not accept financial support; he must therefore find some other way to support himself. Faced with this necessity, Paul becomes a manual laborer. Doing so does involve a step down in status, which is exactly what he wants, as will become clear in his enslavement, not to Christ, but to all in 9:19–23. In other words, as I argue in chapter 1, in Paul's society it mattered less that one was a slave than whose slave one was. Paul's rhetoric capitalizes on this social structure by moving from slavery to Christ in 9:16–18 to slavery to all in 9:19–23. The slaveries in each case, therefore, have different valuations according to the valuations assigned to the parties to which Paul is enslaved.

Verse 18 must be read as an introduction to 9:19–23 and its theme of enslavement to all. Paul's reward or pay as a slave steward is the opportunity for social self-lowering. As we shall see in the next two chapters, self-lowering in Paul's own soteriological scheme has its own consequent reward. But to attain the final reward, Paul must begin by going down. His manual labor, which is made necessary by his refusal of a wage as Christ's slave steward, is the particular way he goes down. Therefore, in a strange way, it is his reward for his being a slave steward and not receiving pay for his services. Thus the reward of verse 18, which comes to Paul as the slave of Christ, leads to the theme of 9:19–23: the self-lowering of the apostle as the slave of all.

3

THE

ENSLAVED

LEADER

AS A

RHETORICAL

TOPOS

The idea that a king or some kind of leader could be called a slave intrigued Greco-Roman authors. Some speculated that, as people are enslaved to kings, so kings are enslaved to the gods.[1] Others, like Plato, spoke of good leadership as being subject to the laws. According to him, such subjection constituted an admirable "slavery to the gods."[2] The theme that rulers were to be slaves of the laws was such a common one that it could be first assumed and then refuted, as when, according to Plutarch, Anaxarchus gives bad advice to Alexander the Great: Anaxarchus encourages Alexander not to be a slave to laws but to be like Zeus, who keeps the Law and Justice seated beside, not above, him. Plutarch argues that this was bad advice because it made Alexander reckless and arrogant. It was a reversal and misuse of the enslavement to the law topos.[3]

Ragner Höistad, in tracing Cynic concepts of kingship, has shown that the image of the leader (in most of his cases, the philosopher) as slave was a Cynic topos. According to Höistad, the Cynic ideal king was the true wise man (*sophos*) who endured hardships and suffering, even slavery, for the good of others. Heracles and Odysseus were examples, among Cynics, of the ideal king, the slave king. Höistad claims that the main point of the enslaved-leader topos in Cynicism "was to show the philosophical inner freedom which is founded on moral perfection and not on outward circumstances."[4]

As these three examples demonstrate, the notion that a leader could be enslaved was not unusual in Greco-Roman rhetoric. In contrast, Paul claims in 1 Cor. 9:19–23 to be enslaved not to Christ or to God but to all; that is, he is enslaved precisely to those he is supposed to lead. In 1 Corinthians 9, Paul is careful to establish his role as a, if not the, leader of the Corinthian church. He begins the chapter insisting that he is an apostle (9:1); he defends his rights as leader of the group (9:1–14); and at the end of the chapter, he again alludes to his role as a preacher of the gospel (9:27). Thus, it is precisely in his role as leader that Paul portrays himself as a slave of all. Here again, his self-portrayal as an enslaved leader has parallels in Greco-Roman rhetoric. In this chapter, I wish to explore the rhetorical topos current in the first century that presented a leader as enslaved to his own subjects. Other elements from Paul's argument in 1 Cor. 9:19–23 also occur in the topos: the leader is said to be a chameleon, changing himself to suit his audience; he lowers himself socially; he is said to do so for gain; he claims to be working not for selfish gain but for the salvation of the people.[5]

In ancient rhetorical contexts, the topos of the enslaved leader was linked to a certain political debate. In Greco-Roman political rhetoric, there were two major models of leadership: the populist model, by which the leader attempted to identify himself with the common people and therefore lowered himself socially to their level; and what I call the benevolent patriarchal model, by which a leader ruled benevolently but from a secure, firm position of social superiority.[6] Populist leaders—or demagogues, as the populists were called in Greek contexts—were those who enslaved themselves to the people. The model of the leader as enslaved to his followers was called democratic (*dēmotikos* or *dēmokratikos*), that is, the enslaved leader was the man of the people (*dēmos*). He took the part of the common people and advanced (or tried to appear to advance) their interests against the interests of the upper class. For this reason, the image of a leader as enslaved to his subjects eventually comes to be a topos associated with populists or demagogues; thus my designation of it as the demagogue topos.

In Cynic thought, the leader as slave may be said to have an "individual-ethical" function, to use Höistad's terminology.[7] Slavery, or the appearance of slavery, is one hardship, among others, which the sophos, as an individual, must endure or overcome through an ethical observation of virtue in spite of adverse circumstances. In such a context, slavery is in appearance only; it is simply, as the philosophers would say, an external "indifferent" (*adiaphoron*). The true wise man internalizes freedom and lives, insofar as is possible, as a truly free individual, even though he may be a slave by legal definition. In the individual-ethical context, slavery may relate to social status, but only to demonstrate that status is purely external and has nothing to do with the true nature of the individual, which is defined inwardly and apart from external circumstances.

Within the demagogue topos, however, the leader-as-slave element relates directly to status and social level. It is used to criticize both upward and downward social movement. In the first case, it derides a person's origin, occupation, education, or activity. The leader's social origin or position demonstrates that he is unworthy of leadership and should remain in his inferior position. In the second case, the leader-as-slave motif censures the downward social movement of one who has abandoned a high position in order to take a position among or even below those ruled. Any such movement is considered, by the critics, inappropriate and shameful. The dominant function of metaphorical slavery in the demagogue topos is thus to point to a change of status.

These two rhetorical models of leadership, the benevolent patriarch and the enslaved leader, and their accompanying moral-political ideologies provide the focus of this chapter. First, I wish to examine the benevolent patriarchal model of leadership and to explain its function as a support for patronal ideology. I will then delineate the opposing, populist model of leadership, reconstructing the demagogue topos and its different elements from a variety of sources. Finally, I will explore the function of these two models of leadership within a wider ideological debate of the Greco-Roman world.

THE LEADER AS BENEVOLENT PATRIARCH

In chapter 1, I discussed the patronal ideology of the Greco-Roman world by which the rigidly hierarchical structure of that society was maintained and by which persons lower on the social scale were encouraged to remain in their places and work within the system in order to improve their lot, if such improvement were allowed at all. As part of that discussion, I noted that persons of the upper class realized the value of benevolent treatment of their social inferiors. These upper-class patrons, as the term itself indicates, cast themselves in the role of the kindly father, who rules the other members of the societal household gently but from a firm position of social superiority. Indeed, the image of the upper-class ruler as the kind father had a long and important history in Greco-Roman rhetoric and ideology.[8]

In the *Nicomachean Ethics*, Aristotle proposes three main forms of *politeia*, or constitution: kingship, aristocracy, and timocracy (8.10.1). Each of these "good" polities is mirrored by a "bad" polity. Tyranny corresponds to kingship, oligarchy to aristocracy, and democracy to timocracy.[9] The difference between the good and the bad constitutions is simply that in the good, whoever has power rules in the interest of the entire population; in bad governments the rulers, whether tyrant, oligarch, or people (as in democracy), exercise their power purely for selfish gain (8.10.2–3).

Each constitution has an analogy in family relationships.[10] The king's relationship to the people is like that of a father to his sons (8.10.4). The leader in this model has the interests of the populace at heart and rules from a position of benevolent superiority, like Zeus. "This is why Homer styles Zeus 'father,' for the ideal of kingship is paternal government" (8.10.4). Aristocracy is reflected in the relationship of husband to wife. The husband rules but hands over to the wife certain matters that she is capable of ruling. If the husband took control of everything and turned it to his own use, he would be like the oligarchs. Timocracy is like the relationship between brothers. They are equal in a way, but they may be of different ages. Aristotle seems to suggest that the amount of power allotted to each brother depends upon factors that relate to the nature and position of each within the family structure. Then Aristotle places democracy into this scheme: "Democracy appears most fully in households without a master, for in them all the members are equal; but it also prevails where the ruler of the house is weak (*asthenēs*), and everyone is allowed to do what he likes" (*hekastō exousia*, 8.10.6).

Aristotle feels that the best constitution is kingship. He is willing to admit that, of the bad constitutions, democracy has the best chance of succeeding as long as the citizens are really equal and equally share all things in common (8.11.8). But Aristotle has little faith in democracy. For him, equality, the watchword of democracies, can only function among those truly equal. Because people of different classes are not equal, a polity based on equality is inappropriate. This allows Aristotle to opt for one of the two other polities, kingship or aristocracy. In either one, a benevolent patriarch, not brotherly equality, is the model of leadership.[11] The leader is modeled directly on the well-intentioned, kind, superior father.

It makes perfect sense, therefore, that Aristotle's *Politics* begins with a discussion of the family and government. Some persons, he realizes, claim that people are by nature equal and therefore have no right to enslave one another (*Politics* 1.2.3). But in his famous argument defending slavery, Aristotle insists that those who are by nature slaves ought naturally to have masters. "To rule and to be ruled are, therefore, not only necessary but also beneficial, and straight from birth some are marked to be ruled and others to rule" (1.2.8, my translation). This does not mean that Aristotle believes that leaders should be like masters ruling slaves.[12] Rather, the statesman is like the physician or pilot of a ship (7.2.8). Government is of two sorts: that carried on for the sake of the ruler (that of the master) and that carried on for the sake of the ruled (that of free men, 7.13.4).

Democracy fails because it is rule by the poor for the poor, instead of rule for the benefit of the entire population, including the rich.[13] Democracy may succeed if the best class of citizens have the best positions (4.4.4). Too often, demagogues arise who flatter the masses.[14] The many then are lords (*hoi polloi* are *kyrioi*, which for Aristotle is an oxymoron, 4.4.4) and conduct themselves as despots over the "best" citizens (4.4.5). The way to avoid such chaos, Aristotle believes, is for those who are by nature superior to rule benevolently but firmly.[15]

At the end of the first century c.e., Aristotle's three constitutions surface again in a speech by Dio Chrysostom.[16] Dio's construction differs somewhat from Aristotle's, which indicates that he is probably drawing from rhetorical traditions rather than directly from Aristotle. In the category Dio calls "mob rule," the degenerate parallel to democracy, he includes references to demagogues. As Dio states, "The next in order is a motley impulsive mob of all sorts and conditions of men (*poikilē* and *pantodapē*) who know absolutely nothing but are always kept in a state of confusion and anger by unscrupulous demagogues" (3.45).

For the most part in this oration, Dio contrasts the king with the tyrant, not the demagogue. But his presentation of the king as the benevolent father still holds as a counterpart for the servile and tricky populist. Dio indicates that the king, here referring specifically to Trajan, is more benevolent toward his subjects than a loving father.[17] The sign of a good king is whether he has the subject's best interest as his own interest (3.39).

Nature itself shows that the greater should govern and care for the lesser, Zeus providing the supreme model (3.50). God has ordered the superior to care for and rule the inferior, the strong over the weak (*beltios . . . bēttōn, dynamis . . . astheneia*, 3.62).

In his discourses on kingship, Dio usually emphasizes that the king, though naturally superior, must be kind. The tyrant is like a harsh master. The king, in contrast, will not want even his own slaves, much less his subjects, to call him "master" (1.22). When contrasting kingship with tyranny, therefore, Dio emphasizes the benevolent aspect of kingship. This does not mean, however, that Dio would allow the true king to humble himself before his subjects.[18] In *Discourse* 2, Alexander the Great discusses kingship with his father. Alexander is noble; there is nothing humble (*tapeinos*) about him (2.7). He prefers Homer over Hesiod: Hesiod is for manual laborers and others who "slave away" (*douleuein*), not for kings (2.9). Alexander argues that, although the leader should not be luxurious, neither should he appear humble or act like the common crowd (*hoi polloi*). That is why Homer has generals wear distinguishing, though not luxurious, dress: to show the superiority of the leader (2.49). In this scheme, the leader saves the people and protects the weak but not by lowering himself (2.69).

When Dio wishes to stress the natural superiority of those who lead, he contrasts the good leader with the demagogue who caters to the masses. In *Discourse* 38, Dio compares the cities Nicomedia and Nicea to two politicians who are struggling for leadership. They court the smaller towns for support in order to enhance their own positions. Like politicians, they serve everyone (*therapeuein*), "even those who are ever so far beneath them" (38.34). Dio thinks this is a bad situation, with the proper statuses of leadership wrongly reversed. The two superior cities should take back their proper statuses (*taxis*) and should behave toward the small ones gently and moderately but not like flattering demagogues. They should maintain their superiority.[19] Dio's preferred model of leadership, therefore, is the benevolent father, the gentle superior.

THE POPULIST MODEL OF LEADERSHIP

The idea that the ruler should be a benevolent patriarch, that is, that leadership should be from a secure position of superiority, is so dominant in ancient sources that one might well suppose it represented the only available ideology of leadership in the Greco-Roman world. As implied in the above analysis of Aristotle and Dio, however, another model of leadership seems to have developed in opposition to the benevolent patriarchal model. The populist model pictured leadership as enslavement to the many or leadership from below. The presentation of the leader as enslaved to those he leads recurs so regularly in ancient sources and contains so many recurring elements that it may be called a topos. In this topos, the following elements are most important: the leader accommodates the people, he lowers himself socially, and his motivation is gain.

Generally, the populist was said to be willing to change himself—that is, his speech style or life-style—to suit his audience or the needs of the political situation. This accommodation was expressed by several different terms: *polytropos, poikilos, polyeidēs, polymorphos, pantodapos,* and so forth.[20] The terms were morally ambiguous in that they may or may not have implied a negative ethical judgment. In many rhetorical contexts, for example, Odysseus, whom Homer called the polytropic man, came to represent the changeable, tricky politician.[21] Homer's use of the word could have been taken simply as a description of the many turns of Odysseus's wanderings. But Horace, when speaking of this Odyssean accommodation, uses the term *dolosus* (2.5.3), thus making the unfavorable connotations explicit.[22] Another Latin translation for polytropos, *levitas,* also reflects the Roman distaste for what was considered fickleness (e.g., Horace 2.7.29; 2.7.38). In much of the ancient world, therefore, *polytropos* was taken to refer to Odysseus's accommodating behavior in different situations, and such accommodation, at least according to more classical or conservative Greek and Roman thought, was felt to impugn Odysseus's character. Thus, Antisthenes felt the need to defend Odysseus's polytropic character, if we are to believe the scholiast on the first line of the *Odyssey.* Odysseus's manner of speech, Antisthenes says, was varied in order to address different kinds of hearers, but his character was not changeable or unscrupulous (scholia on *Odyssey* 1).

In spite of Antisthenes' defense, for many in the ancient world Odysseus represented the changeable, wily opportunist. For example, in Athenaeus's *Deipnosophistae,* Odysseus is introduced as an exemplary advocate of feasting, drinking, and pleasure (from *The Odyssey* 9.5). But then someone suggests that perhaps Odysseus "was only deferring to the exigencies of the moment, in order to appear to be in sympathy with the manners of the Phaecians" (*Deip.* 12.512–13). The mention of Odyssean accommodation leads to a list of similar quotations, all defending the practice. The polyp, someone says, is to be imitated, and one should change one's

thoughts and behavior to accord with one's environment. Some of Athenaeus's collected quotations, including the following line from Sophocles,
contain the same theme but from a philosophical, ethical point of view:
"Be minded, as the polyp changes its body to the colour of a rock, so to
turn thyself before a man whose thought is true."[23] From this section of
Athenaeus two observations can be made: first, the mention of Odysseus's
behavior introduces the subject of accommodation, thus demonstrating
the traditional link between Odysseus and the polyp or chameleon motif;
second, accommodation was sometimes defended as both necessary and
philosophically justifiable.

Odysseus's versatility was often tied to his role as the paradigmatic
populist. W. B. Stanford notes that Pindar viewed Odysseus's behavior as
"a consort of coaxing words, a deviser of guile, an insinuation of mis-
chievous calumnies, always attacking the illustrious and exalting the igno-
minious." Stanford concludes, "It was natural that a poet of [Pindar's]
tradition, training, and inclination, should prefer Ajax, the highborn
prince of Doric Aegina, to the versatile grandson of Autolycus."[24]

Euripides also endowed Odysseus with demagogic traits. In *Rhesus*,
Odysseus slips into Troy in a shameful disguise, thus showing himself to
be a beggar and slave. He is a tricky flatterer in beggar's clothes, he is
guileful (*dolios Odysseos*). In *Hecuba*, Odysseus is explicitly called a "demos
pleaser" (*dēmocharistēs*). He humbles himself (*tapeinos*) and acts basely. He
behaves like demagogues who cater to the many just to procure honors,
and who forsake their own friends in the process. Hecuba, the noblewoman, denounces demagogues because they are ungrateful and be-
tray their "friends," that is, their own class.[25] At the end of the play,
Polyxena dies like a free noblewoman. Her refusal to be a slave or behave
slavishly contrasts with Odysseus's trickery and his begging, servile behavior. Accommodation, then, was a famous Odyssean characteristic,
and Odysseus, precisely as the changeable opportunist, exemplified the
versatile politician, abasing himself in order to win over the masses.

Accommodation was defended by some, as the references in Athenaeus mentioned above show. Later, we shall see how Philo, in his treatise
On Joseph, castigates demagogues who enslave themselves to the masses for
the sake of political expediency; Philo, in the end, chooses the benevolent
patriarchal model of leadership to praise. Before rejecting the demagogic
model, however, he uses Joseph as an example of the politician who must
sometimes alter his behavior to suit circumstances.

Philo's point of departure for discussing demagogues is Joseph's coat of many colors. Joseph's variegated garment represents political life, itself variegated and changeable (*poikilon, polytropon*, 32; cf. *On Dreams* 1.219–225). The politician must be able to change behavior according to context, audience, or the need of the moment, like a ship's pilot or a physician, who suits behavior to the changing conditions or to the individual needs of different patients. Therefore, "the politician must needs be a man of many sides and many forms" (*polyeidēs, polymorphos* 34). For example, the leader may need to act differently when addressing the few rather than the many: he should strenuously and sternly oppose the few but deal with the many by persuasion and easy discussion. In all cases, however, the leader will act for the well-being or salvation (*sōtēria*, 33; cf. 73, 76) of the people, as the physician and pilot are concerned only with the well-being of their charges. The true politician cares only for the common good. Furthermore, the leader will be willing to endure dangers in order to benefit the people. Philo's text is somewhat ambiguous about whether or not the true leader will submit to common labors.[26] In any case, the leader willingly accepts difficult circumstances in order to save the people.

In *Questions on Genesis*, Philo again grants that the philosopher will alter his words according to the ability of his audience to hear. In the best of all possible worlds, he says one could tell all the truth to all the people (4.69), but in the real world discretion must be used. That is why Abraham, in Genesis 20, lied about Sarah his wife and said she was his sister. Abraham's dishonesty was pedagogical. "But the expression 'speak the truth about everything' is the injunction of an unphilosophical and unlearned man. . . . The wise man requires a versatile art [*polytropos*] from which he may profit in imitating those mockers who say one thing and do another in order to save whom they can."[27] In other words, straightforward behavior, though desirable, is not always practical; the philosopher or political leader (ideally they are one for Philo) must sometimes adopt versatility due to necessity.[28]

Maximus of Tyre echoes Philo's sentiments in his speech entitled "That the discourse of a Philosopher is adapted to every subject."[29] Maximus points to Proteus as a Homeric figure who is multiform and various (*polytropos, pantodapos* 1.1). Philosophers also should modulate their tone to fit sorrowful or happy circumstances (1.2). Again, the reason for a change in tone is the necessity of the circumstances: "The necessity of the drama changes the garb of the actors" (1.10).[30] Accommodation, therefore, was defended as a necessary evil by some philosophers. For the most part, however, it was an insult hurled at one's enemies, and especially at demagogues who changed their speech or lifestyle in order to gain influence with the many.[31] When a speaker wished to stress the need for flexibility, he admitted it as necessary, philosophical accommodation. On the other hand, when people wished to castigate the same behavior, they portrayed it as demagogic flattery.

Again, the writings of Maximus demonstrate that servile democratic leaders, as stock rhetorical figures many years after the political debates of classical Athens, were still connected with charges of flattery: "But also, of the constitutions, aristocracy is full of friendship, but democracy is stuffed with flattery. So aristocracy is superior to democracy. There was no Cleon in Lacedaemonia, nor any Hyperbolus, base flatterers of a licentious public [*dēmos*]."[32] Plutarch provides further evidence that demagogic accommodation was taken to be flattery. In the essay "How to tell a flatterer," Alcibiades is the example of the flattering, changing demagogue because he took on different lifestyles in different cities.[33]

In other words, there were two sides to the issue. Leaders who altered their behavior in order to relate to the masses saw their own actions as sincere accommodation based on necessity, while their enemies condemned the same behavior as base flattery. In fact, both points of view appear side by side in a play by Euripides, *The Suppliant Women*. A herald from Thebes criticizes Athenian democracy as mob rule. He prefers the Theban government, as it is less changeable:

> and there is no one
> To puff it up with words, for private gain [*kerdos idion*],
> Swaying it this way, that way. Such a man
> First flatters it with a wealth of favors; then
> He does it harm. . . .
>
> . . . .
> When a wretch, a nothing,
> Obtains respect and power from the people
> By talk, his betters sicken at the sight.
>
> (lines 412–415, 424–425)

Theseus, defending democracy, responds:

> Now [in a democracy]
> A man of means, if badly spoken of,
> Will have no better standing than the weak [*asthenēs*];
> And if the lesser [*hoi asthenesteroi*] is in the right, he wins
> Against the great. This is the call of freedom.[34]

Theseus defends democracy as the great equalizer and the road to justice and praises the democratic politicians as those who look out for the interests of the lower class. The critic, using typical antidemocratic rhetoric, scorns democracy as mob rule and flattery of the base.

A second element of the demagogue topos concerns the populist's social self-lowering. In fact, stepping down to the level of the lower class was the aspect of the demagogues' versatility that most bothered their critics. The problem was not simply that populists changed their speech or style of living but that they lowered themselves socially in order to identify themselves with the lower class.

I mentioned above that a Latin term used to translate *polytropos* was *levitas*. In the political turmoil of early imperial Rome, *levitas* was a slogan turned against *populares*, the populists and their leaders. In these political contexts, it meant both "instability" and "a tendency to flexibility." A politician respected the need for levitas when he spoke one way in the Senate and another way in the Forum or the circus. Yet *levitas* referred not only to manners of speaking but also to one's change of dress, action, or even place of abode.[35] One demonstrated levitas by forsaking one's proper place in society and attempting to assume a lower place in order to appeal to those at the lower end of the social scale.

Self-lowering was, therefore, a recognized political device in Greek and Latin texts. Dio Cassius explains why Marcus Marcellus and Sulpicius Rufus were chosen consuls in 51 B.C.E. instead of Cato: "One special reason was that they, even if they did not employ money or violence, yet showed great deference to all and were wont to appeal frequently to the people, whereas Cato was deferential to none of them. He never again became a candidate for the office, saying that it was the duty of the upright man not to shirk the leadership of the state if any wished to use his services in that way, nor yet to pursue it beyond the limits of propriety."[36] Marcus Marcellus and Sulpicius Rufus serve the people, win them over, and gain office. Cato, in the more aristocratic tradition—that of the benevolent patriarch—insists that the true noble will never abase himself in such a way.

Plutarch again offers a positive assessment of what might be considered by others sham pretense and flattery. He says that Galba, in his rise to power, conducted his interviews and meetings with his inferiors in a kind and democratic manner. He maintained a simplified lifestyle, refusing to use the furniture and luxuries sent to him from Rome. A pernicious advisor, however, argued that Galba's simplicity was just demagoguery (*dēmagōgia*) and "a refinement of delicacy which thought itself unworthy of great things." Persuaded by his advisor, Galba began to use the riches sent from Nero in order not to appear pretentiously humble, that is, in order not to look like a demagogue.[37]

As Galba's example shows, by merely adopting a manner of living that seemed lower, one might be accused of playing the demagogue. For example, Plutarch mentions the opinion that Gaius Gracchus was a self-serving crowd pleaser. Plutarch disputes the charge, claiming that Gaius was led by necessity to a life in politics (1.5). Gaius promulgated laws that favored the poor (5.1ff.), pushed the *politeia* from aristocracy toward democracy (5.3), and showed himself to be a "skillful demagogue" in his kind and considerate relations with the people (6.4).[38] Gaius even goes so far as to move into a "lower-class neighborhood." Plutarch explains the significance of Gaius's move: "On returning to Rome, in the first place Caius changed his residence from the Palatine hill to the region adjoining the forum, which he thought more democratic [*dēmotikōteron*], since most of the poor and lowly [*penēs, tapeinos*] had come to live there; in the next place, he promulgated the rest of his laws, intending to get the people's vote upon them" (*Gaius Gracchus* 12.1). Gaius also defends the interests of the poor when he opposes certain rich persons who had built grandstands where a spectacle was to take place so they could charge admission. Gaius had the seats torn down during the night, saying that the poor should be able to watch the show for free (12.3f).

Plutarch, realizing that these actions make Gaius look like an opportunistic, self-abasing demagogue, defends him by insisting that Gaius, unlike others of that time, acted purely in the interest of the state, though especially of the poor. But, he says, Gaius never got rich from his political activity. Thus Plutarch realizes that Agis, Cleomenes, and the Gracchi are populist leaders in that they lower themselves socially and are thus accused of catering to the masses. But Plutarch defends them by maintaining that they never acted in their own interests—especially financial interests.[39]

Cicero provides some examples of the levitas of the populares. In *Pro Sestio* 109ff., he criticizes L. Gellius Poplicola, whom he calls a "so-called populist." According to Cicero, Poplicola was of noble birth but squandered his wealth. He then affected philosophy, Cicero says with tongue in cheek, because he was already living in "philosophic" poverty. He was also a seditious rabble-rouser. Cicero sneers that Poplicola married a freedwoman—not driven by desire, but to appear a *plebicola*, a friend of the common people.[40] Elsewhere, Cicero ridicules a certain Rullus, who began affecting different behavior when he was elected tribune. At least, that is what Cicero would have us believe: "As soon as he was elected, he practiced putting on a different expression, a different tone of voice, and a different gait; his clothes were in rags, his person was terribly neglected, more hair about him now and more beard, so that eyes and aspect seemed to protest to the world the tribunician power and to threaten the republic" (*De Lege Agraria* 2.13). One easily discerns here a bit of upper-class fear of the power of the populist.

Cicero may have been nervous with good reason. Usually when leaders attempted to identify themselves with the lower strata of society, the upper class assumed it was threatened. Sallust makes an interesting comment when he tells of the popularity of Sulla, who was a nobleman but whose family had declined. Sulla ingratiated himself with the soldiers by being courteous toward them. "He talked in jest or earnest with the humblest [*humillumis*], was often with them at their work [*operibus*], on the march, and on guard duty, but in the meantime did not, like those who are actuated by depraved ambition, try to undermine the reputation of the consul or of any good man" (*The War with Jugurtha* 96.3). "Good" here means, of course, a nobleman. Sulla is the exception that proves what was thought to be a rule: self-lowering in order to identify oneself with the lower class meant disloyalty to the upper class.

Along with calling them slaves, the enemies of demagogues often derided them as manual laborers. Cleon was said to be a tanner, Hyperbolus a lamp maker or potter, Cleophon a lyre maker, Lysicles a cattle dealer. These traditional demagogues, however, were actually not manual workers, as historians have repeatedly pointed out.[41] They were portrayed as workers in servile occupations precisely because they alienated those of the upper class by identifying themselves with the lower class. For example, Cleon seems to have deliberately designed a harsh and vulgar speaking style to indicate that he was a man of the people, in opposition to the more conservative, traditional style of leadership.[42]

Some of the populists may have even cut off relations with higher-status people or avoided close relationships with people of their own class precisely because they wanted to win the loyalty of the lower class. According to Aristophanes, for example, Cleon was a slave usurping power or a manual laborer grasping above himself.[43] But there are several indications that Cleon, in reality, lowered himself socially in order to gain power. Plutarch notes the tradition that Cleon dismissed his friends when he entered politics: "And being rough and harsh to the better classes he in turn subjected himself to the multitude in order to win its favor . . . making the most unpretentious and unsound elements his associates against the best [*aristoi*]."[44] The scholiast of Aristophanes knows this tradition, as shown by the comment on line 7 of *The Knights:* "Observe that Cleon attracted the attention of the Athenians by slandering the rest of the magistrates."[45] By turning to the lower class for support, Cleon alienated the upper class, maybe intentionally.[46] At least this was the way tradition perceived it. This self-abasement was what made Cleon servile.

Cleon's offense, in the eyes of the upper class, was not in trying to move up the social scale, in which case he may have looked ridiculous but not threatening, but in moving down. He affected the lineage, rhetoric, and manner of the lower class and so was easily accused of being a lowly manual laborer, a slave and flatterer. Cleon was not the only populist leader to act and to be portrayed in this way. As Zvi Yavetz has shown, "*levitas popularis* remained important throughout the Julian-Claudian era."[47]

Whatever the real reason for the leader's accommodation to the lower strata of society, opponents could attack any populist by charging that he did what he did from selfish motives, which brings us to the third element of the demagogue topos: gain as the demagogue's motivation. As M. I. Finley states, "From Aristophanes to Aristotle, the attack on the demagogues always falls back on the one central question: in whose interest does the leader lead?"[48] For that very reason, of course, someone could defend any populist by asserting that he acted purely in the interests of the public. As shown above, Plutarch defended Gaius Gracchus from the charge of demagoguery by claiming that he had never acted for his own gain (*Agis and Cleomenes and the Gracchi Compared*, 1.4). Cicero, fighting a new, populist-inspired agrarian law, cries that the people ought to support these leaders such as himself (!) who are populares in reality and not just in speech (*non oratione popularis*). He says that the agrarian law is not, after all, in the best interests of the people but will rob them of their liberty (*De lege agraria* 2.15–17). Cicero claims that Rullus should take himself out of the running for political office if he is really proposing the law for the public good and not merely for his own personal gain (2.22). Cicero, of all people, is attempting to outpopularize the populists. One wonders how many people he actually fooled. Nevertheless, whatever Cicero's own motives, he employed the usual rhetorical criterion for judging demagogues, by asking whose interests they served.

Such, then, are the different elements of the demagogue topos: a populist leader is said to be a slave of the people, primarily of the lower class (*hoi
polloi*), although the leader may simply be said to be enslaved to everyone;
he is a chameleon, accommodating his speech and life to any occasion; he
changes himself in order to appeal, for the most part, to the lower segments of society; he is therefore a flatterer of the base, lower than the low.
In fact, self-lowering is the primary, though not the only, way he alters
himself. The populist's enemies insist that he is motivated purely by
selfish interests for his own private gain. The populist, however, can
defend himself by claiming to act for the salvation of the people or as their
protector.[49]

POSITIVE USES OF THE DEMAGOGUE TOPOS

For Dio Chrysostom, the demagogue topos functioned purely as pe-
jorative rhetoric turned against the self-lowering politician enslaved to the
masses. What did positive appropriations of the topos look like? Were
there populist leaders who adopted enslavement as an intentional self-
characterization of their activity? Did people talk about self-lowering in
positive depictions of leadership? A problem here is that the surviving
literature was almost exclusively written and transmitted by the upper
class. This historical fact is as obvious as it is difficult for many historians
to keep in mind. Few positive portrayals survive of populist leaders from
either the Greek or the Roman political scene. Cleon's portrait, for example, would surely be quite different had leather workers rather than upper-
class comics and highbrow professors written about him and recorded his
words. Yet there are a few indications that populist leaders were willing to
appropriate the demagogue topos for themselves.

Claudius Aelian, who taught rhetoric in Rome in the third century,
relays a story about King Antigonos (probably Antigonos Gonatas, 320–
239 B.C.E.).[50] According to Aelian, Antigonos was a popular and gentle
king (*dēmotikos*). Noticing that his son was behaving harshly and arrogantly toward his subjects, Antigonos said, "Do you not know, son, that
our kingship is but an honorable slavery (*endoxos douleia*)?" Aelian takes
Antigonos's statement as evidence of his mildness and *philanthropia*.[51]

Connected with this idea that the ruler is a slave was the rhetorical
commonplace that the king was like a shepherd. Plutarch, for example,
provides a Sophoclean fragment in which shepherds admit that they are
slaves to their sheep, as they must serve their needs: "Of these, indeed,

though masters, we are yet the slaves" (*Agis* 1). The quotation is Plutarch's starting point for his presentation of Agis, Cleomenes, and the Gracchi, all of whom, as we have seen, he portrays as populist leaders. His use of the Sophoclean quotation, at the very least, shows the traditional link between the enslaved leader and the populists. More important, Plutarch's version of Gaius Gracchus provides an example of someone who likely used populist rhetoric positively. As I mentioned above, Plutarch knew that Gaius was accused of being a demagogue (*Gaius Gracchus* 1.5). Though Plutarch nowhere states approvingly that Gaius enslaved himself to the masses, he clearly narrates how Gaius won over the lower class by his own calculated movement down the social scale. Plutarch feels Gaius is justified in his politics because he really had the interests of the poor at heart (12.3f.), but this does not keep Plutarch from calling him (approvingly?) a "skillful demagogue" because of his kind and considerate relations, especially with lower-class persons (6.4).

Cicero was nothing of a populist, but he quotes an enemy of his who, it seems, attempted to appropriate populist rhetoric for his own use. Cicero ridicules a speech by Lucius Crassus, who appears to be addressing jurists. Crassus says, "Do not allow us to be in slavery to anybody . . . except to your entire body (*vobis universis*), . . . whose servants we both can be and ought to be." Such self-abasement, even rhetorical, infuriates Cicero. Cicero speaks for himself, "We on the contrary, as we have a high and lofty spirit, exalted by the virtues, neither ought to be nor can be; but for your part by all means say that you can, inasmuch as that is the case, but do not say that you ought, inasmuch as no one owes any service save what it is dishonorable not to render" (*Paradoxa Stoicorum* 41). Though Cicero cannot bear the thought of using even a metaphor of self-enslavement for political purposes, it seems others were not as proud, or at any rate not as squeamish.

As argued above, Philo's presentation of Joseph reflects the rhetorical traditions of the enslaved populist. Philo is able to redeem some aspects of the topos, in particular the politician's accommodation to every circumstance. To that extent, he uses the topos as a positive model for necessary, though unfortunate, political behavior.[52] It even appears that Philo, at least for a moment, agrees that the public figure may be said to be a slave (§ 36).[53]

This positive appropriation of the populist model of leadership can be found also in Dio Chrysostom, even though, as we have already seen, he certainly preferred to cast himself in the benevolent patriarchal mold of leadership. Dio was not above playing the demagogue when the need arose. *Discourse* 43 seems to have been delivered before the Assembly in Prusa, Dio's native city. Dio has been accused of assisting an unpopular proconsul, of "torturing the demos," of helping the "tyrant" (the now-deposed proconsul?) take control of the popular government, of being a bad example of luxurious living, and so on (43.11).[54] Last on the list, however, is the accusation that Dio "bribed the masses" to make them forget what he formerly did (during the time of the "tyrant" proconsul?). It seems that Dio is being accused by certain persons in Prusa, probably political rivals who are members of the Council and therefore of his own class, of first acting against the interests of the common people and later bribing them so they would forget his treachery.[55] In other words, Dio was accused of betraying the lower class. Dio defends himself by emphasizing his deep concern and love for the people (43.1–2). His enemies, he says, are merely envious of his popularity with the masses and wish to be rid of him, he tells the common people, so he can no longer be around to protect the demos. Dio, therefore, presents himself as the one true protector of the people. He alone can use frankness (*parrēsia*) with them because he has shared their misfortunes and difficulties (43.7).

After reading *Discourse* 43, no one should be surprised to find Dio in *Discourse* 50 defending himself in the Council against charges that he has sided with the common people against the Council. Here, therefore, he is being accused of demagoguery. Some have even charged Dio with blocking the assembling of the Council (50.10).[56] Dio insists (to the Council, anyway) that he is a friend and kindly to all (50.3). He may have taken pity on the common group (*dēmotikoi*) and attempted to ease its burden, but that does not mean that he is more friendly with the demos than with the Council. Not even the worst demagogue in the most democratic city, such as Cleon or Hyperbolus in Athens, would give less honor to the Areopagus or the Council than to the demos. Dio, then, would certainly honor the Council more than he would the common people. Dio's subsequent praise of the Council is so extravagant that he must go to great lengths to defend himself against possible charges of flattering them. It certainly looks like flattery nonetheless. Dio's main argument, however, is that his protection of the demos does not necessarily mean he is a demagogue and should not be taken to indicate disloyalty to the Council.

Dio and Philo are examples of how speakers in the first century used the two different models of leadership, the demagogue as opposed to the benevolent patriarch. Even when the speaker preferred the benevolent patriarchal model of leadership, as did both Philo and Dio, he could still make use of certain elements of the demagogue topos—such as the claim that he was the true friend and protector of the people—in an attempt to win over the loyalty of the lower class. As one weapon in the rhetorical arsenal, therefore, the topos of the enslaved leader occurred in a variety of rhetorical contexts, from fifth-century B.C.E. Athens through the second century C.E. It can be discerned also in later texts, such as those of the Christian bishop Augustine (354–430 C.E.), the pagan patron Libanius (314–ca. 393 C.E.), and the seventh-century historian Theophylact Simocatta.[57] Sometimes the topos was used as a positive political metaphor. Indeed, two texts from the period under study speak quite approvingly of enslaved leaders: Nicolaus of Damascus's account of Cyrus and Antisthenes' "Odyssean" speech.

Scholars have argued that Nicolaus's Cyrus and Antisthenes' Odysseus represent individual-ethical heroes in the Cynic tradition.[58] Cyrus and Odysseus are examples of true wise men who are really free even though they may exhibit external marks of servility. They are free by virtue of their inward and ethical nobility, thereby exemplifying a thoroughly Cynic virtue. As I have just shown, however, the enslaved leader topos had a wide circulation in ancient rhetoric and was not at all the exclusive property of the Cynics. Furthermore, on the basis of the other traditions examined in this chapter, it is clear that Nicolaus's Cyrus and Antisthenes' Odysseus functioned not only as individualistic philosophical ideals but also as models for political leadership opposed to more conservative models favored by the elite.

In chapter 1, I reviewed the history of Cyrus as recounted by Nicolaus of Damascus. In comparison with Xenophon's account, Nicolaus's highlights some interesting aspects of Cyrus. Xenophon begins his *Cyropaedia* with a potshot at democracy, so one should expect to find nothing of the populist leader in Cyrus, the hero.[59] Xenophon does say that Cyrus endured labor and danger, but there is no hint of self-lowering in this labor. Indeed, Cyrus endures such adversities for the sake of praise, which is evidence of his nobility (1.2.1).[60] According to Xenophon, Cyrus was never a slave, not even, as in Herodotus, in appearance only.[61] Xenophon probably knew traditions that Cyrus was a servant or a cupbearer, but whereas in Nicolaus the head cupbearer is Cyrus's patron, supporter, and, eventually, adoptive father, in the *Cyropaedia* the head cupbearer, named Sacas, is a foolish, evil man, the servile receptionist and favorite of the king. By serving his own grandfather and uncle at meals, Cyrus playfully

mocks Sacas (1.3.8; 1.3.12). Cyrus's mimickry of the servant merely contrasts his own natural nobility with the natural slavishness of the cupbearer.

Cyrus is Xenophon's exemplar of the good leader as the firm, benevolent patriarch.[62] According to Xenophon, people willingly obey a leader
whom they believe will wisely look after their interests, as they obey good
physicians, ship pilots, and guides (1.6.21). But the leader looks after the
interests of the subjects from a secure position above; there is no attempt to
be equal to those below him. Cyrus again provides an explicit example in
the way he treats those whom he is training to be slaves: "He did not
encourage them to practice any of the exercises of freemen; neither did he
allow them to own weapons; but he took care that they should not suffer
any deprivation in food or drink on account of the exercises in which they
served the freemen" (8.1.43–44). Xenophon writes approvingly that
Cyrus treated the lower class like beasts of burden. "And so this class also
called him 'father,' just as the nobles did, for he provided for them well [so
that they might spend all their lives as slaves, without a protest]."[63]
Xenophon will allow not even a taint of lowly origins for his Cyrus: Cyrus
is the quintessential superior, but benevolent, leader.

When contrasted with Xenophon's account, Nicolaus's Cyrus looks
very much like the antitraditional, populist leader. In the first place,
Nicolaus makes no attempt to disguise what he takes to be Cyrus's servile
origins. In fact, he emphasizes Cyrus's rise from those origins. Cyrus is
not a supposed slave (contrary to the history of Herodotus); he is actually
the son of a poverty-stricken robber and a goatherd mother (66.3). He sells
himself into slavery and then rises through the ranks of the imperial
service to become the head cupbearer, though still a slave, of Astyages. In
spite of Cyrus's low birth and servile background, he is by nature noble
and high-minded (66.12).

Once Cyrus attains some power in Astyages' kingdom, he begins plot-
ting to seize the empire itself. Unlike Xenophon's Cyrus, the hero of
Nicolaus's account is not motivated by a love of honor—that ubiquitous
virtue of the Greek and Roman upper classes—but by a sense of injustice.
Although fate has ordained him to take over only Astyages' kingdom,
Cyrus is also concerned that the Medes have oppressed the Persians, who
are "no worse by nature" than the Medes (66.14). Cyrus gains a close ally
when, on a trip for Astyages, he meets and liberates a fellow Persian who
has been beaten and who appears to be a slave (66.13). He eventually

makes this Persian—Hoibaras, also of lowly origins—his right-hand man in the revolution and later in his kingdom. Early on, Hoibaras abets Cyrus's indignation against the Medes' oppression of the Persians. The Medes should be punished, Hoibaras says, for thinking themselves worthy to rule their betters. Hoibaras encourages Cyrus to appeal to other oppressed peoples, such as the Cadusioi, who "hate the Medes but love the Persians" (66.15). Together these two slaves plot a revolution against the Emperor Astyages.

Astyages plays the role of the arrogant noble. Once he finds out about Cyrus's treachery, he regrets treating "base men" (*kakoi*) well. He has been taken in by "useful speeches" (representing a traditional slam against demagogic dependence on rhetorical ploys). He then ridicules Cyrus's background as a "base goatherd" and as being by race a Mardan (66.30). Later, in a confrontation, Astyages derides the previous poverty of Cyrus and his father. He threatens Cyrus and his father with chains and says that if they do not surrender they will be punished as befits base men (66.33). Significantly, Cyrus does not deny his lowly origins. Rather, he rebukes Astyages' arrogance and answers that the gods have now chosen to help these "goatherds" (66.33). In the end, Cyrus is supported by the other peoples oppressed by the Medes and eventually wins the empire.

In Cynic thought, the slavery of a Cynic hero often functions as one difficulty in the education or *paideia* of the wise man. In Nicholaus's account, the hardships through which Cyrus passes do not function as moral education for him, at least not explicitly. His slavery is used as a means for upward mobility and as anti-aristocratic propaganda. Cyrus does not learn from his labors: rather, he uses them to his advantage and through them becomes the liberator of the Persians and other nations mistreated by the arrogant Medes. Cyrus's humble origins, voluntary slavery, and role as liberator present him as an antitraditional leader. These aspects of Nicolaus's Cyrus are especially noticeable when compared to Xenophon's portrait of Cyrus as the upper-class, benevolent patriarchal leader.[64]

Antisthenes, in fifth-century B.C.E. Athens, provides a portrait of Odysseus similar to this one of Cyrus. Antisthenes gives a speech to Ajax, who argues before the Greek warriors at Troy that he ought to be allotted the weapons of the fallen Achilles.[65] Ajax argues that Odysseus has no claim to such noble weapons because he is sneaky and servile. Odysseus is unwilling to fight in the open and to attack straightforwardly; instead, he disguises himself in rags, allows his own slaves to treat *him* like a slave, fights only with words and not with bold actions, and does it all merely for his own gain (*kerdainein*; "Ajax" 5).

In the second speech, Odysseus defends himself not by denying that he has endured humiliations and abasement but by stressing that his actions have benefited the entire army and have furthered its cause against the Trojans. Alone he has endured dangers in order to harm the enemy ("Odysseus" 1,2,9). Ajax, with his impregnable shield, fights only in daylight, on the walls where he can be seen by everyone. Odysseus claims not to care if his own struggling, though shameful, is seen by anyone. "But even if as a slave or a pauper and whipping-boy I was about to harm the enemy I would attempt it, even if no one saw. . . . I do not have weapons already arranged by which I challenge the enemy to battle, but by whatever manner someone wishes, whether against one or many, I am always prepared" ("Od." 9, my translation). He fights, he says, if necessary, in slavish rags, with ragged and makeshift weapons, and even during the night. But it is because of these "shameful, servile" actions that Ajax and the others can sleep securely ("Od." 10).

Odysseus says that because Ajax will fight only in the honored, traditional ways—openly, in daylight, surrounded by fellow soldiers, and with conventional weapons—he thinks he is better, nobler, and more virtuous than Odysseus ("Od." 6). But Odysseus, though not maintaining a secure position above others, is a more effective fighter. He is the scout who sneaks behind enemy lines; he is the captain who guides the ship securely while the others sleep, and in these ways he saves all the others, Ajax included ("Od." 8; for the "saving" motif, see also 5 and 10).

In Antisthenes' version, Ajax represents leadership as traditionally derived from nobility and high social position, and Ajax's speech expresses traditional antidemocratic views. Ajax resents having to submit to judgment by the other soldiers, claiming that the hearers (who become in the speech, for all practical purposes, a jury) are ignorant and have no right to render a decision in the case. The king, he says, is the only one competent to judge matters concerning virtue ("Ajax" 4). Probably like some viewers of Aristophanes' plays, Ajax considers it an outrage that inferiors sit on juries to judge their superiors.[66] Furthermore, Ajax resents being judged alongside Odysseus, whom he considers his inferior. Ajax says, "And if there were any similarity of manner between me and this man it would not matter to me if I lost my case. But as it is there is nothing more dissimilar than his [lifestyle] and mine ("Ajax" 5; my translation).

Ajax wants none of that unequal equality that, according to the more conservative view, plagues democracies.

In contrast with Odysseus's humility, Ajax emphasizes his own strength ("Ajax" 7). He bullies and threatens the jurors to influence the case in his favor ("Ajax" 8) and sneers that Odysseus is the antithesis of nobility. In the first place, he says, Odysseus only came with the army unwillingly (*akōn*, "Ajax" 9), which is itself slavish. In the second place, he voluntarily allows himself to be abused, thereby abasing himself as no nobleman would.

Odysseus's speech plays off these very accusations to demonstrate that he personifies a different kind of leader. There is no mention in Odysseus's speech of kings, and his expressions are not antidemocratic. Ajax insulted and threatened the army, who are the jurists. Odysseus refrains from insulting them. Rather, he says that Ajax knows nothing ("Odysseus" 3–4).[67] Odysseus excuses any prejudice against himself by suggesting that the others may have been unwillingly led astray in their opinions, but he rebukes Ajax for threatening and bullying as if he had not himself been saved by Odysseus's disgraces ("Odysseus" 5).

Odysseus admits that he lowers himself and takes on the form of a slave, a poor man, or anything else, no matter how shameful, but he does it for the sake of all the others. He fights by any manner whatsoever (*tropos*, "Odysseus" 9):[68] with slavish weapons, in rags, and submitting even to beatings by slaves ("Odysseus" 10). Such things, however, should not be despised but used to save others. Finally, Odysseus emphasizes that being strong does not make one manly. (The term *strong* [*ischyros*] functioned as an indicator of social level.)[69]

Ajax's and Odysseus's speeches, therefore, do not simply espouse two different lifestyles or philosophies; they represent two models of leadership. Moreover, these two models, though used by Cynics, also circulated widely outside the circles of cynic philosophy and rhetoric, as has been shown. Antisthenes may or may not have intended the two models to be taken politically.[70] Nevertheless, the speeches are examples of how they may have been used in political contexts by such populist politicians as Cleon, Crassus, Gaius Gracchus, or even by some anarchist Cynic of the first century. This possibility becomes more likely in light of the fact that, for others in Antisthenes' day, Odysseus represented the demagogue.[71] Odysseus's speech or something like it could have been used by any of the upstart populist politicians to counter aristocratic attacks.

CRITICS OF THE POPULIST MODEL OF LEADERSHIP

The demagogue topos outlined above is found not only in contexts that promote the populist model of leadership but also in the writings of those, such as Cicero and Dio Chrysostom, who criticized populist leaders and their democratic ideology. The particular way these two models of leadership battled one another in Greco-Roman rhetoric can be more fully illustrated by analyzing three authors—Aristophanes, Plato, and Philo—who castigate enslaved leaders in order to advocate their own choice of benevolent patriarchalism.

Aristophanes (d. 385 B.C.E.)

The demagogue topos can be traced back at least as far as Aristophanes. His fifth-century comedy *The Knights* satirizes the new populist leaders of Athens, in particular Cleon and his coterie. The play, produced in 424 B.C.E., features a struggle between Paphlagon (a common slave name intended to represent Cleon) and an upstart demagogue, who is called simply "the Sausage-seller." They vie for the attentions of a stupid, gaping-mouthed master called "Demos".[72] From the beginning the slavishness of the populist leaders is advertised. The first character on stage calls Paphlagon "that newly purchased low-life" (line 2), a slave of the master Demos. He is a "bought slave" (44) who caters to the master (*therapeuein;* 59). True to his servile nature, Paphlagon is not straightforward but "of many colors" or "changeable" (*poikilos;* 459, 686, 758; cf. *panourgotatos;* 45). In other words, he quickly changes his behavior to suit his master or to take advantage of any situation.

The servileness of these demagogues is evidenced by their trades and lowly origins. Paphlagon is a leather worker or tanner (44–47); a sausage seller later usurps his position as Demos's lover. Neither Paphlagon nor the sausage seller has any education: they are "agora-trained" (181), of low birth and "brutal voice" (218). In one humorous scene, Demosthenes, another slave of Demos, tries to get rid of Paphlagon by talking Sausage-seller into entering public life (178–233). Sausage-seller answers that he is "not worthy of great power." "O me, not worthy!" Demosthenes cries, "What's the matter now? You've got, I fear, some good upon your conscience. Are you of noble stock?"[73] Sausage-seller answers that he is from the basest of stock. That is all the more fortunate for a start in public life,

Demosthenes says. Sausage-seller counters that he has no more than an elementary education. Demosthenes assures him,

> The mischief is that you know ANYTHING.
> To be a Demos-leader is not now
> For lettered men, nor yet for honest men,
> But for the base and ignorant. Don't let slip
> The bright occasion which the gods provide you.
>
> (190–94)

The play here ridicules the Athenian demagogues as both ignorant and anti-intellectual. Like many of the self-made new men of Greco-Roman satire, they feel they've made their way just fine without the burden of formal education.[74] As Demosthenes congratulates Sausage-seller, "A nobody today, tomorrow everything! O mighty ruler of Imperial Athens!" (158–159).[75]

By winning the favor of Demos, Paphlagon or Sausage-seller would become the "Savior of the City" (149; 458; cf. 1017). Both contrive to become, not just lowly slaves, but the slave overseer of the entire demos, the steward (212; 948; 959). Their ambitions and activities lead to accusations that they are acting with a view only to their own greed and gain (802–835). But each can counter such accusations by showing that he has acted purely for the well-being of Demos; their only motive is their love for him (821; 789–800). Paphlagon defends himself even against the charge of stealing by saying that he did it only "for the good of the city" (1226). The scene then proceeds with a farcical competition of bribery and petty flattery. Sausage-seller finally wins by convicting Paphlagon of selfish gain and then by showering Demos with such simple gifts as shoes and a tunic. The implication, of course, is that the Athenian populist leaders have both enslaved themselves to the people of Athens and have bought off the people with petty bribes.

Aristophanes speaks elsewhere as well of the demagogue as enslaved to the masses. In *Wasps*, for instance, one character, Cleon-hater, tries to convince his father, Cleon-lover, that the current Athenian jury system is slavery for the people.[76] The father counters that, on the contrary, under the current, populist government, Cleon and the other demagogues are the slaves of the dicasts, the jurors (596–602). The system gives these old men a veritable lordship over their own rulers. It was this topsy-turvy situation of government, according to the view from above, anyway, that fueled Aristophanes' aristocratic wit and constituted the primary focus of his critique of the demagogues' leadership.[77]

Plato (ca. 429–347 B.C.E.)

Plato, though no friend of Aristophanes, used the same topos when depicting populist leaders in his aristocratic philosophy. Book 8 of *The Republic* criticizes democracies and tyrannies. According to Plato, democracies arise out of oligarchies when the perennial struggle between the upper class (the "haves" or the rich in Plato's terminology) and the lower class (the "have-nots" or the poor) comes to a crisis.[78] The lower class is inherently weak (*asthenesteros*, 569b); it therefore puts forth leaders who will advocate for its interests against the upper class. These populist leaders are eventually able to overthrow the oligarchy and establish democracy, which, according to Plato's view, is the rule of the many against the few rich. According to Plato, however, democracies carry within themselves the seeds of their own destruction in their excessive freedom and equality. Soon a strong leader arises who looks for all the world like a gentle populist ruler but who turns the democratic chaos to his own advantage and eventually ensconces himself in power as a vicious tyrant.

In this section of *The Republic*, Plato is not concerned solely with political constitutions. His depiction of the democratic man, for example (*dēmokratikos*, 558c–562a), serves as a moral paradigm of the soul which is not properly ruled by its own higher elements but which succumbs to the rule of its passions. Nevertheless, the section appropriates common themes about populist leaders and applies them to both democratic and tyrannic constitutions and politicians.[79] Tyrants as well as demagogues put themselves forward as populist leaders defending the interests of the lower class (see, for example, 565c).

According to Plato, the democratic constitution and populace lack consistency. In addition to having too much freedom and equality, the democratic city resembles a variegated garment (*poikilon*, 557e). Boys and women might find such a garment pleasing, but true men and philosophers scorn it. The democratic man, however, is "manifold" (*pantodapos*) and "displays the greatest diversity in personal qualities and life styles."[80] Part of what bothers Plato about this changeableness is that it bestows leadership status regardless of the social status or inherent nature of the person. "The democratic city cares nothing for the past behavior of the man who enters public life. He need only proclaim himself a friend of the people, and he will be honored." Plato then states his unforgettable aristo-cratic maxim: "In its diversity and disorder [democracy] proceeds to dis-pense a sort of equality to equal and unequal alike" (558c; trans. Sterling and Scott). Instead of providing true freedom, democracies only overturn proper social hierarchy. The people insist that its leaders be gentle and forebearing (562d). Rulers act like subjects and subjects like rulers. Chaos invades every home. Parents imitate and fear their children; citizens, aliens, and strangers are all equal; teachers fear and flatter their students. All of society imitates the democratic leadership. "The old respond by descending to the level of youth. Exuding charm and amiability, they mimic the young in turn so that they may not be looked upon as arbitrary or unpleasant" (563a–b, trans. Sterling and Scott). Slaves are no longer slaves but are just as free as their masters. Even horses and asses no longer give way to their superiors but rudely bump into whomever they meet in the street (563a–d). The democratic leaders take advantage of the class hostility and confusion: they rob from the rich and give to the poor, sidetracking most of the funds into their own pockets (565a).

In this excess of liberty, the tyrant enters political life claiming to be the protector of the people.[81] He begins by condescending to the masses and defending their interests (566a). He insists that he is no tyrant and tries to prove it by grinning at whomever he happens to meet in the street, work-ing for the public good, canceling debts, and distributing land.[82] He flatters the lowly and is gracious and gentle to everyone (566e). In the end, according to Plato, the tyrant destroys himself in the same way he de-stroyed the society. He himself becomes a slave to those whom he must flatter in order to stay in power (579e). Before he destroys himself he will have already turned the proper structure of society upside down: "People who have fled the smoke of being enslaved by slavery to freemen, as the saying goes, are now consumed by the fire of conquest by their own slaves. In exchange for excessive and unmanageable liberty they now wear the garments of their own slaves, as it were, in doubly cruel and bitter servitude."[83] Of course, from the slave's point of view such a result might not look bad.

In *The Republic*, the depiction of the leader as enslaved to those who are being led is limited to Plato's criticism of populist leaders, either the demagogue or the tyrant who gains power as a demagogue. The topos occurs in his discussion of democracy, and, as comments above empha-sized, the problem of democracy for Plato lies in its disruption of the social scale and confusion of statuses (see 562d; 563a–b; 569c). Plato's criticism of the demagogic model of leadership makes perfect sense in light of his praise of the true king as the proper model for leadership.

According to Plato, both the populace that rules the democratic city and its leaders are weak (*asthenesteros*, 569b). In a properly governed city, however, the philosopher is the ruler and governs from a position of strength (*ischyros*; 376c). The good ruler might do something that *appears* wrong, such as lying, but only for the good of the city (389b). Behavior that is wrong for the people may be right for the leader, but only the leader has this freedom and only for the sake of the public interest (389c).

Plato approves of rule by free men. The fact that they are free excludes any changeableness in their own lives and in the constitution of the city. They will do nothing humiliating, nor will they ever indulge in imitation or pretense (395c–e). They certainly will not alter their behavior to suit the lower class or anyone lower in status than they (boys, women, slaves). Furthermore, they will do nothing that would appear unseemly for a free gentleman, so manual labor is out of the question.[84]

Plato's two styles of leadership are paralleled by two styles of speaking. One style has little variation and is simple and straightforward. It is the better of the two styles, though it may not please boys or mobs. The more popular style uses many variations and is base and pleasing to the masses (397a–c). In the city where the first style prevails, people stick to their social places. Cobblers stick to cobbling and do not try to become ship captains (397e). The moral of the story is that in a well-governed city the rulers will stick to ruling and the subjects will stick to obeying.

There is much in *The Republic* about people staying with their own trades and not "leaving their own businesses and taking on the others'."[85] Plato's real worry, however, is with people changing not jobs but classes. "So any person from one class who meddles in another does his city the greatest wrong" (434b; see also 435b). People from the artisan class should not attempt to be leaders.[86] Conversely, those who are by nature leaders should not attempt to ingratiate themselves with the lower orders. Some politicians debase themselves, according to Plato, by flattering and fawning on the people; they serve (*therapeuein*) the crowds and so are praised by the many (426c–d). But the true rulers, the strong, while ruling benevolently, will never debase themselves in this manner.[87] Plato's approved model for leadership is Ajax, the brave, strong man who maintains his nobility and superiority and justly, then, receives the lion's share of the rewards (468d).[88] For Plato, the problem of democracies and their populist leaders is that the roles of ruler and ruled are precariously reversed.

The topos of the ruler enslaved to the masses is Plato's way of expressing his frustration.[89]

Philo (ca. 30 B.C.E.–45 C.E.)

The Genesis account of Joseph's role in the Egyptian government makes him a useful exemplar for Philo's views on politics and politicians in his treatise *On Joseph*.[90] Joseph, as Potiphar's slave steward (*oikonomos*), had been prepared for politics by his training in household management (*tois kat' oikonomian*, 38). The ruler as household manager was a commonplace in Greco-Roman rhetoric.[91] As shown above, Philo speaks of demagogues in much of the treatise. Eventually, however, he insists that Joseph is not a demagogue but a positive example of the true politician in the benevolent patriarchal mold.[92]

Up to a point, Philo uses elements of the demagogue topos, especially the chameleon motif, to provide a positive example of the way political leaders must behave due to political realities. Suddenly, however, Philo changes his tone and begins to ridicule leaders who cater to the crowd: "However, it is well said that such a person is sold. For the demagogue or popular orator goes up upon the platform, just like slaves who are sold in the slave market. And he becomes a slave instead of a free man for the sake of honors he thinks he will receive. He has been captured by a thousand masters" (35, my translation). The popular orator, by catering to the masses, humbles himself to the point of slavery. But instead of one master, he serves thousands. And demagogues change masters frequently, because they and the crowd are equally fickle. The last accusation can now be seen to be a piece of antidemocratic rhetoric bemoaning the same kind of political chaos that bothered Plato so much.[93] In the last analysis, the demagogue is distinguished from the valid leader by this self-lowering and by the fact (or accusation) that the demagogue changes for the sake of honors or empty glory, whereas any self-adjustment by the true politician is done for the common good.

Philo is not entirely comfortable with the idea that a leader ought to submit to the vicissitudes of political necessity. Later in this treatise, his discomfort surfaces when he is forced to admit that even the true politician knows that the demos holds despotic authority. "Yet he will not confess himself a slave, but a freeman and [he will act only] to please his own soul."[94] The true leader will not be a demagogue; he will be a good guardian (*agathos epitropos*) or a benevolent father (*patēr eunous*) and will use no despicable pretense. Philo's model leader, in the end, will refuse the role of slave, insisting that he is nobly born.[95]

Philo is well aware that the fickle populace may chafe under the rule of his virtuous leader. The strict, parental governor is rarely accepted by the spoiled, childish populace, which cries, "Obey me, wait on me and do all that gives me pleasure. The stern, strict, uncompromising friend of truth, stiff and solemn and inflexible in all his dealings, who clings to the beneficial only and pays no court to his audience, is to me intolerable" (65). But the true leader will pay no attention to such whinings. He will stand aloof from any unfree service or slavelike flattery (*therapeuein aneleutherō kai sphodra douloprepei kolakeia*, 79). That is just the kind of nobility, according to Philo, that the common herd cannot abide. For Philo, the mob may be master, but the true politician will be no slave. He will be the concerned physician or the benevolent father, strict and unbending but acting for the good of the entire city, not just for the poor.[96]

As we have seen, Philo is able to appropriate some elements of the demagogue topos as part of his positive portrayal of a good leader. In the end, however, he opts for a benevolent patriarchal model of leadership. That is why Philo insists that Joseph's slavery is only apparent. He is really a man of free and noble birth (*eleutheros, eugenēs*, 106), as the benevolent patriarchal leader usually is. Even after the section on the necessity for flexibility in the politician, Philo maintains that Joseph's way of acting does not change with the times (263). Therefore, although Philo knows the tradition that the leader, in a democratic situation, is slave to the masses, his true leader will never admit that he is enslaved, will maintain complete inner freedom, and will work for the benefit of all social levels of the society, not just for the rich or the poor. The treatise is Platonic with regard to political views and Stoic with regard to the ethics of slavery and freedom and the outer and inner person. It is also antidemocratic.

CONCLUSION

In many different rhetorical contexts, the topos of the enslaved leader was used in ideological debates about proper forms of leadership. Speakers desiring to maintain or reinforce the prevailing structures of authority—and it is from such persons that most of our surviving literature comes—insisted that proper leaders should be like kind fathers. Leaders should treat their social inferiors well and tend to their needs but at the same time maintain traditional positions of social superiority, which meant that leaders had to manifest the traditional badges of high social status: sufficient income, leisure, avoidance of manual labor, education, and appropriate dress and demeanor. Upper-class fear of social instability was regularly hypostatized in the character of the unstable democratic man or populist leader, who disrupted the structure of society either by attempting to move up from the lower class into a position of leadership or by moving down from a high-status position and betraying his own class's interest in identifying with the lower class. The fickleness of democratic polity was personified in the chameleon-like behavior of the demagogue. It was this threat of instability, perceived from the rumblings of the populace and projected onto the person of the populist, that most antagonized conservative authors.

The topos of the enslaved leader could be used positively even by someone of the upper class, who could actually gain power by seeming to give it up in a move down the social scale. Cleon, for example, gives up some of the traditional symbols of status and power but does so in order to appeal to the power that could be derived from the support of the lower class. Gaius Gracchus, to hypothesize further, extricates himself from the traditional patronal structure of upper-class society, in which he can depend on his friends for support, in order to become the patron of the people, a broader, if perhaps more precarious, power base.

In each of these cases, the function of the topos of the enslaved leader is to question the traditional link between leadership and the normal badges of high status. Upper-class persons may bemoan the breakdown of this link, whereas lower-class persons, or their populist patrons, may attempt to exacerbate it. Among such upper-class authors as Aristophanes, Plato, and Philo, the image of the self-lowering populist unambiguously condemns the populist. Such behavior is considered catering to the masses and, like any attempt to modify one's behavior to suit those lower on the social scale, it is castigated. Not surprisingly, not many coherent examples exist of the positive appropriation of the topos; neither do we have actual speeches of populist politicians. It is not difficult to imagine, however, a positive use of the topos. The populist would argue that the good of the entire community, its salvation, required that someone come forward to protect the interests of the common people. That person might well be someone from the upper class, but he must be willing to give up his immediate interests in order to advance the interests of the majority of the population, the masses. The populist presents himself as just such a person, willing to change his own lifestyle for the good of the people, just as a polyp changes its color to save itself. The populist would say, as had Cicero's enemy, Crassus, "I will be no one's slave except yours, whose servant I ought to be."

It is clear, at any rate, that in the first century these two dominant models for political leadership opposed one another: the populist model of leadership as self-enslavement to the people and the benevolent patriarchal model of leadership as the kind but superior father-king. Both models were appropriated positively by public speakers, although sources have tended to preserve only the latter model due to the upper-class bias of the surviving ancient literature itself. The populist model, however, represented a counterpart to more conservative Greco-Roman models of leadership from above. The antitraditional voices, using a positive appropriation of the demagogue topos, suggested a model of leadership from below, leadership by the person who had identified himself with the lower class.

4

SLAVE

OF

ALL

IN

1 CORINTHIANS 9

In 1 Corinthians 9, Paul not only depicts himself as a slave of Christ; he also says he has made himself a slave of all. It is a mistake to read the two different kinds of slavery as evoking the same evaluative response from Paul's contemporary readers. Given the context of Paul's rhetoric, that is, a context in Greco-Roman, urban, early Christianity, Paul's slavery to Christ in 1 Cor. 9:16–18 does not represent self-abasement. Rather, it establishes Paul's authoritative role, although that authority must be heard as a different kind of authority from that of the wise man, or sophos, in moral philosophy of Paul's society. According to moral philosophical discourse, the sophos is the only good leader—the only true king—because he is truly a free man. He completely controls his will and never acts against it. He rules by virtue of his natural superiority, which he maintains in order to serve as a model for those below him. Moral philosophy theoretically allowed that any person could be such a wise man, but actually the concept was firmly tied to the model of leadership I have called benevolent patriarchalism, which functioned ideologically to maintain the traditional status hierarchy of Greco-Roman society. Paul's self-portrayal as Christ's managerial slave, who must preach the gospel by compulsion and not from free will, is a clear rejection of the moral philo-

117

sophical discourse that spoke of the leader as the benevolent, patriarchal wise man. Yet Paul's slavery to Christ does not yet function to represent self-lowering on Paul's part. Indeed, it establishes beyond dispute (or at least it hopes to preclude dispute) that Paul is the authoritative, high-status representative of Christ.

Immediately after establishing his authority, however, Paul abruptly turns from the image of slavery to Christ and introduces an image of low social status by insisting that he is a slave not only of Christ but of all (9:19–23). At first sight, these verses are problematic and appear foreign to Greco-Roman concepts of leadership. As I have shown, however, the image of the leader as enslaved to those whom he leads is a known rhetorical topos. Recognizing that Paul is here employing a topos solves several exegetical problems of these verses that have occupied the attention of many commentators: for instance, Paul's admission of chameleon behavior, changing himself to suit his audience; his use of *gain* (*kerdainein*) to refer to his practice of winning converts; and his admission that he has become weak to win the weak.[1]

Analysis of these verses reveals that these different exegetical problems are of a piece; they are not to be addressed, as has sometimes been done, as disparate issues. Furthermore, this analysis shows the necessary rhetorical connections between the various motifs of 9:19–23 and 9:1–18, where Paul is preoccupied with status and forms of financial support; in the process, the analysis offers a coherent explanation of the several issues as they all relate to rhetoric, power, and social status. Indeed, the special importance of status for the interpretation of 1 Cor. 9:19–23 becomes obvious in an examination of Paul's "weakness" toward those who are weak.

PAUL'S SUBMISSION TO THE "WEAK"

Paul first says that he enslaves himself to all in order to gain more. Yet when he then lists the different categories of persons he "becomes," the categories for the most part turn out to be Jews and Gentiles. He becomes a Jew to win Jews; he becomes someone "under the law" in order to win those "under the law"—presumably Jews again, or perhaps now more specifically law-abiding Jews. He then says that he becomes "without the law," which refers to Gentiles. The next category, however, does not seem to fit this Jew-Gentile schema: He becomes weak in order to win the weak. By mentioning the weak last, Paul emphasizes that category and makes his submission to the weak the rhetorical goal of the list. But it is unclear who exactly Paul means by the weak and why he privileges that group.

Scholars have offered various suggestions. Most identify the weak of 1 Corinthians 9 as those who are weak in conscience, or whose faith, in some way, is weak.[2] That is, many scholars have tended to center on theological concepts that are unrelated to any particular social conflict. Gerd Theissen, on the other hand, moves the discussion to another plane. He argues that the dispute engaged in by the strong and weak, though fundamentally the-ological, was also a conflict that can be analyzed sociologically, a conflict between groups of different social—and specifically class—positions.[3] In the first place, Theissen has shown that the terms *weak* (*asthenēs*) and *strong* (*dynatos* and *ischyros*) have definite social implications and often correspond to the lower and higher classes, respectively. In the second place, the particular conflict between the weak and the strong over eating meat can be understood as a conflict between lower- and higher-status Christians. Urban dwellers of low social status had few opportunities to eat meat, and if they did it was usually in a public, cultic setting. Only members of the higher strata had many chances to eat meat outside the context of a pagan cult. Whereas low-status Christians likely received few invitations to din-ners hosted by important Corinthian citizens, higher-status Christians (such as the city-treasurer Erastus?) may have felt it absolutely necessary to give and receive dinner invitations.[4] To avoid meat in such situations meant committing a social faux pas, which could scarcely be afforded by a Chris-tian concerned with convention and social advancement. Furthermore, the strong seem to defend their freedom by appeal to general philosophical arguments. "We all have knowledge!" (1 Cor. 8:1); "An idol is nothing! There is but one God!" (8:4); "All things are permitted!" Those more likely to have access to such arguments, and the education these arguments imply, are the wealthier members of the Christian groups. One does not usually expect Cynic or Stoic phrases from the uneducated masses.[5]

Theissen's arguments substantially advance our understanding of Paul's vocabulary in 1 Corinthians 8–10. His recognition that strong and weak correspond to categories of social status at Corinth helps solve sever-al exegetical problems of 1 Corinthians 9. As noted above, Paul gives the weak the privileged last position in his list of those whom he seeks to gain by changing his own behavior. Moreover, even though up to this point his list has mentioned a pair of groups to which he accommodates himself, Paul fails to mention strong as something he becomes, thus highlighting even further his concentration on the weak. Paul's striking emphasis on his submission to the weak makes good sense when the overall strategy of 1 Corinthians 9 is understood.

In 9:12, Paul says that he has not made use of his right to financial support but has instead "endured everything" in order not to cause any "hindrance" to the gospel. This is normally taken to mean that Paul wished to avoid appearing as a charlatan who only preached the gospel for his own personal gain.[6] By refusing to accept the Corinthians' money, Paul hoped to avoid offending anyone. This may likely be one of the reasons Paul sometimes refused financial support. In 2 Cor. 11:12, for example, Paul offers his self-support as evidence that he is not like others who preach the gospel (for their own gain, by implication). Yet 2 Corinthians also reveals that at least some people at Corinth were offended not by a preacher accepting money but by Paul's refusal of their money (11:7–11; 12:13–15). If Paul took on manual labor in order not to offend those people, he blundered badly; they were offended by the very actions Paul undertook to avoid causing offense. Obviously, for many people at Corinth, a leader's manual labor, and not church support of that leader, was an obstacle.

If, however, *strong* and *weak* include meanings of social status, Paul's statement in 9:12 makes perfect sense in its context. In order to see exactly what Paul means by "hindering the gospel" in 9:12, we must recognize that the construction of 9:12 is parallel to 8:8–9. In 8:8, Paul admits the indifference of eating meat offered to idols and so agrees with the fundamental correctness of the position taken by the strong: "Food will not commend us to God. If we abstain we are at no disadvantage; if we eat we have no advantage." Paul thereby establishes the right of the strong to eat. But then comes Paul's qualifier: "See that this very 'right' [*exousia*] of yours does not become a stumbling block to the weak." The same pattern occurs in 9:12. First, Paul claims a share in "this *exousia* of yours": "If others share in this 'right' of yours, shouldn't we even more so?" The presence of "yours" is important. Up to this point in chapter 9, Paul has been speaking of his own exousia (9:4–6). In 9:18, he again mentions his exousia. In 9:12, however, Paul speaks of sharing in *their* exousia, that is, sharing in the right and authority (*exousia* meant both at the same time) of the strong at Corinth.[7] He connects his right with theirs. He has the same exousia as do the other apostles and as do the strong themselves.

Yet Paul has been willing to do what the strong have heretofore resisted: he has not made use of his right but has "endured everything." His strategy for giving up this right has been to avoid placing a hindrance before the gospel of Christ. Paul's word for "hindrance" in 9:12 is *egkopē*. The corresponding term in 8:9 is *proskomma*. But as Gerhard Dautzenberg insists, *egkopē* (according to him the key to the entire passage) must be read on analogy with similar terms in this context: "to cause to stumble" (*skandalizein;* 8:13), "to be an 'unstumbling' block" (*aproskopon einai;* 10:32), and "stumbling block" (*proskomma;* 8:9).[8] Furthermore, the function of *egkopē* in 9:12 is precisely that of *proskomma* in 8:9. In 9:12, the hindrance is to the "gospel of Christ," whereas in 8:9 it is to the weak, but, as 8:12 shows, the result of the two hindrances is nevertheless the same: when the strong put up a stumbling block before the weak, they are actually sinning against Christ himself.[9] Likewise, Paul fears that accepting financial support and thereby being able to avoid manual labor would result in a hindrance to the gospel itself. In Paul's scheme of things, to hinder the weak is to hinder the gospel. Therefore, the phrase "to be a stumbling block [or hindrance] to the weak" of 8:9 finds its parallel in 9:12: "in order that we might not provide any hindrance to the gospel of Christ." What Paul means here by a "hindrance to the gospel" is the possibility that his acceptance of financial support would be a stumbling block to someone. That someone is the weak one.

I have noted that most interpreters believe 9:12 expresses Paul's wish to avoid offending people in general. Paul refused money, it is said, in order to avoid any appearance of wrongdoing. Such an interpretation does not adequately consider the overall rhetorical thrust of chapter 9, which, like most of the surrounding material, is directed primarily at the strong.[10] Paul begins with terms of high status: "Am I not a free man [*eleutheros*]" (9:1). Three times he repeats the rhetorical question that is meant to establish his own status: "Do we not have authority?" (9:4–6). Günther Bornkamm, to name only one example, completely misunderstands the thrust of Paul's language when he says that Paul "calls on *each* [i.e., the strong and the weak] to renounce for the sake of the other the use of his own *exousia*."[11] On the contrary, Paul calls not the weak but the strong to do this. The term *exousia* refers to a social prerogative and is directly related to freedom, high status, and power.[12] Low-status persons, the weak, by definition have no exousia to surrender. Telling the weak to give up exousia is like telling a slave to give up his or her *eleutheria,* "freedom." Paul's pointed surrender of his eleutheria and exousia (as one of the strong) is therefore not intended to serve as a general call to action but is directed precisely at those who have these things and resist giving them up, that is, those of higher status.

That this is the goal of Paul's rhetoric is borne out by a comparison with similar texts. In 1 Corinthians 4, Paul addresses certain persons at Corinth who are "filled," "rich," and who "reign like kings" (4:8).[13] In contrast to these people, Paul says that he and his co-workers are of low status: they are foolish instead of wise, weak instead of strong, dishonored instead of famous. Paul juxtaposes these different pairs of terms in an obvious play on status positions. It is no accident that the next sentence mentions very real indicators of Paul's low status: hunger, thirst, nakedness, abuse, homelessness, and manual labor. Yet after contrasting certain Corinthians' high positions with his own lowly one, Paul then lays claim to a self-description that establishes his role as authoritative: he is not a mere pedagogue (implying that some others are), but their "father" (4:15). This constitutes a blatant claim to authority and status not just equal to those at Corinth who are kings but actually above them. After setting himself up as their father, Paul tells them to imitate him (4:16). Note, however, that the aspect in which the kings are to imitate him is in his lowliness. In this section, therefore, Paul addresses "certain ones" who are "puffed up" (4:18). To them Paul makes a claim to authority and then offers his acceptance of low status as that which they are to imitate. In response to their pride in their speaking ability ("the speech of those who are puffed up"), a high-status indicator, Paul offers the power of God (4:20).

In 1 Corinthians 9, Paul manifests the same rhetorical agenda. He does not advocate self-lowering as a general ethical value; he has a specific goal of persuasion with a specific audience in mind. In 1 Corinthians 4, Paul contrasts the apostles' weakness with the strength of "certain" people at Corinth. His assertion of his authority and his call to imitation are directed at those "certain ones" who judge their own positions by normal criteria of social status. Likewise, in 1 Corinthians 9, Paul first establishes his authoritative position (9:1–18) and then speaks of his self-abasement (9:19). Within his argument contained in chapters 8–10, Paul also offers his own behavior as an example (10:32–11:1). Indeed, the first-person voice of 8:13, which introduces chapter 9, already implies that Paul is again about to offer himself as a model. The example in 8:13 is his willingness to forgo meat; in chapter 9 it is his willingness to forgo financial support. At this point, however, what is important is that the pattern of Paul's rhetoric in 1 Cor. 8:13–11:1 parallels that of 4:8–24: Paul balances a claim to high status with an admission of self-abasement and then directs his high-status readers to follow his example. It is clear why Paul does not include the strong in his list of 9:19–23: he is directing this instruction primarily to *them*. In 1

Corinthians 9, as in 4:8–24, Paul targets the ones on top, the wise, rich, strong, and free.

Romans 15 contains another parallel to 1 Corinthians 9. Here also Paul links himself firmly with the strong: "Now, we, the strong, ought to bear the weaknesses of those who are not strong, and not please [*areskein*] ourselves" (15:1). The Greek term *areskein* occurs in popular usage, such as epigraphs, to mean "to render service."[14] It therefore has status implications. In fact, the related word *areskoi*, when used by such upper-class authors as Aristotle, is a term of shame, referring to servile or fawning people.[15] In the ancient world, one rendered service only to those higher up the social scale. As chapter 1 showed, one element of patronal ideology was the assumption that freedom and high status meant acting in one's own interest. To act for the interests of another was servile and belied one's status as a free man (*eleutheros*). Therefore, when Paul calls upon the strong to act in the interest of the weak, to render service to them, his demand challenges the normal social structure and its expectations about the proper behavior for persons of different social ranks.[16]

Paul's main goal in 1 Corinthians 9 is to persuade the strong to modify their behavior to avoid offending the weak. Seen in this light, the overall issue of the chapter is one of status. Within the context of Greco-Roman society, acting in the interest of another or giving in to another constituted an admission of lower status, indeed, servility. It is quite appropriate, therefore, for Paul to use his own means of financial support as an example to those unwilling to lower themselves in status for the sake of others in the church.

That Paul uses his manual labor as an example in chapter 9 of his social self-lowering indicates clearly that he views working with his hands as degrading and humbling.[17] This important point has been made recently by both Ronald Hock and Abraham Malherbe. Hock notes that Paul's trade would have caused him to appear weak and slavish. Because of his manual labor, Paul knew the trials of low status, "of being bent over a workbench like a slave and of working side by side with slaves; of thereby being perceived by others and by himself as slavish and humiliated; of suffering the artisan's lack of status and so being reviled and abused."[18] Malherbe also argues that "Paul's decision to engage in manual labor was a sacrifice, for he did not belong to the working class."[19] Paul's traditional Greco-Roman view of labor originated, then, not in the lower class but in the upper class.

Hock and Malherbe imply that the negative view of manual labor prevailed throughout the different strata of Greco-Roman society. I have argued that members of the lower class, for the most part, did not share the antibanausic attitudes of the upper class and the intelligentsia. The implication that manual labor was despised in general within Greco-Roman society is not sufficiently class-sensitive.

The point of 1 Corinthians 9 is that Paul takes on manual labor *because* of (not in spite of) his view that it is demeaning; he takes it on in order to gain the weak. If *weak* here is understood in its social sense, Paul's argument throughout chapter 9 is coherent. He lowers himself in order to gain those who are themselves of lower status.[20]

Paul gives up his right to financial support in order to present no hindrance to the gospel. But as we have seen, those who shared upper-class attitudes toward manual labor would have taken offense not at Paul's acceptance of money but at his self-support by means of a servile trade. They were likely those who wanted Paul to accept their financial support, especially if doing so allowed him to cease the practice of his craft, which to them was an embarrassment. Therefore, when Paul takes up manual labor in order not to offend someone, he must have in mind those people who do not find his manual labor offensive: the manual laborers themselves. Had Paul maintained his higher-status position as a nonlaboring free man, he might have lost the opportunity to gain the weak. By rejecting that form of life and becoming a manual laborer, Paul appeals to the weak—the lower class. He removes a possible hindrance to the spread of the gospel. For those who have no prejudices against manual labor—the laborers themselves—Paul's self-lowering is an invitation to Christianity. To those who despise manual labor, Paul offers his own self-lowering as an example for them to follow.

SELF-LOWERING WITHIN THE DEMAGOGUE TOPOS

Within the demagogue topos, as outlined above, self-lowering functions to express concerns about status reversal or status confusion. The leader challenges the assumptions about the givenness of prevailing status indicators and may well be castigated for causing status chaos by not remaining in his traditional social position. Like Antisthenes' Odysseus, the self-lowering leader says that normal status indicators are indifferent if not downright harmful and that the salvation of the community may necessitate social self-lowering on the part of the leader. The leader takes on a humble role in order to save or elevate those whom he leads. In these contexts, self-enslavement symbolizes the social self-lowering of the leader in his attempt to win over the lower class.

This is also precisely the function of Paul's self-enslavement to all and especially, in 1 Corinthians 9, to the weak. Paul gives up his high status as an eleutheros, a free man, and enslaves himself to all. There is, incidentally, little distance between Paul's *all* (*pas*) and the *many* (*hoi polloi*) who are the masters of demagogues and populists. Like the populists, Paul changes his behavior to suit his audience, indeed, to win it over; also like the populists, he does it in order to gain (9:19).

Here Paul manipulates the rhetorical commonplace. The bad demagogues were accused by their opponents of becoming chameleons and enslaving themselves in order to gain money or political power. Paul's gain, however, is only the conversion of his listeners. He gains no money; he gains *them*. Like any good leader, whether king or populist, Paul claims to have only the interests of his followers at heart.

The previous chapter has also shown that the model of the enslaved leader usually functioned in opposition to the model of the leader as the benevolent patriarch.[21] The fatherly, kingly figure leads compassionately but from a secure position above his people. His moral and social superiority are the direct results of his superior nature. Therefore, to depict him as an equal with those whom he must lead is ludicrous. To depict him as enslaved to them, in a *lower* position, is the height of folly. Everyone is much better off, according to benevolent patriarchal ideology, if people remain in their rightful places. Inferiors are happiest when they respect and follow those who are their natural superiors. Paul's rhetoric, however, rejects the benevolent patriarchal model of aristocratic leadership. By portraying himself as enslaved to those whom he is supposed to lead, he opts for the demagogic model over that of the benevolent patriarch or king. Paul refuses to lead from the secure position of social superiority.

Did Paul intend to portray himself as a demagogue or populist? Did he self-consciously choose this model of leadership and reject the other? These questions are unanswerable and ultimately unimportant for this study. If his listeners were familiar with common rhetorical conventions, if they were accustomed to listening to speeches in the amphitheater, if they listened to Cynic preachers in the markets or at the games, then they likely recognized Paul's language as familiar fodder. Certainly to educated persons, but probably to many more as well, 1 Cor. 9:19–23 represents Paul as a populist leader who aligns himself with persons of lower status. Further-more, it would be understood that he was rejecting the benevolent pa-triarchal model, with its careful maintenance of existing social hierarchy.

Because Paul sets himself up here as an example, the implication is that any of the Corinthians who intend to be leaders must follow Paul's exam-ple and model their leadership on that of the self-enslaving leader. Their leadership cannot simply shore up the existing status hierarchy. By enslav-ing themselves to their social inferiors, they challenge that hierarchy. By using rhetoric about the self-lowering leader, Paul does just what conser-vative Greco-Roman leaders wanted to avoid when they portrayed leaders as benevolent fathers: he throws normal social hierarchy and status indica-tors into disarray.

1 CORINTHIANS 9 AND LOVE-PATRIARCHALISM

Gerd Theissen correctly located the problem of the weak and the strong at Corinth as one of status and conflict between low- and high-status groups, particularly between poorer and wealthier Christians. He also correctly noted that Paul aligned himself with the interests of the weak and directed his rhetoric toward changing the behavior of the strong. Theissen claims, however, that Paul advocated a compromise between the strong and the weak as a solution to the problems surrounding eating meat offered to idols and the observation of the Lord's Supper.[22] Paul's solution to these problems, according to Theissen, reflects his general ethic of "love-patriarchalism." Theissen defines love-patriarchalism as that ethos prevalent in primitive Christianity by which status differences were to be maintained and yet mitigated by committing people of high-er status to greater responsibility toward people of lower status. In Theissen's words, "This love-patriarchalism takes social differences for granted but ameliorates them through an obligation of respect and love, an obligation imposed upon those who are socially stronger. From the weaker are required subordination, fidelity and esteem."[23]

According to Theissen, in early Christianity equal status was granted to all within the community on a theoretical or mythological level. "At the same time, however, all of this was internalized; it was true 'in Christ.' In the political and social realm class-specific differences were essentially accept-ed, affirmed, even religiously legitimated" (109). Love-patriarchalism was therefore moderately conservative from a social point of view. It functioned ideologically to maintain the normal hierarchical structure of society while defusing conflict by integrating the different strata of society into one interrelated whole. The socially weak are to be content with their subordination; that contentment is reinforced by the attention to their needs provided by the socially strong. Theissen claims that historically this ethos tended to work for social integration and stability first within the early church and later within the late empire.

Theissen is surely correct to suggest that the strong at Corinth likely did not view their own practice of eating meat as socially irresponsible. They probably had a concept of imitation, as did Paul, and because they were the socially superior, they would have expected the weak to follow their morally superior example.[24] As we have seen, in patronal ideology imitation played an important role in that the patron provided an example of wise and liberated living for social inferiors.[25] Thus Theissen suggests, "Was it just cynicism if some of the strong in Corinth believed that under the circumstances they could 'edify' the weak by their example (1 Cor. 8:10)? Could they not have believed, with a very clear conscience, that the lower classes should not further curtail their already limited possibilities in life with such religious scruples?" (140). This is not only a possibility; it is a probability, given the normal function of imitation in benevolent patriarchalism. In that conceptual system, the leaders, who are socially and therefore morally superior, provide a model for the weak by their behavior. To modulate their behavior to fit the whims of the weak means not only a denial of their own status but also a surrender of truth to the caprices of the masses, who may be pitied but cannot be trusted and certainly must not be obeyed.

Theissen maintains that Paul himself advocates love-patriarchalism as his solution to the problems in Corinth. The ethos, he says, became even more important in deutero-Pauline literature and in the Pastoral Epistles. Later, according to Theissen, the love-patriarchalism that originated in the primitive Christian communities became the dominant mode of conceiving and structuring society in general. "In the context of late antiquity this love-patriarchalism became significant for society as a whole. It offered a new pattern for direction and shaping social relationships in contrast to that of Greco-Roman antiquity" (108). In Theissen's view, the egalitarianism of the polis became more and more unworkable and was gradually replaced with an ethos informed by love-patriarchalism. Originally developed within a small religious movement of house churches, love-patriarchalism eventually provided late antiquity with a "new pattern of integration" (109).

Theissen's analysis of love-patriarchalism is quite insightful, yet it fails to describe the function of that ideology in 1 Corinthians. What he calls love-patriarchalism I have called benevolent patriarchalism. It was not an invention of primitive Christian communities or of Paul but was prevalent in Greco-Roman rhetoric and philosophy as an ideology for social control and integration. Theissen believes that Greco-Roman antiquity "sought to solve the problems of social integration by means of a noble vision of a citizenry enjoying equality of status" (108). According to him, it was this polis-centered concept of equality of status that finally gave way to early Christian love-patriarchalism. Contrary to Theissen's suggestions, the egalitarian emphasis in Greco-Roman concepts of the polis was part of one particular conceptual system that in the ancient world was called democratic. Benevolent patriarchalism was an alternative ideology that rejected equality of status and held that social hierarchy was both necessary and beneficial to all as long as those of lower status respected their superiors and those of higher status conscientiously cared for their inferiors.

Benevolent patriarchalism likely characterizes the views of the strong at Corinth, who probably saw their role as providing moral leadership for the weak. By following the example of the strong in freedom, wisdom, and strength, the weak could be liberated from their oppressive and misinformed religious opinions. But for the strong to alter their own behavior to conform to the opinions of the uneducated amounted to self-enslavement and endangered any chances the strong might have for social advancement. According to benevolent patriarchalism, leaders must lead from a position of strength and freedom.

In opposition to such a view, Paul presents himself as the enslaved leader. Once we recognize that Paul's self-lowering is part of a rhetorical topos we might be tempted to depict it as nothing more than a rhetorical ploy. But Paul actually had become a manual laborer, although that role seems to have been below his normal social level.[26] Within benevolent patriarchal ideology, such action is almost always censured. Paul does not imply that those of high status should simply care for those of low status; by offering his very real social self-lowering as a model to the strong, Paul implies that they should respond in kind. Modern persons imbued with ideas similar to the democratic ideology of Paul's world may not find Paul's implication radical, but to those Greeks and Romans whose symbolic universe was more informed by benevolent patriarchalism, Paul's advice was disturbing and unacceptable.[27] On the other hand, it may have been just the leadership model that appealed to members of the lower class, as we may gather from the remarks of aristocratic authors who opposed the democratic leaders.

In any case, the above analysis of Paul's rhetoric in 1 Corinthians 9 suggests that love-patriarchalism is not the solution offered by Paul. On the contrary, he counters the benevolent patriarchal models of social structure and leadership held by the strong with his own alternative model of the enslaved leader. He uses traditional democratic rhetoric to call into question the benevolent patriarchal maintenance of normal social hierarchy and the appropriateness of normal status indicators. Further, he offers his own activity as a manual laborer as the concrete support for his rhetoric.

PAUL'S SELF-ENSLAVEMENT AS HIS SALVATION

Thus far in this chapter I have analyzed Paul's self-enslavement both as a practical strategy for missionary activity, that is, social self-lowering in order to appeal to low-status persons, and as a rhetorical strategy for portraying to the strong at Corinth Paul's own model of leadership. This exegesis of 1 Cor. 9:19–23 would be incomplete, however, if it did not emphasize that Paul's self-enslavement is for him not only pragmatically and rhetorically strategic but also theologically important. *Enslavement* as a metaphorical expression for social self-lowering and social advancement serves as scaffolding for Paul's soteriology.

I have already examined in chapter 2 how the expression *slave of Christ* functioned in early Christianity to represent salvation. The theme occurs also in 1 Corinthians 9. Paul's enslavement works to gain others or to save them, but it also provides gain for himself. After mentioning that he has done all this in order to save others (9:22), he points out that the end in view is that he will also "share" in the gospel. Paul's comment later (9:27) shows that he believes the end result of his self-enslavement will be his own salvation. He subjects his own body to slavery so that, having preached to others, he will not himself be found unworthy.

At work here is a common Pauline soteriological structure. In Paul's scheme of salvation, the glory of eschatological salvation must be preceded by debasement; one must descend in order to ascend. This down-up soteriology is important for Paul's theology as a whole and is too pervasive in Paul's thought to allow full treatment here (cf. Rom. 15:1–12). Yet in order to see how slavery functioned in Pauline Christianity as a metaphor of salvation we must see how it played a role within Paul's theolo humiliation and exaltation. One place where that metaphor plays an important role is in Paul's letter to the Philippians.

Slave terms actually occur only a few times in Philippians. Paul begins the letter by referring to himself and Timothy as "slaves of Christ Jesus" (Phil. 1:1), and later Paul says that Timothy has worked like a slave for the gospel (2:22). The most famous use of slave language in Philippians, and the most important, is the designation of Christ as a slave (*doulos*) in the hymn of 2:6–11. The movement of Jesus in that passage is downward and then upward. He lowers himself, becoming a slave, and even suffers a slavish death. "*Therefore* [*dio*], God has highly exalted him." The last half of the hymn, then, describes the exaltation of Jesus (2:9–11).

Ronald Hock, in an unpublished paper, argues insightfully that the humiliation-exaltation christology of the hymn finds its basis for plausibility within Greco-Roman slavery and particularly within depictions of slavery in the ancient romances.[28] Hock shows linguistic and structural parallels between the Philippians hymn and the ancient romances. Heroes and heroines in these stories endured slavery and then were highly exalted by the master to a position of power. In Chariton's romance, for example, Callirhoe is tragically sold into slavery, though she is actually a noblewoman. Later, however, she becomes the mistress of the household of her former master, now husband, Dionysius.[29] In Xenophon's *Ephesiaka*, the hero Habrocomes also becomes a slave, suffers unjust treatment, and then gains his freedom and becomes the manager of the entire household.[30]

Although Hock's examples do not show anyone taking on slavery voluntarily en route to exaltation, as is the implication of the Christ hymn in Philippians, I have given such examples in chapter 1. Hock's suggestions, therefore, provide a plausible literary and social context for reading the movement of Jesus in Phil. 2:6–11. As Hock says, "The author of the hymn made sense of the principal 'facts' of the gospel, namely the death and resurrection of Christ (cf. 1 Cor. 15:3–5), less by appealing to, say, the figure of the Suffering Servant than by pointing to widely-shared experience. The hymn in effect says that the closest analogy to what the gospel says of Christ's death and resurrection is the dramatic reversal in status of a slave whose obedience and unjust punishment are recompensed by an exaltation to a position of authority. Functionally speaking, the analogy makes the claims for Jesus' death and resurrection meaningful and true."[31]

Hock capitalizes on the humiliation-exaltation theme in Paul to analyze the christological significance of the Christ hymn. The same theme also provides a framework for Pauline soteriology and ethics. In Philippians, the central paradigm of Jesus' humility and exaltation shapes the rest of the letter. Paul holds up Jesus the onetime slave as a model for the Philippians to emulate. Like Jesus, they should look to the interests of others rather than to their own (2:4). Paul does not stop with his call to humility. He pictures this downward movement as the precursor to upward movement for the Philippians, as well. This is the way they will "work out their own salvation" (2:12). By following Christ down, they will also eventually follow him up.

All the good characters, the heroes, of Philippians are involved in this same down-up movement. Paul gives up his own interests for those of the Philippians. He would rather depart and be with Christ, but for their sake he will stay (1:1–26). He is poured out for them (2:17). He has given up everything for Christ (3:4–7). Consequently, he expects to move upward as Christ did (3:8–11). Analogously, both Timothy, serving like a slave, and Epaphroditus show their genuineness by looking out for the interests of others (2:19–22, 29–30).

The Philippian Christians also participate in humility and exaltation. They are to take Paul (and presumably Timothy and Epaphroditus) as examples (3:16–17). Paul speaks of "our" glorification, which will follow the pattern set by Christ. Phil. 3:19–21 hearkens back to 2:6–11. The passage that promises eschatological transformation for the Christians reuses terminology from the hymn. They await the exalted Lord Jesus Christ (3:20; cf. 2:11). He will "change their form" (*metaschēmatizein* 3:21; cf. *schēma* 2:7), which is now, as Jesus' was then, one of lowliness (*tapeinōsis* 3:21; cf. *etapeinōsin heauton* 2:8). Instead of the slave form that Jesus assumed (*morphē* 2:6), he will give them at that time a form like the body of his glory (*symmorphon* 3:21; see also 2:11). God subjected everything to him (*pan* 2:9; *pan* 2:10; *pasa* 2:11), and so Christ has power to make everything subject (*ta panta* 3:21). The enemies of the cross of Christ, whose minds are set on earthly things (*ta epigeia* 3:19), will be among those earthly beings (*epigeioi* 2:10) who will bow the knee to Christ. This brief survey suggests that a large portion of the letter to the Philippians hangs on this humiliation-exaltation movement of Christ, imitated by Paul and then by the Philippians.

Elsewhere, Paul uses the down-up pattern to speak of his ministry as self-humbling in order that others might be exalted (2 Cor. 11:7). Sometimes the self-abasement is accompanied by slave language (2 Cor. 4:5, 12). The humiliation, however, is followed by exaltation, thus linking humility and self-abasement to such soteriological images as resurrection, glory, and upward movement in general (2 Cor. 4:13–18). This is not to say that in every occurrence of the down-up thematic pattern Paul has metaphorical slavery in mind. The theme of humility and exaltation is part of Paul's apocalyptic worldview and his theological use of crucifixion and resurrection and can occur quite apart from any analogy to slavery.[32] Often, however, in Philippians, Paul's theology of the cross does find ready metaphorical representation in images of slavery. This was possible because Greco-Roman slavery was multifaceted and ambiguous. Popular myths about slavery in the ancient world provided a plausibility structure for portraying both abasement and exaltation, humiliation and the possibility of honor. In sum, precisely because the social institution of slavery carried different connotations in different contexts, references to slavery could represent self-abasement as well as upward mobility and access to high status.

Thus in 1 Cor. 9:19–23, Paul appropriates the soteriological meaning of slavery in early Christianity. He has already depicted himself as Christ's slave steward (9:16–18), which functions as a claim to authority. He then offers himself as a model for the voluntary self-abasement of a leader (9:19–22). Finally, he again plays on the soteriological meanings of metaphorical slavery by showing that his own self-lowering will bring not only the salvation of his converts but his own eschatological salvation as well (9:23,27). In 1 Corinthians 9, Paul has taken the common early Christian language of slavery, which represented salvation in terms of social mobility, and turned it to an ethical demand based on his theology of the cross.

SLAVE OF CHRIST AND SLAVE OF ALL

I have analyzed 1 Corinthians 9 by focusing on two different aspects of slavery in Greco-Roman society and rhetoric. In both 9:16–18 and 9:19–23 Paul uses slavery as a metaphor. The difference between the meanings of slavery in the two sections lies in the different masters. As I pointed out in chapter 1, in Greco-Roman society it mattered less that one was a slave than whose slave one was. The slavery to Christ to which Paul alludes in 9:16–18 can be understood as a claim to high status by association and therefore authority, for it draws on forms of slavery in which a managerial slave exercised power and enjoyed some social mobility due to his or her connections to a powerful patron. In 9:19–23, however, the "slavery to all" takes its meaning from common rhetoric that portrayed leaders as gaining power by giving up their normal high status and enslaving themselves to the masses. This kind of slavery does include low status and unconditional obedience. Therefore, in these few verses, slavery depicts both high status by association and low status. The two sections, however, are connected by a significant "for" (*gar*, 9:19). Precisely what is the import of this connective particle? In other words, what is the connection between these two apparently contradictory uses of slavery as a metaphor?

Paradox may explain the connection between the two slaveries. One might say, that is, that Paul is paradoxically combining high-status with low-status symbolism. Paradoxically, he finds high status in his acceptance of low status. Along these lines, interpreters of 9:19 often take Paul's phrase *eleutheros gar ōn ek pantōn pasin emauton edoulōsa*—translated as, "For, although I am free I have enslaved myself to all"—as a representation of paradoxical freedom in slavery. Paradox, however, is not a satisfying way to explain Paul's combination of freedom and slavery in 1 Corinthians 9 unless we also explain what paradox would have meant in Paul's situation and how his audience would have heard his language as paradoxical.

There was a philosophical tradition of freedom in slavery, particularly in the Stoic paradox of the *doulos eleutheros*, the "free slave." Therefore, this is one possible context in which Paul's language could have been heard. But there are a couple of reasons to reject the philosophical paradox as the explanatory framework for Paul's use here of slavery and freedom. For one thing, as we have seen, Paul has already done himself damage in 9:16–18 if his language is interpreted within the discourse of moral philosophical concepts of freedom: his admissions that he serves "unwillingly" and "under compulsion" would be quite out of place in any moral philosophical defense of his actions. It would not then make sense to interpret 9:19 as representing an appeal to paradoxical freedom in slavery along the lines of philosophical paradox when Paul's language of 9:16–18 has already rejected that philosophical discourse. Second, the pervasive issue of chapter 9 (and chapters 8–10) is one of status and the inappropriateness (from the upper-class perspective) of persons of high status behaving like persons of low status. In this context, the *eleutheros* of 9:19 recalls not images of philosophical freedom of the soul or will but the social position of the free man as a person of high status.

For these reasons, the interpretation of 9:19 should not be "For, although I am free of all I am also a slave of all" but "For it is exactly from a position as a free man—a man of high status—that I became enslaved to all." In other words, the *ōn* of 9:19 should be taken not as indicating present time but as cotemporal with the aorist verb *edoulōsa.* The first translation takes the language as indicating a state: paradoxical freedom in slavery, or the free slave. The second translation indicates a linear movement from high position to low position. "Paradox," therefore, is a misleading way to describe the rhetoric. Paul does not use the philosophical commonplace of the paradoxically free slave or the enslaved free man; rather, his argument effects a linear movement from high status to low status. The movement from high to low is indicated within verse 19 by the movement from "free from all" to "enslaved to all."

The same movement from high to low is represented by the shift from slavery to Christ in verses 16–18 to slavery to all in verses 19–23. This may seem to imply that in 9:19–23 slavery represents humility and abasement. But to suppose that two different slaveries are represented here, one powerful and one powerless, is to oversimplify the function of the demagogue topos. The populist who lowers himself does not really give up power or cease to be a leader. The enslaved leader actually gains power by a step down in status. The populist does not completely give up the patronal form of social structure but steps outside the normal patronal structures of status and authority to appeal directly to the masses. He becomes the patron of all the people, the patron of those without patrons. The leader becomes the protector of the populus; thus his designation as popularis. He is the savior not just of the high class, the *beltistoi* or the *kaloi k'agathoi,* but of all the people, the *plēthos,* the demos (though this was usually understood to mean the lower class in particular); thus his designation as demagogue. Paul's self-enslavement to all, therefore, advocates not general self-denial or the relinquishment of authoritative leadership; rather, it argues for a certain kind of authoritative leadership: one from a social status position among the lower class. In 9:19–23, the issue is not giving up power but lowering status. The power is shifted, not lost.

In both 9:19–23 and 9:16–18, slavery provides a model of leadership that is different from the normal benevolent patriarchal model. The slave of Christ does have authority, but it is a subtle form of authority, an authority derived from status by association. The slave of all also has authority: the authority gained by appealing directly to the people. It comes not from the maintenance of the leader's high social position but from the strength given the populist by popular support itself. Again, it is a derived authority and not dependent on normal status indicators. Nevertheless, it does constitute power.

Therefore, though it may appear that these two slaveries are disparate and unconnected, one representing high status and one representing low status, there is a rhetorical movement binding together the two sections: a step-by-step move away from the position of the strong. In 1 Cor. 9:16–18, by depicting his leadership as slavery to Christ, Paul takes one step away from their position. They think of Christian leadership as modeled on the benevolent, free, high-status sophos. Paul, however, depicts his leadership as the derived authority by association with his master Christ. This does constitute a claim to authority but one different from that of the strong. Then, in verses 19–23, Paul takes a further, more radical step away from the position of the strong. By using the demagogic model of the leader as slave of all, Paul more specifically rejects the status-maintaining leadership of benevolent patriarchalism. Again, he still claims leadership, but it is leadership from below. It is an exercise of authority, but a more subtle, ambiguous authority that is not based on normal social position and normal status hierarchy. In both sections, slavery represents leadership. The purpose of neither is to depict humility. They are different ways of picturing abnormal structures of authority—abnormal, that is, from the point of view of the sophos leader.

My discussion of freedom and slavery in 1 Corinthians 9 should not be taken as a rejection of paradox as a category for understanding Paul's language elsewhere. The theme of strength in weakness is prominent in the Corinthian letters. Paul's theology of the cross as the representation of God's power resident in a humanly despicable form may well lie behind Paul's willingness to embrace low status in 1 Corinthians 9. Indeed, the centrality of the crucified Messiah in Paul's thought was likely one reason that Paul, a person of relatively high status, could use rhetoric that seemed so radical to high-status persons. This central image, the slavery of Jesus, ruled Paul's worldview, as can be seen from its role in Philippians. For Paul, the stumbling block of the cross challenged any easy acceptance of the usual connection between normal status indicators and leadership. Therefore, though paradoxical freedom in slavery—or, for that matter, high status in low—is not the way to understand the function of slavery in 1 Corinthians 9, the theological paradox of the crucified Messiah does lie in the background of Paul's argument. Paul uses rhetoric about leadership that would have seemed radical coming from a person of high status. His own theological reasons for doing so, reasons he does not mention in 1 Corinthians 9, are that all high-status indicators have been challenged by the cross of Christ.

5

THEOLOGY

AND

IDEOLOGY

IN

CORINTH

Fredric Jameson, in an essay on interpreting texts within social historical contexts, speaks of the difference between two meanings of *meaning*.[1] Recalling recent hermeneutical theories, Jameson differentiates the sense (*Sinn*) of a text from its "historically operative function" (*Bedeutung*). The sense of the text is its inner structure and syntax. Translation attempts to arrive as close as possible to this limited meaning of the text. The Bedeutung, which I will call the *significance* of the text, refers to the larger meaning of the text within its context, its effects and functions as part of a larger narrative, history, or ideology. Although the sense may be arrived at, more or less, without a great deal of attention to the situation of the text, the significance of the text, which is the further goal of interpretation, cannot be ascertained without constructing, at least tentatively, some believable narrative or history within which the text could function. Jameson rightly urges us, however, to recognize that we place the text in a historical context of our own creation. In Jameson's words, "The text's meaning then, in the larger sense of *Bedeutung*, will be the meaningfulness of a gesture that we read back from the situation to which it is precisely a response."[2] According to these statements, we cannot arrive at the meaning, in the fuller sense, of a text or terminology until we construct a historical context for the language.

I have suggested three different contexts within ancient ideology and culture for the use of slavery as a metaphor. Slavery worked in the Roman Empire as a means of social mobility. Attachment to an important person, even as that person's slave, often gave one opportunities—or at least the hope—for status improvement. Drawing on this concept, slavery to Christ was able to function as a positive, soteriological image for early Christians even in a Greco-Roman, urban environment. Second, the managerial slaves of a powerful person themselves enjoyed a certain amount of power and prestige. They wielded authority, although that authority was derivative and not normal authority, that is, the slave's authority did not carry the usual badges, such as wealth, high legal status, and patronal position. Within early Christianity, *slave of Christ* signified authority by analogy to the authority of the managerial slave. Third, rhetoric that designated leaders as slaves of the masses or slaves of all functioned within a particular ideology of leadership. Slavery to all served as a leadership model challenging conservative patronal assumptions about leadership and its automatic connections to high social status, patronal position, and the manifestation of the usual status indicators.

All these meanings of slavery functioned within the patronal structure of society and depended, to some extent, on patronal ideology for their effect, but each invokes different values and presuppositions.[3] Slavery as upward mobility connotes loyalty to the master and the slave's occupancy of a reasonably secure position within the household. The metaphor therefore tends to encourage loyalty to the master, in this case, Christ, and solidarity with other members of the household, in this case, the church. The connotations attending slavery to Christ as a designation of leadership were similarly outlined in chapter 2. Likewise, the designation *slave of all* as a model of leadership functions to challenge benevolent patriarchal leadership based on normal status indicators. When a leader used this terminology, he necessarily placed himself within the ideological context attending the terminology. He identified himself as a leader in the populist mold and by that identification challenged both the benevolent patriarchal model of leadership and the givenness of status positions as understood by the upper class.

THE "CORINTHIAN SITUATION"

What began as an analysis of Paul's slave language has become an analysis of a social conflict. Paul's metaphors of slavery function within a particular ideological debate, a debate about status, leadership, monetary support, and manual labor. We cannot interpret Paul's metaphors of slavery without positing a plausible reconstruction of his conflict with the Corinthian Christians. Peter Marshall, in a study of Paul's rejection of the Corinthians' financial support, suggests one possible reconstruction. He shows how the giving and receiving of money functioned symbolically in Greco-Roman society. For one thing, Paul's refusal of the Corinthians' money was necessary if he was to maintain his own independence from the patronage of certain powerful people at Corinth. His status as a leader would be compromised if he were perceived as the dependent client of powerful Corinthian patrons. At the same time, Marshall argues, by refusing their money, Paul risked offending those wealthier citizens.[4]

Paul's rejection of their support, however, could be interpreted differently even by different people of his own culture. In the symbol system of patron-client ideology, it could be interpreted as a refusal to become a client of the donors, a gesture to differentiate himself from sophists and charlatans, or a refusal to enter into a "friendship" relationship with the donors. These different possible meanings of Paul's self-support imply three different status relationships. In the first case, by refusing to make himself the dependent of the donors, Paul insists that he is not lower in status than they.[5] In the second, Paul's rejection of the sophist's fees indicates that he rejects the sophist's high status also. (Sophists were of high status even though it had become fashionable in Paul's day for people who fancied themselves philosophers, such as Dio Chrysostom, to run them down.) In the third case, Paul's refusal implies that he rejects friendship with the donors on a more or less equal basis (granting the unspoken understanding that such relationships included an account of debits and credits).

We cannot choose one of these interpretations as *the* meaning of Paul's rejection of support; all were simultaneously possible. Thus there is not one answer to the question, what did it mean for Paul to insist on supporting himself by manual labor? It meant several things, and different things to different people. Paul himself noted that his self-support permitted him to differentiate himself from other preachers (2 Cor. 11:12). He also acknowledged that it represented his refusal to enter into a relationship of dependence on certain powerful patrons at Corinth. He expresses this by insisting that parents should support their children, not vice versa (2 Cor. 12:14), implying his superior position to those at Corinth who wish to support him financially. As Marshall points out, however, the prospective donors at Corinth probably interpreted Paul's actions to mean that he was refusing to enter into a friendly relationship with them. This would explain their strong indignation and sense of hurt reflected so clearly in 2 Corinthians 10–13.

Building on an analysis of the topos of the enslaved leader in Greco-Roman antiquity, I have suggested that Paul's rhetoric in 1 Corinthians 9 raises another possibility for the significance of Paul's self-support. Paul claims that he willingly gave up his right to be supported by the Corinthians, characterizing this move as self-enslavement to all. By using rhetoric associated with populist leaders, Paul indicates that his self-enslavement is an intentional social self-lowering. He recognizes that both his relinquishment of his exousia (*right* or *authority*) and his activity as a manual laborer, which was necessitated by that relinquishment, constitute downward social movement. He thus descends voluntarily in order to appeal to those of low status: he becomes weak to win the weak. In other words, Paul gives as one reason for his rejection of financial support a missionary strategy of appealing to lower-class persons.

As argued above in chapter 1, manual labor had different meanings to people in different locations in Greco-Roman society. Paul's assumption of manual labor, therefore, likely appealed to lower-class persons, those who were themselves manual laborers. On the other hand, Paul's actions probably offended persons of higher status, who shared the antibanausic attitudes of the upper class. They would have been embarrassed to see their leader joining those below his station at the workbench. Furthermore, Paul's characterization of his action by means of the topos of the populist leader would only have exacerbated their discomfort. It seems Paul was admitting that he sought to flatter the masses. Paul looked like the indiscreet and unprincipled demagogue, who shamelessly deserts his true position to cater to the worst elements of society. Viewing his self-support in this way, this segment of the Corinthian church urged their leader to let them support him. Otherwise, his shameful appearance indeed reflected negatively on them as he was the recognized leader of the group.

Thus both Paul's manual labor and his explanation of his actions in 1 Cor. 9:19–23 had at least two different meanings: to those of lower status Paul's activity and his rhetoric about it were not only acceptable but attractive; to those of higher status they were likely threatening or embarrassing. This difference in the perception of Paul's actions and language helps explain the misunderstandings and tensions reflected in 2 Corinthians 10–13. Although Paul goes to great lengths to explain that his actions were not meant as an offense to the Corinthians, some of them were certainly offended. At times, Paul admits that his actions suggest his own low status and weakness, sometimes capitalizing on this motif in order to expound his theology of the strength of God manifested in weakness (2 Cor. 12:9–10). At other times, however, Paul insists that the weakness is only apparent and that, if necessary, he will manifest for the Corinthians the strength that God can work in him (2 Cor. 10:2–6, 13:1–4). Sometimes Paul attempts to characterize his self-support in terms of high status: he does not accept their money because parents should not be supported by their children (2 Cor. 12:14); his self-support enables him to differentiate himself from charlatans (2 Cor. 11:12–15). At other points, however, he accepts the low-status indications of his activity, admitting that it shows him to be weak (2 Cor. 11:7). The complexities of Paul's argument are a result of the ambiguity of Paul's self-support as a manual laborer. The confusion could scarcely be helped, however, because what seemed like solidarity to those of lower status seemed like flattery to those of higher status.

Just as Paul's actions meant different things to different people, so his language about self-enslavement to all was heard differently, according to how much of its accompanying ideology was grasped by the listener. At the very least, persons understood that Paul recognized his self-support as constituting social self-lowering. But to those more familiar with the topos of the enslaved leader, Paul's language was heard as the appropriation of a particular model of leadership opposed to the benevolent patriarchal model. Paul's self-enslavement to all meant that he rejected benevolent patriarchalism with its careful maintenance of status hierarchy arranged according to traditional criteria of social status: wealth, legal status, and patronal position. Possibly, the very people most likely to have access to these rhetorical motifs were those who were themselves more educated, that is, those of higher status. Paul's antipatriarchal rhetoric, therefore, may have had a greater chance of being understood precisely by those who were most likely to disagree with it.

CHAPTER 9 WITHIN THE ARGUMENT OF 1 CORINTHIANS 8–10

1 Corinthians 9 is Paul's fictitious defense, his apologia. Within the argument of 1 Corinthians 8–10, however, it functions more to set forth Paul's actions as an example than simply to defend them. His apology is a rhetorical pretext for the more immediate goal of establishing himself as a

model for the strong. He gives up his right for the good of the weak; his manual labor, therefore, is an example to the strong of self-lowering. Social abasement is here one instance of giving up one's own interests for the sake of the other.

We have seen that Paul's call to the strong to follow his example of social self-lowering constitutes a more radical ethic than is often realized. Paul calls on the strong to be willing to suffer material social disadvantages by giving up their right to eat meat. Therefore, his advice constitutes not merely a theological construction unrelated to actual social behavior, but a particular social action with important consequences for the social positions of the strong. In patronal ideology, to alter one's behavior to meet the expectations and demands of low-status persons was usually perceived as offensive social self-abasement. Paul, by his own example and rhetoric, advocates precisely such a course for the strong.

The accommodation of the strong to the weak, which means a reversal of the normal statuses, is theologically defended by appeal to the theology of the cross. The strong must have no less concern than Christ for the weak one, "the brother for whom Christ died" (1 Cor. 8:11). In Rom. 15:1–3, the crucifixion of Christ is even more explicitly the theological grounding for seeking the interests of the other rather than of oneself. In 2 Cor. 8:9, Paul uses the status reversal significance of the cross to motivate the Corinthians to contribute to the collection. Jesus, though rich, became poor for them; his poverty made them rich. Paul's own "weakness" about which he "boasts" in 2 Cor. 11:30–12:10 is his embodiment of the weakness of the cross (1 Cor. 2:2–5). It is this rejection of the traditional badges of power and status that Paul takes from Christ and intends to pass on to the Corinthians (1 Cor. 11:1).

Proceeding from the logic of Paul's cross-centered theology, one would expect the complete rejection of patriarchalism. Yet Paul, as has often been both bemoaned and celebrated, does not go that far. His use of patriarchal language and structures is not always clear and has led some scholars to paint Paul as a visionary egalitarian while others have insisted that he was a patriarchal conservative. Either conclusion, if stated without severe qualification, is incorrect. Paul does urge the submission of Christians to patrons of the church, such as Stephanas (1 Cor. 16:15–18). He himself uses patronal ideology to solidify his own position (e.g., 1 Cor. 4:15–16; 2 Cor. 12:14). But here one must be careful to recognize not just the occurrence of the patriarchal language but also its final function for Paul's argument. As discussed in chapter 4, Paul often sets himself up as a strong, authoritative figure precisely to insist that other high-status Christians follow his example of social self-lowering. He uses patriarchal rhetoric to make an antipatriarchal point.[6] Certain aspects of Paul's appearance, specifically his financial self-support by manual labor and his questionable speaking ability (2 Cor. 10:10; 11:6), were seen by some at Corinth as inconsistent with their blueprint of the proper leader. Paul disrupts their concepts of leadership and status by employing, among other things, traditional patronal ideology. This explains why Paul insists in 1 Cor. 4:15–16 that he is their "father." As argued in chapter 2, it is also why he calls himself Christ's authoritative slave representative in 1 Cor. 9:16–18. In both these contexts, the ultimate goal of Paul's rhetoric is to challenge the traditional linkage between high-status indicators and leadership within the church.

Sometimes, therefore, patriarchal language in Paul's letters is in the service of antipatriarchal status reversal. This observation does not, however, explain all the occurrences of patriarchalism. For example, though Paul attempts a theological undermining of the difference between master and slave, he never pursues the logical end of rejecting the actual social structure of slavery.[7] He is willing to allow the patronal household as the dominant form for the social embodiment of the church. Thus, in spite of his rhetoric in 1 Corinthians that severely questions the validity of traditional status indicators, status reversal in itself does not seem to be Paul's goal. Paul's cross-centered theology, with its paradoxical strength in weakness, is not the sole reason for his rhetoric. His rhetorical challenge to the strong and his ethic of status reversal must have another goal besides that of expressing ethically his christology or his theology of the cross.

That final goal of Paul's rhetoric in 1 Corinthians is the unity of the church, a theme that pervades the entire letter. Paul begins with a plea that the Corinthians heal their divisions "in order that you all might agree and that there be no schisms among you, but that you may be reconciled in the same mind and in the same opinion" (1:10). Part of this statement recurs almost verbatim in 12:25. Elsewhere, in his discussion of the Lord's Supper, schisms are again Paul's central concern (11:18). The particular way Paul argues for the unity of the church is by affirming the abasement of the high and the elevation of the low. For example, the line of argument stretching from 1:18 through 2:5 maintains that God's status values are the opposite of traditional status values ("not of this age" 2:6). Paul stresses the relative insignificance of Apollos and himself in order to convince the Corinthians not to be "puffed up" for one against the other (4:6). In other words, the status language serves to discourage division. Later, Paul uses the common rhetorical analogy of the body and its different members to represent the group. Epictetus uses the same analogy, but whereas for Epictetus the point is simply the interdependence of the different members of the body, Paul stresses the status differences among these members.[8] The status differences are mitigated by the greater honor given the least honorable. The weak members are more essential; the dishonorable are given greater honor. God accomplishes all this "in order that there be no schisms in the body" (12:22–25).

For Paul, the church, the *ekklēsia*, is an eschatological, cosmological community. His concern is the building up (*oikodomē*) of that community. The Corinthians are not just a group of people; they are the building of God (3:9). The preachers are those who build upon the foundation laid by Paul (3:12,14). The criterion for Paul's valuation of prophecy over speaking in a tongue is upbuilding (14:3–4,12). Indeed, everything should be done with this goal of upbuilding in mind (14:26).

In 10:23, *oikodomein* (*to build up*) is in parallel construction to *sympherein* (*to benefit*). Paul ends the section on eating meat offered to idols with an argument that the Corinthians should seek not their own private benefit but that of the other (10:23–11:1). This is the way to avoid placing a stumbling block before any segment of the church, Jews or Gentiles, or indeed before the church itself (10:32). He uses himself as an example of one who seeks not his own private benefit (*sympheros*) but that of the many (10:33). The final benefit he has in mind, of course, is their salvation.

Paul's use of *sympheros* should be compared with the function of *to sympheron* in rhetorical contexts dealing with *homonoia*. Both Greek and Latin rhetoric knew the rhetorical topos of *homonoia*, or concord, a regular element of which is the concern with what is profitable (*to sympheron* or *ta sympheronta*).[9] Of course, anyone delivering a deliberative speech might need to argue that the advice therein benefits the listeners. Orators addressing a variety of topics frequently claim that they are about to suggest the most advantageous course. Further, orators speaking on homonoia often specifically contrast private with public benefit. For example, in Xenophon's *Memorabilia*, Pericles, discussing homonoia with Socrates, says that the Athenians should work together for the benefit that would accrue to all of them (*heautois ta sympheronta*). As it is, they selfishly profit off one another rather than benefiting mutually.[10]

Isocrates' speech *On the Peace* seems to have become a model of the homonoia speech for later orators. Isocrates begins by insisting that he will show his readers what is to the advantage of the city. He assumes, with his audience, that all people pursue their own interests.[11] His goal is to convince them that conflict, in spite of the normal view, does not really advance their interests. Selfishly pursuing their advantage, they miss their true advantage (*to sympheron*). Much of Isocrates' speech depends on the rhetorical opposition of private and public advantage. Only by seeking the second can people gain the common well-being (*koinē sōtēria*).[12]

The epistle by Demosthenes on homonoia follows a similar line of argument. He begins in a typical way by urging his normally impatient audience to hear him out, as he will point out what is beneficial to them.[13] He closes his introduction with the same assurance (note *sympherein*, 1.4). Specifically introducing homonoia as his theme "toward the city's common benefit," he urges his listeners to lay aside disputes, give up their private benefits, and pursue the common good (*ta koinē sympheron*). Demosthenes gives himself as an example of one who has done so.[14]

The theme of benefit as part of the topos of homonoia occurs in a wide variety of contexts, showing that it was a readily available mode of argument. It appears in Aristotle, Dio Chrysostom, Plutarch, and Marcus Aurelius.[15] Even the individualistic Epictetus insists that the duty of the citizen is "to treat nothing as a matter of private profit" (*idia sympheron*). After recalling the analogy of the body, Epictetus insists on the importance of giving in to the other in order to maintain unity. In these different texts, *sympherein* regularly occurs, playing off private benefits against the public well-being. Furthermore, the public good is often expressed as the salvation of the community.[16]

As noted above, the unity of the church is the overarching theme for all of 1 Corinthians. In chapters 8–10, the particular threat to that unity comes from the issue of eating meat offered to idols. Paul here uses the themes of upbuilding and benefit to counter the insistence by the strong on their prerogatives as free individuals. Just as Greco-Roman rhetoricians urge unity by insisting that individuals give up their own private interests for the benefit of the whole community, so Paul insists that the strong at Corinth give up their right to eat meat offered to idols for the upbuilding of the church. Paul even turns the upbuilding motif to ironic use when he says that the free person's exercise of the right to eat meat may "build up" a weak person to eat the idol meat also, against his or her conscience (8:10). In other words, one person's freedom may ironically "build up" another to fall down.

This emphasis on unity is not meant to suggest that Paul is concerned with the church merely as an institution or an ordinary social group. Causing another to sin does not simply divide the social group; the consequence of such provocation is, one might say, a cosmic event in that the Christian who is induced to eat meat against his or her conscience sins and is destroyed. One's eternal fate hangs in the balance. Moreover, because the social group is understood as a transhistorical, supernatural entity— the body of Christ, the eschatological community—to place a stumbling block against it, divide it, or fall out of it constitutes an action of transhistorical significance. Causing another person to stumble is, therefore, equivalent to placing a hindrance against the gospel itself (1 Cor. 9:12). Conversely, to aid in the salvation of another is to become a partner in the gospel (1 Cor. 9:23). Thus, when Paul argues in chapter 10, based on his own example given in chapter 9, that the strong ought to concern themselves with what benefits and builds up the other (10:23), the end result, in Paul's view, will be the building up of the church, the salvation of the many, the *hoi polloi* (10:33). Seeking the interest of the other rather than one's own interest is the way to build up the body of Christ. The desired social expression of this theological emphasis on upbuilding is the unity of the Corinthian church.

THEOLOGY AND IDEOLOGY

This chapter represents something of a departure from traditional ways of interpreting Paul's letters. Paul's interpreters tend to give theological explanations for his rhetoric. Paul may have appropriated political ideology, they admit, but only because that form of rhetoric adequately expressed Paul's theology of the cross. Interpreters assume, moreover, that the theology was prior and the ideology consequential.[17] I have insisted, on the contrary, that one cannot explain Paul's rhetoric simply as an ethical expression of his cross-centered theology. In other words, one cannot draw a straight line from a prior theology to a consequential appropriation of a certain political ideology. Paul has a very practical goal: the unity of the church. To accomplish that goal he is willing to use a certain ideology of leadership and a theological interpretation of the crucifixion. I do not mean to suggest that Paul's theology is therefore unimportant or that it is merely pressed into service to support a prior commitment to an ideology of leadership. It seems to me that all arguments about priority—that one's theology is simply a reflection of one's ideology or vice versa—are fruitless. How can we possibly know the answer to such a question? How could we ever sort out so exactly the intricate workings of another person's mind, when we can never be sure why we ourselves believe certain things? Some Marxists insist that religious beliefs are nothing more than secondary reflections of a given ideology. Many religious people, conversely, believe that the true reality lies in theological statements, which then find, or ought to find, expression in one's ethics. Both positions, however, are dogmatic answers that try to settle the question by fiat. As with chickens and eggs, so with theology and ideology: we cannot know which comes first.

My interpretation of Paul's rhetoric is not intended to imply that Paul's theology of the cross is nothing more than a religious prop for ideology. I do insist, however, that Paul's theology itself cannot be shielded from ideological analysis. We cannot be content to outline Paul's language purely in theological terms; we must also examine how that theological language relates to social structures, conflicts between groups of people, and struggles for power. The conflict at Corinth was not a debate about abstract theological concepts. It was a struggle between different groups of people with different ways of viewing the world, indeed, different ways of actually structuring the world. Paul entered that struggle, a struggle for the right to define reality and therefore a struggle for power, using whatever weapons he could. One powerful weapon in Paul's rhetorical arsenal was his surprising self-portrayal as a slave of Christ and a slave of all.

CONCLUSION

Surprising as it may seem to modern readers, Paul's slavery to Christ did not connote humility but rather established his authority as Christ's agent and spokesperson. Even Paul's slavery to all was not unambiguously humbling, for it evoked in the minds of Paul's contemporary audience a model of leadership in which the leader exercised power by stepping down to the social level of those whom he was to lead. The way Paul uses both these rhetorical strategies sheds much light on the historical reconstruction of the Corinthian letters and the role of those letters in the conflicts within the church at Corinth.

Recent studies of the Corinthian correspondence take the problems at Corinth, to a large extent, to be due to divisions within the church along lines of social status and economic class. My analysis supports such studies but argues that the ideology of benevolent patriarchalism does not reflect Paul's own position. Paul himself exploits the antibanausic prejudice of the higher-status Christians, admitting the servility of his labor and then calling on the strong to imitate it. This is a radical challenge to patronal ideology because following Paul's example necessitates social self-lowering on the part of these high-status Christians. Such social fluctuation was censured by patronal ideology. The radicalness of Paul's actions and rhetoric can be gauged by the harsh reaction from certain persons at Corinth reflected in Paul's later correspondence with them (2 Corinthians 10–13). But for Paul, the unity of the church demanded that those of high status be willing to place themselves below those of low status. His own leadership is an example of the self-lowering leader, the leader who leads from below.

To be sure, Paul did himself use patronal ideology and benevolent patriarchal language. His argument that the strong submit to the weak had as its ultimate purpose not social revolution but church unity, but when viewed against the range of options available to him, Paul's rhetorical strategy appears much less conservative. There were other ways to advocate unity, as is clear from an analysis of the homonoia topos in various contexts. Within benevolent patriarchalism, the theme of unity was quite popular, but in that ideology the unity was achieved by maintaining normal status hierarchy and convincing those on the bottom to resign themselves happily to their protected inferiority. In contrast, Paul sides with those on the bottom of the social scale, and, in a move perceived as radical in his day, he calls on other higher-status Christians also to give up their own interests and to identify themselves with the interests of those Christians of lower status. Paul does not advocate social revolution; but he does deconstruct the presuppositions that make hierarchical structure unassailable. Though allowing, for the most part, the patriarchal structure to stand, Paul undermines the ideological supports for that structure with his labor and rhetoric.

Words mean different things to different people. Even our everyday experience with words convinces us that important factors affect the way people hear words: social level, education, and position in an economic class, for instance. In Paul's day, in the chaotic, crowded shops and street corners of Corinth, the differences between classes were even more pronounced and important. Only a small segment of the population was well educated, and these people were almost all from the small upper class, the leisured class, the nonworking class. There is no reason to suppose that language was heard by lower-class persons in the same way as by these upper-class, educated persons.

There are no such things as ideologically neutral words.[1] All words, at least as soon as they are actually used by someone in some real context, are value-laden, that is, they all carry evaluative baggage. The values of those words, however, do not inhere in the words themselves but are assigned to the words by their users, by the listeners' own appropriations of the words and the ways the listeners construe the intentions of the speaker. Thus, to learn what effect Christian language had on early Christians, that is, to learn what such language meant for them, we cannot analyze language in the abstract or list the lexical meanings of the words—meanings that, in any case, have been gleaned from the writings of a rather homogeneous upper class. Rather, we must hear with several different sets of ears: the ears of the strong at Corinth, the ears of the moral philosophers of Paul's day, the ears of manual laborers, the ears of low-level slaves, and the ears of those moving up the social ladder, whether free people or upwardly mobile slaves.

By imagining the different ways Paul's language may have been heard in his society, we discover that the ideological functions of his manual labor and his metaphors of slavery were anything but simple. The very actions Paul took up in order to identify himself with the lower class offended his higher-class converts. His rhetoric explaining and defending those actions only confirmed their picture of him as wily, deceptive, and changeable. On the other hand, the very same rhetoric was a signal to lower-status members of the church that Paul was their defender, the patron of the patronless. He took their side in their disputes with the higher-status members of the Corinthian church. Not only that, but Paul, the upwardly mobile slave of Christ, was also their model, the assurance that they need not be trapped forever in the slavery of obscurity, for they also would eventually overcome the oppressions of hierarchy to reach high positions in the household of Christ.

APPENDIX

TABLES

OF

INSCRIPTIONS

The lists of inscriptions used in this study make no pretense of completeness. I have concentrated on Asia Minor, Greece, and Macedonia (including the islands and Thessaly), but inscriptions from other areas are occasionally cited. For Asia Minor, I have attempted to collect all the slave and freed inscriptions from the five volumes of *TAM* and the eight volumes of *MAMA*. Various other sources supplement those lists, as will be evident in the tables below. The inscriptions for Greece and Macedonia have been collected primarily from *IG* 2–3, *IG* 4, *IG* 5, *IG* 9, *IG* 10, *IG* 12, *Corinth* 8, and *CIL* 3. (For the most part I have not included manumission inscriptions, as these have received quite a bit of attention in other studies.) These lists have been also supplemented by various sources.[1] Therefore, although my collections of funerary inscriptions are not exhaustive by any stretch of the imagination, they are representative.

I have based my study on several hundred inscriptions not in order to evoke anything like statistical confidence in my claims. Percentages of inscriptions in the tables, for example, do not imply any claim about percentages of population. What can be learned about slaves and freedpersons from funerary inscriptions is, in the end, quite limited, but the inscriptions can be used to correct and enrich an interpretation of ancient slavery based purely on literary sources. The use of several hundred inscriptions, though not giving the study a quantitative validity, can help guard it from being purely intuitive.

1. I am much indebted to Elizabeth Meyer, who allowed me complete access to her collections of slave and freedperson inscriptions from Greece and Macedonia and has helped me in countless other ways to collect and analyze the inscriptions.

Most of the time I have counted as slaves or freedpersons only those people who explicitly call themselves such. I do include, however, some inscriptions that contain the names of persons I believe, for a variety of reasons, to be slave or freed even though they do not say so explicitly. Using names to decide whether or not someone is a slave is problematic, but some judgments can be made on this basis. For example, sometimes we can be confident that the person is a slave when he or she has only one name while the other persons named in the inscription have two or three. In one inscription, for example, a pragmateutes has only one name while the two donors of the inscription have three: "M. Aurelius Zenon and M. Claudia Juliana, asiarchs twice, (made this) for Zotikos (their) pragmateutes, for the sake of memory."[2] Zotikos is probably a slave, especially as pragmateutai are usually slaves or freedmen. In another example I have taken P. Anterota to be a freedman because he shares the first name of the man whom he serves as a pragmateutes.[3] The shared name could be a coincidence, but it seems more likely that he was the man's freedman. In other words, I have used names to decide slave or freed status only where other factors in the inscription or in the geographical and chronological location of the inscription provide clues about the relation of names to status.

In other cases, there are additional indications that the person is a slave. For example: "L. Septimios Appianos for Meneas, (his) pragmateutes (who was) pleasing to him [*aresanti*], for the sake of memory."[4] The term *pleasing*, along with the single name, indicates that Meneas is probably a slave. In another case, an oikonomos is honored for his "good life and work-loving slavery" (*ant' agathou de biou kai doulosynēs philoergou*).[5] I think it safe to call the man a slave, though he does not explicitly call himself such.

All dates are Common Era unless otherwise stated. An ordinal number alone (1st, 2d, etc.) indicates century (e.g., 2d means second century c.e.).

2. Smyrna, 386.
3. Robert *EA* 241.
4. *IGR* 3.257 (*MAMA* 1.40).
5. *SEG* 28.1033.

Table A
115 Slave Funerary Inscriptions from Asia Minor

Letters under "Type" refer to the type of family structure evidenced in the inscription.

A, B, C, and D refer to different family types:

    A = husband and wife alone.

    B = husband, wife, and at least one child.

    C = extended family (blood and marriage relations including slave and freed dependents).

    D = nonrelated persons included along with family.

F = inscription too fragmentary to ascertain family type.

M = a man and offspring.

N = no evidence of family in the inscription.

S = special; that is, there is a possibility of some kind of familial structure that does not fit the four basic categories. For example, some inscriptions include the names of *threptoi*, a term that may indicate an adoptive family relationship but may also simply indicate some other nonfamilial relationship of dependence.

W = a woman and offspring.

Place names are listed here as they appear in the editions of the inscriptions. Regions or Greek equivalents of Turkish names are often added in parentheses.

Reference	Type	Place	Date
BCH 5 (1881), p. 346, no. 8	C	Aidin (Lydia)	—
CIG 2831 (*BCH* 52 [1928]: 414)	B	Aphrodisia (Caria)	—
IGR 3.252 (*MAMA* 1.41)	B	Laodicea (Galatia)	—
IGR 3.256	B	Laodicea (Galatia)	—
IGR 4.235	B	Kebsud	—
IGR 4.530	S	Dorylaeum (Phrygia)	—
IGR 4.538	B	Cotiaeum (Phrygia)	—
IGR 4.543	W	Nicoleae (Phrygia)	—
IGR 4.921	D	Cibyra (Phrygia)	145
IGR 4.1221	N	Thyatira (Lydia)	—
IGR 4.1573 (*CIG* 3095)	N	Teos (Lydia)	—
IGR 4.1576 (*CIG* 3104)	B	Teos (Lydia)	—
Landvogt p. 26 (*CIG* 3793)	N	Chalcedon	—
Landvogt p. 48 (*IGR* 3.279)	A	Ak-Kilisse (Isauria)	—

(*continued*)

Table A
(*Continued*)

Reference	Type	Place	Date
Landvogt p. 48	N	At-karasi (Galatia)	—
MAMA 1.26 (*IGR* 3.251)	B	Laodicea (Galatia)	—
MAMA 1.27 (*IGR* 3.253)	A	Laodicea (Galatia)	—
MAMA 1.28	A	Ladik (Phrygia)	—
MAMA 1.29	A	Serai önü (Phrygia)	—
MAMA 1.30	C	Serai önü (Phrygia)	2d (184?)
MAMA 1.31a	A	Ladik (Phrygia)	2d?
MAMA 1.40 (*IGR* 3.257)	N	Laodicea (Galatia)	2d–3d C.E.?
MAMA 1.295	B	Atlandy (Phrygia)	—
MAMA 4.114 (*IGR* 4.753)	A	Lysias (at Oinan)	no date?
MAMA 5.3	F	Eskisehir (Dorylaeum)	—
MAMA 5.201	M	Seyit Gazi (Nacolea)	1st (ca. 18)
MAMA 6.222	C	Dinar (Apameia, Phrygia)	247/8
MAMA 7.45	B	Laodicea Combusta	—
MAMA 7.200a	N	Aksehir (Philomelion)	—
MAMA 8.70	F	Akören (Lystra)	—
MAMA 8.341 (*IGR* 3.243)	N	Kirik-Kassaba (Galatia)	—
MAMA 8.361	B	Donarsa	—
MAMA 8.379	W	Salir	no date?
MAMA 8.399	A	Cavundar	—
MittAth 24 [1899], p. 360	C	near Thyatira (Akhisar)	no date?
Robert H 13. pp. 105–106. (no. 385)	N	Armutlu (Salir)	—
SEG 28.1015	N	Dakibyza (Bithynia)	—
SEG 28.1033	N	Nikaia (Bithynia)	1st
SEG 28.1034	N	Nikaia (Bithynia)	—
SEG 28.1111 (*IGR* 4.665)	B	Diocleae (Phrygia)	241–242
SEG 29.1186	A	Saittai (Içikler, Lydia)	165–166
SEG 29.1303	A	Nikaia (Bithynia)	—

(*continued*)

Table A
(*Continued*)

Reference	Type	Place	Date
SEG 31.1282	N	Antiocha (Baladiz)	—
Smyrna 225 (*CIG* 3382, *IGR* 4.1477)	D	Smyrna	2d
Smyrna 386 (*CIG* 3324, *IGR* 4.1481)	N	Bornova	2d–3d?
TAM 2.59	B	Termessus	—
TAM 2.217	N	Termessus?	—
TAM 2.289	B	Termessus	—
TAM 2.322	N	Xanthus	—
TAM 2.338	S	Xanthus	—
TAM 2.437	C	Patara	2d?
TAM 2.438	D	Patara	before 2d
TAM 2.466	N	Patara	—
TAM 2.518	N	Pinara	—
TAM 2.611 (*IGR* 3.569)	C	Tlos	—
TAM 2.627	N	Tlos	—
TAM 2.636	C	Termessus	—
TAM 2.693	N	Cadyanda	—
TAM 2.696	N	Cadyanda	—
TAM 2.898 (*CIG* 4321e)	N	Acalissus	—
TAM 2.967	C	Olympus	—
TAM 2.990	N	Olympus	—
TAM 2.1000	D	Olympus	—
TAM 2.1005	C	Olympus	—
TAM 2.1019	C	Olympus	—
TAM 2.1020	D	Olympus	—
TAM 2.1023	D	Olympus	—
TAM 2.1026	C	Olympus	—
TAM 2.1032 (*CIG* 4325k)	D	Olympus	—
TAM 2.1044	D	Olympus	—
TAM 2.1062	C	Olympus	—
TAM 2.1068	C	Olympus	—
TAM 2.1080	D	Olympus	—
TAM 2.1089	D	Olympus	—
TAM 2.1103	W	Olympus	—
TAM 2.1150	B	Olympus	—

(*continued*)

Table A
(*Continued*)

Reference	Type	Place	Date
TAM 2.1151	C	Olympus	—
TAM 2.1156 (*CIG* 4325h)	B	Olympus	—
TAM 3.215	M	Termessus	—
TAM 3.269	B	Termessus	—
TAM 3.276	B	Termessus	2d–3d?
TAM 3.282	B	Termessus	—
TAM 3.310	A	Termessus	2d?
TAM 3.338	B	Termessus	—
TAM 3.346	B	Termessus	—
TAM 3.357	C	Termessus	—
TAM 3.421	B	Termessus	—
TAM 3.429	B	Termessus	—
TAM 3.483	W	Termessus	—
TAM 3.485	C	Termessus	—
TAM 3.490	B	Termessus	—
TAM 3.495	N	Termessus	no date?
TAM 3.514	N	Termessus	—
TAM 3.518	B	Termessus	—
TAM 3.541	B	Termessus	—
TAM 3.567	B	Termessus	—
TAM 3.577	B	Termessus	—
TAM 3.637	B	Termessus	—
TAM 3.663	N	Termessus	—
TAM 3.702	N	Termessus	—
TAM 3.743	N	Termessus	—
TAM 3.747	W	Termessus	—
TAM 3.762	A	Termessus	—
TAM 3.764	B	Termessus	—
TAM 3.769	C	Termessus	no date?
TAM 3.772	B	Termessus	no date?
TAM 3.794	B	Termessus	—
TAM 3.811	B	Termessus	—
TAM 3.815	B	Termessus	—
TAM 4.147	N	Nicomedia	—
TAM 4.199 (*CIL* 3.329)	B	Nicomedia	—

(*continued*)

Table A
(*Continued*)

Reference	Type	Place	Date
TAM 5.57	B	Silandus	92–93
TAM 5.71	B	Thermae Theseos	140–141
TAM 5.88	N	Saittae	194–195
TAM 5.745 (*IGR* 4.1296)	B	Julia Gordus	—

Table B
92 Freedperson Funerary Inscriptions from Asia Minor

See table A for explanation of "Type" symbols.

Reference	Type	Place	Date
IGR 3.250	S	Laodicea (Galatia)	—
IGR 3.256	B	Laodicea (Galatia)	—
IGR 3.259	N	Iconium-Laodicea	—
IGR 4.544	N	Nacolea (Phrygia)	2d?
IGR 4.762	N	Duman (Phrygia)	—
IGR 4.828	A	Hierapolis (Phrygia)	2d–3d?
IGR 4.1600 (*CIL* 3.14192,17)	N	Metropolis (Lydia)	—
MAMA 4.336	N	Ishiklu (Eumeneia)	2d–3d
MAMA 5.89	A	Ilkburun (Dorylea)	—
MAMA 6.18	C	Eskihisar (Phrygia)	225?
MAMA 6.170	C	Davas (Phrygia)	120–135
MAMA 6.202 (*IGR* 4.804)	N	Dikiei (Apameia)	—
MAMA 6.272 (*IGR* 4.660)	N	Susuz (Akmonia)	—
MAMA 7.49	A	Laodicea Combusta	—
MAMA 8.136	A	Dorla (Isauro-Lykaonia)	—
MAMA 8.267	N	Köpekler (Perta)	—
Robert *EA* p. 242 (*BCH* 17 [1893]:540–541)	A	Çeltikci	—
SEG 28:1154	S	Eumeneia	—
SEG 29.1306	N	Nikaia (Bithynia)	—
TAM 2.52	N	Telmessus	—
TAM 2.289	B	Termessus	—
TAM 2.357	C	Xanthus	—
TAM 2.431	S	Patara	—
TAM 2.438	N	Patara	not after 1st
TAM 2.454	N	Patara	—
TAM 2.459	A	Patara	2d
TAM 2.460 (*IGR* 3.676)	N	Patara	2d
TAM 2.486 (*CIL* 3.12131)	F	Patara	1st?
TAM 2.611 (*IGR* 3.569)	N	Tlos	—
TAM 2.627	N	Tlos	—
TAM 2.859	N	Idebessus	—
TAM 2.861	W	Idebessus	—

(*continued*)

Table B
(*Continued*)

Reference	Type	Place	Date
TAM 2.872	C	Idebessus	—
TAM 2.941 (*SEG* 6.772)	D	Corydalla	—
TAM 2.986	C	Olympus	—
TAM 2.1003	B	Olympus	—
TAM 2.1023	D	Olympus	—
TAM 2.1028	D	Olympus	—
TAM 2.1103	D	Olympus	—
TAM 3.214	A	Termessus	—
TAM 3.221	S	Termessus	—
TAM 3.224	B	Termessus	—
TAM 3.228	M	Termessus	—
TAM 3.236	A	Termessus	—
TAM 3.258	C	Termessus	—
TAM 3.259	A	Termessus	—
TAM 3.275	W	Termessus	—
TAM 3.284	C	Termessus	—
TAM 3.293	A	Termessus	—
TAM 3.295	M	Termessus	—
TAM 3.310	D	Termessus	—
TAM 3.350	C	Termessus	—
TAM 3.359	C	Termessus	—
TAM 3.365	B	Termessus	—
TAM 3.374	A	Termessus	—
TAM 3.381	C	Termessus	—
TAM 3.421	B	Termessus	—
TAM 3.429	B	Termessus	—
TAM 3.430	B	Termessus	—
TAM 3.444	A	Termessus	—
TAM 3.467	B?	Termessus	—
TAM 3.481	N	Termessus	—
TAM 3.484	B	Termessus	—
TAM 3.497	B	Termessus	—
TAM 3.505	B	Termessus	—
TAM 3.509	N	Termessus	—
TAM 3.519	A	Termessus	—
TAM 3.528	B	Termessus	—

(*continued*)

Table B
(*Continued*)

Reference	Type	Place	Date
TAM 3.539	A	Termessus	—
TAM 3.540	C	Termessus	212–223
TAM 3.542	N	Termessus	—
TAM 3.557	A	Termessus	—
TAM 3.558	M	Termessus	—
TAM 3.576	B	Termessus	—
TAM 3.578	N	Termessus	—
TAM 3.649	A	Termessus	—
TAM 3.662	A	Termessus	—
TAM 3.682	F	Termessus	—
TAM 3.723	N	Termessus	—
TAM 3.728	C	Termessus	—
TAM 3.747	W	Termessus	—
TAM 3.758	C	Termessus	—
TAM 3.760	N	Termessus	—
TAM 3.765	N	Termessus	—
TAM 3.772	B	Termessus	no date?
TAM 3.790	N	Termessus	—
TAM 3.826	A	Termessus	—
TAM 3.828	A	Termessus	—
TAM 3.841	N	Termessus	—
TAM 4.276 (*CIG* 3777)	B	Nicomedia	—
TAM 4.466	A	Termessus	—
TAM 5.712	C	Julia Gordus	109–110

Table C
Family Types in Slave and Freed Funerary Inscriptions

In this table, funerary inscriptions for slaves and freedpersons have been categorized according to what type of family structure is evidenced in the inscription. See table A for explanation of Type symbols. Numbers in parentheses are percentages. When two percentages are separated by a solidus (/), the first is the percentage of all funerary inscriptions for that category (e.g., funerary inscriptions for slaves from Asia Minor); the second is the percentage of those inscriptions of that category that give some evidence of family. For example, under "Asia Minor, slave, Type A" below, 11 is 10 percent of 115 and 15 percent of 74.

Some inscriptions are too fragmentary to enable confident categorization. Other inscriptions, for one reason or another, do not fit the family categories used in this reckoning. For example, in *IGR* 4.530, a group of brothers provides an inscription for their slave father. In *TAM* 3.211, a freedman provides for himself and his "descendants;" but he may not yet *have* any descendants. Such inscriptions I label *special cases*.

	Asia Minor		Macedonia		Greece	
Family Type	Slave	Freed	Slave	Freed	Slave	Freed
No family	30	26	10	30	7	18
shown	(26)	(28)	(62)	(70)	(100)	(56)
Evidence of	74	54	3	11	0	7
family	(64)	(59)	(19)	(25)		(22)
Type A	11	19	2	7	0	4
	(10/15)	(21/35)	(12)	(16)		(12)
Type B	36	16	1	1	0	1
	(31/49)	(17/30)	(6)	(2)		(3)
Type C	17	14	0	2	0	0
	(15/23)	(15/26)		(5)		
Type D	10	5	0	1	0	2
	(9/14)	(5/9)		(2)		(6)
Man + child	3	3	0	0	0	0
	(3)	(3)				
Woman +	5	3	2	1	0	0
child	(4)	(3)	(12)	(2)		
Too frag-	2	2	1	0	0	7
mentary						
Special cases	1	4	0	1	0	0
Total	115	92	16	43	7	32
	(100)	(100)	(100)	(100)	(100)	(100)

Table D
Funerary Inscriptions from Greece (including the Greek islands)

Reference	Place	Date
SLAVES		
Dessau 7390	Athens	—
IG 2–3.13224	Athens	3d–4th
IG 5.1235 (L p. 23)	Taenarum	3d?
IG 12.3.1232	Melos	—
L p. 24	Cos	—
L p. 24	Cos	—
SEG 28.674	Rheneia (Delos)	1st B.C.E.
FREEDPERSONS		
CIL 3.525	Patras	—
CIL 3.541, add. p. 984.	Corinth	—
CIL 3.544	Corinth	—
CIL 3.575	Nicopolis	2d
CIL 3.582	Epirus	43 B.C.E.?
CIL 3.6107	Athens	—
CIL 3.7166	Casos	1st?
CIL 3.7305	Calydon	—
Corinth 8.2.76	Corinth	—
Corinth 8.2.140	Corinth	—
Corinth 8.2.142	Corinth	—
Corinth 8.3.240	Corinth	1st
Corinth 8.3.280	Corinth	—
Corinth 8.3.281	Corinth	—
Corinth 8.3.321	Corinth	Augustus
IG 2–3.3936	Athens	1st
IG 2–3.7091	Athens	early 1st
IG 2–3.7155	Athens	1st
IG 2–3.10935	Petralona	1st–2d
IG 2–3.12223	Athens	1st
IG 2–3.12590–591	Athens	—
IG 4.634	Argo	1st B.C.E.?
IG 12.3.1232	Melos	—

(*continued*)

Table D
(*Continued*)

Reference	Place	Date
IG 12.5.426	Paros	—
Kos 7	Mytilene	1st
Kos 17	Cos	3d
Kos 44 (*CIL* 3.2076, p. 1310)	Dyme (Achaia)	1st
Kos 75	Patras	—
Kos 82	Sicyon	2d
Kos 83	Sicyon	1st
SEG 17.123	Athens	1st B.C.E.–1st
SEG 27.234	Nicopolis	—

Table E
Funerary Inscriptions from Macedonia

Reference	Place	Date
SLAVES		
Demitsas no. 849, pp. 700f.	Amphipolis	25
Dessau 7479	Diamam	—
IG 9.2.856	Larisa	—
IG 9.2.871	Larisa	—
IG 9.2.873	Larisa	—
IG 9.2.874	Larisa	—
IG 9.2.875	Larisa	—
IG 9.2.876	Larisa	—
IG 9.2.972	Larisa	2d
IG 10.284	Thessalonika	ca. 2d
IG 10.338	Thessalonika	5th or later
IG 10.409	Thessalonika	2d–3d
IG 10.666	Thessalonika	—
IG 10.740	Thessalonika	2d–3d
IG 10.784	Thessalonika	4th or later
SEG 27.221	Phalanna (Thessaly)	1st B.C.E.
FREEDPERSONS		
AD 1973–74, p. 548	Thessaly	—
AE 1969–70.584 (1964.274 rev.)	Ljuboten	—
AE 1980.845	Thessalonika	1st
ArchEph 1910, pp. 354–361, no. 6	Thessaly	before 16
CIL 3.665	Philippi	—
CIL 3.675	Philippi	—
Demitsas no. 970, p. 752	Philippi	1st
IG 9.2.295	Gomphi (Thessaly)	—
IG 9.2.851	Larisa	—
IG 9.2.852	Larisa	—
IG 9.2.853	Larisa	—
IG 9.2.854	Larisa	1st B.C.E.–1st
IG 9.2.855	Larisa	—

(*continued*)

Table E
(*Continued*)

Reference	Place	Date
IG 9.2.856	Larisa	—
IG 9.2.857	Larisa	—
IG 9.2.858	Larisa	—
IG 9.2.859	Larisa	—
IG 9.2.860	Larisa	—
IG 9.2.861	Larisa	—
IG 9.2.862	Larisa	—
IG 9.2.863	Larisa	—
IG 9.2.864	Larisa	—
IG 9.2.865	Larisa	—
IG 9.2.866	Larisa	—
IG 9.2.867	Larisa	—
IG 9.2.868	Larisa	—
IG 9.2.925	Larisa	—
IG 9.2.1166	Demetries (Thessaly)	—
IG 10.310	Thessalonika	ca. 1st
IG 10.339	Thessalonika	1st
IG 10.354	Thessalonika	ca. 1st
IG 10.378	Thessalonika	ca. 1st
IG 10.380	Thessalonika	ca. 2d
IG 10.386bis	Thessalonika	2d
IG 10.451	Thessalonika	2d–3d[a]
IG 10.535	Thessalonika	2d–3d
IG 10.580	Thessalonika	—
IG 10.691	Thessalonika	147
IG 10.701	Thessalonika	ca. 2d
IG 10.723	Thessalonika	2d–3d
IG 10.829	Thessalonika	ca. 2d
IG 10.878	Thessalonika	1st
SEG 28.537	Amphipolis	ca. 100?

[a]Either 145–46 or 261–62 c.e.

Table F
Jobs in Large Roman Households

This table presents results of studies by Susan Treggiari. In the first part, 120 inscriptions from the Roman *columbarium* of Livia (Treggiari, "Jobs in the Household of Livia") are arranged into categories according to job type:

Administrative and managerial;[a] Clerical;[b] Medical and support staff;[c] Craftspersons and laborers;[d] Household servants (excluding those engaged in more personal service);[e] Personal servants.[f]

The second part of the table presents jobs from a study by Treggiari of the household of the Statilii, an aristocratic Roman family (Treggiari, "Domestic Staff at Rome in the Julio-Claudian Period, 27 B.C., to A.D. 68".

Job Type	Slaves	Freed	Total
Household of Livia			
Adminstrative and managerial	5	5	10
Clerical	11	3	14
Medical and support staff	10	5	15
Craftspersons and laborers	21	10	31
Household servants (not personal)	17	8	25
Personal servants	16	9	25
Total	80	40	120
Household of the Statilii			
Administrative and managerial	1	3[g]	4
Clerical	4	2	6
Medical and support staff	3	1	4
Craftspersons and laborers	17	4	21
Household servants (not personal)	1	0	1
Personal servants	5	1	6
Entertainers	3	0	3
Total	34	11	45

[a]*Dispensator* (bursar), *arcarius* (treasurer), *atriensis* (steward), *supra cubicularios* (head chamberlain), *supra medicos* (head physician).

[b]*A manu* (secretaries and short-hand writers) *insularii* (rent collectors and superintendents of apartments?), *libraria* (store clerk), *ad possessiones, rationis* (accountant?), *tabularius, lector* (reader).

^c*Medici* (doctors), *obstetrices* (midwives), *ad valutudinarum* (workers in a "sick area"), *nutrix* (nurse), *paedagogus*.

^d*Aquarius* (plumber?), *aurifices* (goldsmiths), *calciator* (shoemaker), *colorator* (furniture polisher?), *faber* (craftsperson in general), *sarcinatrices* (menders), *lenipendi* (wool weighers), *margaritarius* (pearl or gem setter), *mensores* (surveyors), *pictor* (painter, probably of murals), *pistores* (millers), *a purpur* (perhaps dyers of purple), *structores* (construction workers).

^e*Argentarius* and *ab argento* (in charge of silver), *opsonator* (caterer), *ab ornamentis* (in charge of ceremonial dress), *ostiarii* (doorkeepers), *a specularibus* (window keepers or cleaners?), *ab suppelectile* (in charge of valuable furniture), *a tabulis* (in charge of pictures or tablets?) *ad unguenta* (in charge of oils), *a vest/ad vestem* (in charge of clothes), *a sacrario* (in charge of sacred garments), *stratores* (could be grooms or persons to saddle and make ready mounts, Treggiari, "Jobs in the Household of Livia," 56.).

^f*Cubicularii* (chamberlains), *capsarius* (one who carried a small box of personal items?), *delicium* (a pretty slave for ornamentation), *ornatices* (dressers), *a pedibus*, *pedisequi/pedisequae*, *a sede* (the last three all attendants to one's person in some way), *rogatores* (inviters or announcers?), *unctrix* (masseuse).

^gIncluding a "supervisor of litter bearers."

Table G
The So-called Athenian Manumissions

Merchants and dealers[a]	38
Craftspersons[b]	28
Woolworkers[c]	54
Farmers and vinedressers	11
Animal keepers[d]	5
Laborers[e]	2
Musicians[f]	3
Clerical workers[g]	2
Doctor	1

Note: I am indebted to Elizabeth Meyer for a careful listing of the different professions found on the inscriptions along with a catalogue of the sex and domicile of the "freedpersons." She allowed me to see as yet unpublished research of her own.

[a]Including merchants, traders, ironmongers, and sellers and dealers of various specified commodities (frankincense dealer, myrrh seller, etc.).

[b]Including smiths, goldsmiths, seamstresses, bakers, tanners, millers, carpenters, builders, etc., as well as those specified by what they make: bed maker, shoemaker, etc.

[c]These may all be women; in some cases the sex cannot be ascertained. They seem to have had low status. They are given here as a separate group because there are so many of them.

[d]Two donkey drivers, two muleteers, one keeper of a yoke of draught animals (for lease or rent?).

[e]Water carrier, hired servant.

[f]Two flutists, one kithara player.

[g]One clerk, one underclerk.

Table H
Professions of Slaves and Freedpersons from Eastern Inscriptions

An asterisk (*) refers to imperial-slave or freed status.

Profession	Place	Date	Reference
		SLAVES	
		Greece	
oikonomos	Sparta	—	L p. 23 (*CIG* 1276)
Public slave[a]	Sparta	ca. 100	*SEG* 27.42
oikonomos	Taenarum	3d?	*IG* 5.1.1235
oik. of 5% tax	Athens	2d?	*IG* 2–3.11492
Public slave	Athens	302–301 B.C.E.?	*IG* 2².502
Public slave	Athens	101 B.C.E.	*IG* 2².1335.58
unguentarius[b]	Ithaka	35	Kos 169
		Macedonia	
*oikonomos**	Thessaly	—	L p. 22 (*IG* 9.2.1124)
public slave	Larisa	—	*IG* 9.2.871
slave of *comes*[c]	Thessalonika	ca. 5th	*IG* 10.338
		Asia Minor	
*oikonomos**	Galatia	161–180	Anderson
*oikonomos**	Patara	2d?	*TAM* 2.437
oikonomos	Nikaia	1st	*SEG* 28.1033
oikonomos/*actor*	Apollonia	3d	L p. 48
dispensator	Julia Gordus	—	*TAM* 5.745
dispensator/ *oikonomos**[d]	Chios (Bithynia)	—	*IGR* 4.235
prostatēs[e]	Dorylaeum	(late?)	*IGR* 4.530
pragmateutēs	Olympus	—	*TAM* 2.1020
pragmateutēs	Telmessus	—	*TAM* 2.59
pragmateutēs	Kuyucak (near Dorylaeum)	—	*MAMA* 5.185
pragmateutēs	Aidin (Lydia)	—	*BCH* 5 (1881): 346, no. 8
pragmateutēs	Teos (Lydia)	—	*IGR* 4.1576

(*continued*)

Table H
(*continued*)

Profession	Place	Date	Reference
pragmateutēs	Karoaba	—	*TAM* 5.442
pragmateutēs	Tyriaion	2d	*SEG* 28.1242
pragmateutēs	Cyzicus	—	*IGR* 4.152
arcarius*	Julia Gordus	1st?	*TAM* 5.692
arcarius*	Julia Gordus	110/11	*TAM* 5.713
tabularius*	Synnada	54–68	*MAMA* 4.53
tabellarius* (courier?)*	Thyatira	—	*IGR* 4.1221
votarius*	Kebsud	—	*IGR* 4.235
kankellarios*f	Laodicea	—	*IGR* 3.256
eirenarchēs*g	Hadrianopolis	—	*MAMA* 7.135
palaestra guardh	Patara	1st	Raffeiner no. 40
hippeus*i	Lysias	—	*IGR* 4.753
hippeus	Laodicea	—	*IGR* 3.253
hippeus	Laodicea	2d	*MAMA* 1.30
gladiator	Saittae	—	*TAM* 5.140
weaverj	Nicea	1st?	Raffeiner no. 39
shepherdk	Donarsa	—	*MAMA* 8.361

Syracuse

epitropos	Syracuse	410	Raffeiner no. 37

Moesia Superior

oikonomos*	Nais	—	*IGR* 4.1699
muleteerl	Singidunum	1st–2d	Raffeiner no. 41

Thrace

kynēgos (huntsman?)m	Tomi	2d–3d	Raffeiner no. 43

Sicily

personal servant (*therapaina*)	Morgantina	1st B.C.E.?	*SEG* 29.931

(*continued*)

Table H
(*Continued*)

Profession	Place	Date	Reference
		FREEDPERSONS	
		Macedonia	
nutricula	Ljuboten	—	*AE* 1969–1970.584
phrontistēs[*m]	Thessaly	before 16	*ArchEph* 1910 no. 6
slave dealer[o]	Amphipolis	1st–2d	*SEG* 28.537
		Asia Minor	
epitropos/procurator[*]	Patara	2d	*TAM* 2.459
epitropos[*]	Stectorius (Phrygia)	2d	*IGR* 4.749
epitropos[*]	Lycaonia	—	*IGR* 3.243
epitropos a cubiculario[*f]	Claudiopolis	—	*IGR* 3.75
vice procurator[*q]	Patara	2d	*TAM* 2.459
adiutor procuratorum[*r]	Tyanollus (Lydia)	—	*IGR* 4.1317
oikonomos[s]	Nicomedia	—	*TAM* 4.276
oikonomos?[t]	Termessus	—	*TAM* 3.258
pragmateutēs	Atjilar	—	Robert *EA* p. 241
pragmateutēs	Termessus	—	*TAM* 3.123
tabularius[*u]	Ancyra (Galatia)	3d	*IGR* 3.168
instrumentarius tabularorum	Insuyu (Phrygia)	2d	*MAMA* 7.524
grammateus	Karaoglania (Lydia)	—	*IGR* 4.1347
heimatistēs[v]	Davas, Phrygia	120–135	*MAMA* 6.170
		Cos	
epitropos[*]	Cos	3d	Kos 17

(*continued*)

Table H
(*Continued*)

Profession	Place	Date	Reference
Moesia Inferior			
librarios*	Tomi	3d	*IGR* 1–2.623
Thrace			
*tierarchios?*ʷ	Heraclea	88–90	*IGR* 1–2.781
Syria			
architabularius/ *epitropos*ˣ	Tyre	2d	*IGR* 3.1103

[a]This public slave, Philodespotos, is probably the same as the oikonomos from Sparta.

[b]Dealer in perfumes.

[c]Philoxenos is the slave of a *comes* (a tutor). His master may also be a slave.

[d]Genealios' title is *dispensator ad frumentum/oikonomos epi tou seitou.*

[e]*Prostatēs epi tou sitou/dispensator a frumento.*

[f]*cancellarius* (accountant or auditor).

[g]Keeper of the peace, or policeman.

[h]*Palaistrophylax.*

[i]Groomsman, keeper of the stables or horseman.

[j]*Histōn/textrina.*

[k]A decree from Dionysopolis (ca. 250 c.e.?) also mentions slave shepherds in general (*poimenas . . . doulous*): *MAMA* 4.297.

[l]*Oreōkomos* is a mule driver.

[m]Raffeiner believes this is a slave who was a huntsman in the amphitheater, somewhat like a gladiator.

[n]*Phrontistēs ho epi tōn klēronomiōn.*

[o]*Sōmatanporos.*

[p]Chamberlain.

[q]The Greek equivalent of *vice procurator* in this bilingual inscription is *antepitropos.*

[r]Assistant to the procurators. The Greek in the bilingual inscription is *boēthos epitropou.*

sGaius Tryphonos was a public slave, it seems, and was then freed by the city.

tI take Apelles to be an *oikonomos*, though he does not explicitly say he is, because he is a freedman and carries the nickname "Oikonomikos."

uEditor: "Tabularius in officio procuratoris." The Greek is *taboularios*.

vClothes maker or clothes merchant.

wI am not sure if this signifies some kind of job, an honor, or a civic position.

xThis imperial freedman was architabularius of Egypt and *epitropos . . . prosodōn Alexandreias*.

Table I
Status of oikonomoi

An asterisk (*) indicates imperial slave or freed; A.M. = Asia Minor; "Roman" = Roman Imperial Period.

Reference	Name	Place	Date
	SLAVES		
Anderson p. 19	Eutyches*	Galatia	161–180
IGR 3.25	Genealios*	Chios (A.M.)	—
IGR 4.1699	Arteimetos*	Nais	—
SEG 28.1033	Italos	Nikaia (Bithynia)	1st
TAM 4.57	Markos Skreibonios	Bithynia	—
	PROBABLY SLAVES		
IG 2–3.11492	Philetus	Athens	2d?
IG 5.1.40 (*CIG* 1276)	Philodespotos	Sparta	ca. 100
IG 14.688 (*IGR* 1.464)	Sagaris	Apollonia (Phrygia)	3d
IGR 3.279 (L p. 48)	Kallistos	Isauria (A.M.)	—
L p. 48	Gallikos	Galatia	—
MAMA 1.7	Eu——	Laodicea Combusta	—
MAMA 6.246	Onesimus	Asia Minor	—
Robert *EA* p. 242	Doryphoros	Bithynia	—
SEG 28.1015	Sosylos	Bithynia	—
SEG 28.1034	Philon	Nikaia (Bithynia)	Roman
SEG 28.1045	Soteris	Prusa	2d?
TAM 2.437	Zosimos*	Patara (A.M.)	Roman
TAM 2.518	Symphoros	Pinara (A.M.)	—
TAM 2.1151	Dionysios	Olympus (A.M.)	—
TAM 5.88	Epiktetos	Saittae (A.M.)	194–195
	PROBABLY SLAVE OR FREED		
IG 9.2.1124	Philol——*	Thessaly	—
L p. 24	Demetrios	Cos	Roman
L p. 30	Pulcher	Iasos (A.M.)	—
L p. 50 (*CIG* 2088)	Diomedes	Thracia (A.M.)	1st
	PROBABLY FREED		
Robert *EA* p. 242	K. Karikos	Çeltikci	—
SEG 29.1306	Claudius Thallos	Nikaia	—

(*continued*)

Table I
(*Continued*)

Reference	Name	Place	Date
FREED			
MAMA 8.386	unknown	Armutlu (A.M.)	—
TAM 3.258	Apelles III	Termessus	—
TAM 4.276	Gaius Tryphonos	Nicomedia	—
FREE AND PROBABLY FREE			
IG 12.2.499	unnamed	Lesbos	—
IGR 4.1435 (*CIG* 3151)	Bassos Hermogenous	Smyrna	2d–3d
L p. 25	Cl. Seeros Ophalion	Bithynia	—
L p. 27	Hegesippos Opi——	Lydia (A.M.)	2d–1st B.C.E.
L p. 27 (*CIG* 3162)	Pamphilos	Smyrna	2d–3d
L p. 31 (Kern 98)	unnamed	Magnesia (A.M.)	2d B.C.E.
L p. 38	unnamed	Priene	1st B.C.E.
L p. 44 (*CIG* 2811)	Menander	Aphrodisias	Roman
L p. 45	unnamed	Mylasa (A.M.)	2d B.C.E.
L p. 45 (*CIG* 2717)	Philokalos II	Stratonicea	3d
L p. 45	Hernias and Jason	Mylasa (A.M.)	—
L p. 49 (*CIG* 4132)	Gaius Andromenous	Galatia	—
UNKNOWN STATUS			
IG 5.1.1235	Eutychus	Taenarum (Greece)	3d?
IG 10.150	Zosimos	Thessalonika	3d
IG 12.7.287 (L p. 25)	Diad——	Minoa (Amorgos)	—
IGR 1–2.464	Sagaris	Venusia (Italy)	—
L p. 23	too fragmentary	Lusoi (Greece)	4th B.C.E.
L p. 24 (*CIG* 2512)	Dionysios	Cos	—
L p. 24	Philetos	Cos	—
L p. 26 (*CIG* 3793)	Dionysios	Chalcedon	—
L p. 27 (*IGR* 4.1630)	Antonios	Philadelphia	Roman
L p. 27 (*CIG* 3357)	Neilos	Smyrna	1st

(*continued*)

Table I

(*Continued*)

Reference	Name	Place	Date
		UNKNOWN STATUS	
L p. 29	Nikomachos	Ionia	ca. 252 B.C.E.
L p. 30 (*CIL* 3.447)	unknown	Ionia	Roman
L p. 32 (Kern 99)	unnamed	Magnesia (A.M.)	2d B.C.E.
L p. 32 (Kern 100a)	unnamed	Magnesia (A.M.)	2d B.C.E.
L p. 32f (Kern 101)	unnamed	Magnesia (A.M.)	2d B.C.E.
L p. 33	unnamed	Magnesia (A.M.)	2d B.C.E.
L p. 33	unnamed	Magnesia (A.M.)	2d B.C.E.
L p. 33f.	unnamed	Magnesia (A.M.)	—
L p. 34	unnamed	Magnesia (A.M.)	—
L p. 36	unnamed	Priene	3d B.C.E.
L p. 36	unnamed	Priene	4th B.C.E.
L p. 37	unnamed	Priene	ca. 100 B.C.E.
L p. 37	unnamed	Priene	after 129 B.C.E.
L p. 37	unnamed	Priene	ca. 120 B.C.E.
L p. 37–38	unnamed	Priene	1st B.C.E.
L p. 38	unnamed	Priene	ca. 130 B.C.E.?
L p. 38	unnamed	Priene	1st B.C.E.
L p. 47	Tatianos, Diokleus	Hieropolis	—
L p. 48	Amerimnos	Phrygia	—
L p. 49	unknown	Laodicea	—
L p. 49	Kallistos	Galatia	—
L p. 49	unnamed	Apollonia (Thracia)	2d B.C.E.
MAMA 7.1	Eukarpos	Laodicea Combusta	2d–3d
MAMA 8.136	Aurelios Thalais	Dorla	—
MAMA 8.399	Eirene (female)	Cavundar	—
SEG 28.1019	Ennis Glykon	Bithynia	Roman
SEG 30.725	unknown	Serdica (Thrace)	150–250
TAM 2.1163	Makarios	Olympus (A.M.)	—
TAM 4.150	unknown	Bithynia	—
TAM 5.224	Agathephoros	Philadelphia (A.M.)	189–190
TAM 5.743	Phainos	Julia Gordus (A.M.)	2d

Table J
Status of Pragmateutai

Reference	Name	Place	Date
		SLAVE	
BCH 5 (1881): 346, no. 8	Dadouchos	Aidin (Tralles)	—
IGR 4.152	Metrodoros	Cyzicus	—
IGR 4.1576	Dionysios	Teos (Lydia)	—
MAMA 5.185	Attikos	Kuyucak	—
SEG 28.1242	Phlegon	Tyriaion (Lycia)	2d
TAM 2.59	Agathopous	Telmessus	—
TAM 2.1020	Abaskontos	Olympus	—
TAM 5.442	Eutyches	Karoaba	—
		PROBABLY SLAVE	
CIG 2831	Achilleus	Aphrodisia (Caria)	—
IG 10.409	Zosimos	Thessalonika	2d–3d
IGR 1–2.627	Kastresios	Tomi (Moesia Inf.)	—
IGR 3.257	Meneas	Laodicea	2d–3d
IGR 3.1434	Euelpistos	Cytori	115
MAMA 6.222	Auxanon Helladios	Dinar (Phrygia)	247–248
MAMA 8.182	Demetrios	Almassun	—
MAMA 8.385	Dionysios	Armutlu (Salir)	—
SEG 31.1143	Blastos	Antioch Pisidia	—
Smyrna, 386[a]	Zotikos	Bornova	2d–3d
		FREED	
TAM 3.123	Aurelios Soterichos II	Termessus	—
		PROBABLY FREED	
MAMA 6.204	Aurelios Hermogenes	Dinar (Phrygia)	—
Robert *EA* p. 241	P. Anterota	Atjilar (Bithynia)	—

[a]The same inscription also appears in *CIG* 3324 and *IGR* 4.1481.

NOTES

INTRODUCTION

1. Aaron Kirschenbaum, *Sons, Slaves and Freedman*, 15–16 n. 48. Slaves are spoken of as both human beings and things or tools also in Jewish and Near Eastern sources; see Feeley-Harnik, "Is Historical Anthropology Possible?" On torture of slaves, see Robinson, "Slaves and the Criminal Law"; Brunt, "Evidence Given under Torture in the Principate."

2. Sophocles, *Oedipus the King* 410. See M. Smith, "Review." Smith's reference to Diogenes Laertius 8.34 as providing a similar occurrence of slavery to a god is incorrect. Robin Lane Fox believes that calling a human being a servant of the god is not really a conceptual innovation from language found even as early as the *Iliad*. See Fox, *Pagans and Christians*, 109, 701 n. 20.

3. Plato, *Phaedo* 85B. For Philemon, see "Thebans," in Meineke, *Fragmenta Comicorum Graecorum*, 4:11, lines 4–5. See also Philo, *On the Cherubim* 107: "For to be the slave of God (*douleuein theō*) is the highest boast of man, a treasure more precious not only than freedom, but than wealth and power and all that mortals cherish."

4. Apuleius, *The Golden Ass*, 11.15.

5. *MAMA* 4.279. It is not certain, but the steward may himself be a slave, as he speaks of his lord (*kyrios*). For a different interpretation of this inscription, see Sokolowski, "The Real Meaning of Sacral Manumission," 180. Sokolowski says that the slave confessing is the same one wanted by the god.

6. Bömer, *Untersuchungen* 2:89; Pleket, "Religious History as the History of Mentality." A. Cameron (quoted by Bömer), Bömer, and Pleket all take Strato and others who willingly call themselves slaves of a deity to be freedpersons rather than free-born persons. Their reasons for doing so, however, are based not on information in the inscriptions themselves but on their assumption that free people of the Greco-Roman world resisted calling themselves slaves of a deity. The following statement by Bömer, for example, is quoted approvingly by Pleket: "Dass sich eine freie Person als *doulos theou* = *servus dei* (oder gar *Dei*) fühlt oder bezeichnet, widerspricht dem antiken religiösen Empfinden diametral" (Bömer 2.89; Pleket, 170). In other words, Bömer and Pleket decide that free people do not call themselves slaves of the deity and on this basis conclude that the persons who put up these inscriptions must not have been free persons. I believe their initial assumption to be invalid and prefer to leave the status of these dedicants in question.

7. Bömer, *Untersuchungen*, 3.106; Pleket, "Religious History as the History of Mentality," 170. Other examples of persons calling themselves slaves of the deity, especially in

inscriptions, have been noted by scholars. Besides the study by Pleket, see Nock, *Essays on Religion and the Ancient World*, 1.46 n. 92.

8. Adolf Deissmann, *Light from the Ancient East*, 329–332.

9. See, for example, the general agreements by Westermann, "The Freedmen and the Slaves of God," esp. 55–56.

10. Bömer points out that in sacral manumission, the Greek word used for the buying of the slave by the god is *priasthai*, which never occurs in the New Testament, and not *agorazein*, the word used by Paul. For this and other reasons, Bömer concludes that there is no evidence that sacral manumission of the Delphic or any other variety had any influence on Paul's language or on his ideas of salvific redemption. See his *Untersuchungen*, 2.138–139. Bömer's work is taken by commentators to have closed the case on Deissmann's thesis: Elert, "Redemptio ab hostibus," 267; Conzelmann, *Commentary on 1 Corinthians*; Bartchy, *Mallon Chresai*, 121–125.

11. The following interpretations are representative: K. Russell, "Slavery as Reality and Metaphor in the Pauline Letters"; Sass, "Zur Bedeutung von *doulos* bei Paulus." Russell and Sass agree that the language comes from the Old Testament. They disagree on the evaluative function of the language, Russell claiming that *slave of Christ* is a designation of humility and servanthood, while Sass says that it is an honorific title.

12. Conzelmann, *Commentary on 1 Corinthians*, 128. See also Cranfield, *Commentary on the Epistle to the Romans*, 50: "For the Greek in the classical tradition it was well-nigh impossible to use a word of the *doulos* group without some feeling of abhorrence"; Johnson, *The Freedom Letter*, 24; Beare, *Commentary on the Epistle to the Philippians*, 50; Wilckens, *Der Brief an die Römer* 1.61. The study by Wayne G. Rollins typically stresses the negative slavery images: slavery is not recognized as representing salvation, but rather salvation is depicted as deliverance from slavery. See Rollins, "Greco-Roman Slave Terminology and Pauline Metaphors for Salvation."

13. Tabor, *Things Unutterable*, 5.

14. Regarding the fascination with origin, a remark by Michel Foucault is apropos: "History is the concrete body of a development, with its moments of intensity, its lapses, its extended periods of feverish agitation, its fainting spells; and only a metaphysician would seek its soul in the distant ideality of the origin" (*Language, Counter-memory, Practice*, 145; see also 139–140).

15. The most famous advocates of the complexity of ancient slavery have been Moses Finley and those influenced by him. See especially Finley, "Between Slavery and Freedom"; *Ancient Slavery and Modern Ideology; Slavery in Classical Antiquity*. For a comparable study of the complexity of modern slavery in South Asia, see Lionel Caplan, "Power and Status in South Asian Slavery."

16. Historians now generally acknowledge that surviving Greek and Latin literature is a product, for the most part, of the upper class of Greco-Roman society. As Emilio Gabba points out, "Thus, we can only with enormous difficulty understand the mentality of a slave or a member of the lower classes, since we perceive it as represented by the literature of the upper classes, in other words of owners or patrons" ("Literature," 40). For this study I assume that most Greco-Roman literature reflects the ideologies and biases of the upper class. I attempt some correction of this tendency in the sources by treating the literary sources with suspicion while still using them as historical sources. I have also attempted, when possible, to rely on less literary types of literature or on writings of a more popular nature such as

Artemidorus's *Oneirocritica* (Dream Handbook), speeches made to the general public, and popular romances. I have also used some inscriptions to ascertain both actual social structures and social ideology.

17. Kent, *Inscriptions*.

18. I am assuming Wittgenstein's famous argument that "meaning is use." See, for example, Wittgenstein, *Philosophical Investigations*, 14–15 and esp. 20e: "For a *large* class of cases—though not for all—in which we employ the word 'meaning' it can be defined thus: the meaning of a word is its use in the language." See also p. 8e: "To imagine a language means to imagine a form of life."

19. Theissen uses the terms *Plausibilitätsstruktur* and *Plausibilitätsbasis* in analyses of Pauline Christianity; see his *Studien zur Soziologie des Urchristentums*, 318–330. He translates the terminology from Berger, *The Sacred Canopy*, 45–47, 196 n. 20; *Rumor of Angels*, 43: "The plausibility, in the sense of what people actually find credible, of views of reality depends upon the social support these receive."

20. *Topos* is difficult to define because it has been used differently by modern and ancient literary critics. In this book, I follow modern critics, who define it as "a motif which takes the form of a literary commonplace or rhetorical set-piece: e.g., the comparison between nature and a book or between the world and the theater" (Levin, "Motif," 3.243). By this usage, a topos is a piece of rhetoric that is recognizable in a variety of contexts because it uses the same recognizable images, arguments, and comparisons. For example, among ancient rhetoricians, concord was regularly illustrated by analogy with a beehive. The analogy usually included certain elements, such as the industriousness of the worker bees, the lack of selfish competition in the hive, and the propriety of having a "king bee" (they had the sex wrong) who did not work in the same way as the other bees. Some modern literary critics, though not usually the ancients, call this a topos. The subject of concord itself could be called a topos because rhetoricians so often dealt with it in set, predictable ways (see chapter 5 below). For contemporary usages of topos along these lines, see Wellek and Warren, *Theory of Literature*, 259; Emmerson, *Antichrist in the Middle Ages*, 53. For attempts to ascertain ancient definitions of *topos*, see Grimaldi, "The Aristotelian *Topics*," and Donovan J. Ochs, "Aristotle's Concept of Formal Topics." The way Theon uses topos is quite unlike my usage; see Theon, *Progymnasmata*, 76–78, 93–94. Burke, *A Rhetoric of Motives*, recognizes the limited, ancient use of the term (56–57) and then proceeds to broaden its meaning (along the lines of the modern critics) in his own analysis of "timely topics" in modern journalism (62–63).

21. For rhetorical analyses of topoi, see Jehn, *Toposforschung*; Bornscheuer, *Topik*; Wuellner, "Toposforschung und Torahinterpetation bei Paulus und Jesus."

1. ANCIENT SLAVERY AND STATUS

1. A classic history of Roman slavery along these lines is the famous one by Barrow, *Slavery in the Roman Empire*. A more recent work that also presents a more benevolent view of slavery is Vogt, *Ancient Slavery and the Ideal of Man*. For an opposite point of view, see Bradley, *Slaves and Masters in the Roman Empire*. In a more recent article, Keith Bradley misrepresents Alan Watson and some other scholars as implying that "Roman slavery can be regarded as mild or unoppressive" ("Roman Slavery and Roman Law," 485). An attempt, however, to emphasize the complexity of Roman slavery should not be taken as a defense of that struc-

ture. On the ideology of modern treatments of slavery, see Finley, *Ancient Slavery and Modern Ideology*; E. Wood, *Peasant-Citizen and Slave*, 5–41; and Garlan, *Slavery in Ancient Greece*, 1–14.

2. Ascertaining the status of persons in inscriptions—that is, slave, freedperson, or free person—is difficult, and debates have raged among scholars about how to do so. See the Appendix for a discussion of my use of inscriptions to provide status information about slaves and freedpersons. Besides the simple determination of the person's legal status, an inscription can also sometimes provide evidence for informal status. For example, I claim below that some persons listed in a funerary inscription are social dependents of other persons in the same inscription, judging from the position of the names in the inscription. Usually, though not always, names were given in an order of descending social status, with dependents' names following names of those who enjoyed higher status. The only way observations like this can be made is by comparing many inscriptions within a given area and establishing what were the conventions of giving names on inscriptions of that area and that time. Such is the procedure I have tried to follow.

3. *Epitome Ulpiani* 5.5; A. Watson, *Roman Slave Law*, 46–47. See also Hopkins, *Conquerors and Slaves*, 165.

4. Barrow, *Slavery in the Roman Empire*, 152.

5. See especially Flory, "Family in *Familia*, 89–90, as well as her "Family and '*Familia*'"; and "Where Women Precede Men." See also the essays collected in Rawson, *The Family in Ancient Rome*.

6. Flory, "Family in *Familia*," 79, 91 n. 6.

7. *Digest* 5.1.19.3. See also Buckland, *The Roman Law of Slavery*, 155. All of part 1, chapter 6, of Buckland's study is devoted to laws relating to slaves doing business for masters. For slaves in Greece living independently of masters (*choris oikountes*), see Elena Perotti, "Una categoria particolare di schiavi attici," and Garlan, *Slavery in Ancient Greece*, 71.

8. Rawson, "Family Life among the Lower Classes at Rome," 72, 76; see also Rawson, *The Family in Ancient Rome*, 171. In her claim that slaves most often married slaves within the same household, Rawson's studies agree with those of Weaver (see *Familia Caesaris*, 127); see also Flory, "Family in *Familia*," 82, 93 n. 24.

9. Saller and Shaw, "Tombstones and Roman Family Relations" 124; see also B. Shaw, "Latin Funerary Epigraphy."

10. Saller and Shaw, "Tombstones and Roman Family Relations," 145.

11. Ibid., 151, 149.

12. See the Appendix for explanation of sources and method of collecting inscriptions. My figures should not be compared directly with those of Saller and Shaw; the methods of organizing the data and counting differ and so the numbers and percentages should not be expected to agree completely.

13. In 23 cases (22 percent of 103), the slave owner is the provider or a provider. Sometimes an owner or patron provides an inscription along with the slave's family or other persons. In *MittAth* 24: 360, for example, the lord (*kyrios*) seems to join the family of Dionysios, a young boy, in providing the funerary inscription for him. In 9 cases (9 percent), a slave provides for self with no mention of family. In 3 cases, a collegium provides (*IGR* 4.1221; *TAM* 5.71 [140–141 c.e.]; *TAM* 5.88 [194–195 c.e.]); once several *syndouloi* (fellow slaves) furnish the inscription for a male slave (*TAM* 2.466); in one case a free or freed man allows a slave cousin or nephew, along with that slave's wife and children, to share his own

tomb (*TAM* 3.485); in two cases sacred slaves (*hierodouloi*) and their wives and children are provided for by other (free?) men (*TAM* 2.1000; 2.1089).

14. In 21 cases (25 percent of 84), the patron is the or a provider. Eight times (9 percent), a slave provides for self with no family connections mentioned. In 52 cases (62 percent), family members provide for one another. Some other configurations: the heirs of a freedman provide his funerary inscription (*MAMA* 6.202); in another instance, two freedmen of an imperial freedman join his heirs in providing the inscription (listed in both *TAM* 2.460 and *IGR* 3.676); and in one case, a lone freedwoman is allowed a place in the tomb of a free man along with his family (*TAM* 2.859).

15. For example, this number includes instances in which a slave specifically says the tomb is to be occupied alone (in which case the person probably had no immediate family), instances in which a slave is included in an inscription with other persons of no relation (as far as one can tell), and instances in which only the name of the deceased is given. Obviously, in this last category, many of those so commemorated may have had families, but the customs of providing inscriptions did not encourage giving other information.

16. I have excluded these inscriptions from the familial category because conceivably it would not be difficult for a slave to maintain relationships with offspring. On the other hand, more social stability (and therefore probably more power on the part of the slave) would be required to maintain a family that exceeded the parent-child structure. I have also not included in the familial category those epitaphs in which a child provides for parents. In these cases, the fact that a slave could maintain some sort of relationship with her or his parents (perhaps only the knowledge of who they were) is little evidence for the stability of family structures.

17. *TAM* 2.1020; *IGR* 4.921.

18. This guess might find support in one inscription I find humorous: Aurelius Leukis, a freedman, provides a sarcophagus for himself and his wife; he then notes that his daughter, Armasta, and son, Apollonios, may be buried in it also "if they are unable to supply other coffins for themselves" (*TAM* 3.576). Perhaps, like many fathers, he suspected his children might be less independent than he would like.

19. I have presented figures for inscriptions from Asia Minor. I have collected far fewer freedperson and slave inscriptions from Greece and Macedonia. Furthermore, out of 7 funerary inscriptions for slaves from Greece (including the islands), none provides evidence for familial relationships. Out of 16 from Macedonia (including Thessaly), only 10 (62 percent) offer any information about family. The lack of information, however, seems to be due to conventions of providing the inscriptions and cannot be taken as evidence of the lack of family structures among slaves. This can be seen when the figures for freedpersons are compared. Of the funerary epitaphs from Macedonia I have examined, family connections can be ascertained in only 11 out of 43 (25 percent). Out of 32 inscriptions for freedpersons from Greece, only 7 (22 percent) offer any information about family. Therefore, if the dearth of familial epitaphs from Greece and Macedonia is taken to indicate the absence of family for slaves, the same conclusions must obtain for freedpersons. It is more likely that funerary conventions did not encourage the inclusion of such information. The figures for Greece and Macedonia are given on the tables, however, for the sake of comparison between the slave and freed inscriptions within the same area. For slave families in ancient Athens, see Garlan, *Slavery in Ancient Greece*, 41; and Biezunska-Malowist, "La vie familiale des esclaves," *Colloque Camerino 1978*, *Ceti dipendenti e schiavitù nel mondo antico*, *Index* 8 (1978/1979), 140–143.

20. No statistical confidence can be placed in such a small number of inscriptions. That is, the percentage of inscriptions denoting the presence of families should not be taken as representing a percentage of slaves throughout the society who maintained family structures. We have no way of knowing how representative these inscriptions are of the entire slave population of the empire.

21. Talmudic sources may be taken to imply that slave families existed also among slaves of Jews of the period: Solodukho, "Slavery in the Hebrew Society" 6; Urbach, "Laws Regarding Slavery" 15–16.

22. Gaius, *Institutes* 2.96; Kirschenbaum, *Sons, Slaves and Freedmen*, 10–11. For a concise discussion of the legal aspects of peculium see A. Watson, *Roman Slave Law*, 95–96. See also Buckland, *Roman Law of Slavery*, 131, 184–187; Kaser, *Roman Private Law*, 77, 86f. It is important to remember that legally children of the paterfamilias—no matter how old they were—were under this same legal restriction of ownership. They could also own money only as a revocable peculium allowed by the paterfamilias. See Kaser, 69 (11.2.1a); Kirschenbaum, 16. Some scholars have argued, certainly correctly, that this legal situation rarely prevailed as social reality, and when it did it affected only the upper class. The majority of the free population was probably not affected by these laws. Whatever money they could get was completely under their own control and not under that of their father. See Daube, *Roman Law*, 75, 92; see also Daube, "Dodges and Rackets in Roman Law," and Rawson, *The Family in Ancient Rome*, 16–17. Talmudic references suggest similar conditions for Jews in the East, with slaves carrying on business for the owner, controlling funds and property, making loans, and owning slaves themselves (Solodukho, "Slavery in the Hebrew Society," 5; Urbach, "Laws Regarding Slavery," 33–35, 46).

23. Sometimes the very wording of laws related to the peculium shows that, though from a strictly legal point of view the master owned all the slave's assets, the Romans seemed to think of the peculium as the slave's. For example, *Digest* 15.1.17 (Ulpian) poses this question: "If my ordinary slave [*ordinarius*] has *vicarii*, may I deduct from the *peculium* of the *ordinarius* whatever the *vicarii* owe me?" (quoted from A. Watson, *Roman Slave Law*, 99). Posing the question in this way ("may I?") seems ridiculous if the legal fact of the paterfamilias's full ownership correctly reflects the full social situation. See also Kirschenbaum, *Sons, Slaves and Freedmen*, 31–38.

24. Dessau 1514 (*CIL* 6.5197). See also Ste. Croix, *Class Struggle*, 143. These slaves were, of course, *vicarii*, underslaves, and as such were legally property of Musicus's own master, the emperor.

25. Note the references in Pliny, *Natural History*, 33.145; Suetonius, *Otho* 5. See also *CIL* 6.5197. Pliny (*NH* 7.129) mentions also a wealthy slave actor who he says made 500,000 sesterces a year.

26. Athenaeus, *Deipnosophists*, 13.593–596; see also *Greek Anthology* 6.332 for the wealthy prostitute Polyarchis.

27. Classical Greece: Garlan, *Slavery in Ancient Greece*, 75. Roman period: Hopkins believes that in some cases family members provided the funds, but he admits that we do not know where most slaves obtained the money for their manumission price (*Conquerors and Slaves*, 167–168). For legal references to slaves purchasing their own freedom, see Ulpian in *Digest*, 33.8.8.5; Marcellus in *Digest*, 37.15.3. For the church practice, see Ignatius, *Epistle to Polycarp*, 4.3.

28. Dessau 7812 (date uncertain).

29. Hopkins, *Conquerors and Slaves*, 146 n. 24: "A poor peasant family needed one ton of wheat equivalent for minimum subsistence, which includes a bare allowance for heat, housing and clothing."

30. The cost of a simple monument in western provinces could be as low as a hundred sesterces or even in the tens of sesterces, according to estimates by Saller and Shaw, "Tombstones and Roman Family Relations," 128; see also Duncan-Jones, *Economy of the Roman Empire*, 99–101; and Rawson, *The Family in Ancient Rome* 55 n. 116.

31. *TAM* 3.811 (probably from the second to third century c.e.).

32. *AD* 1971, p. 337 (name of slave: Soton); L p. 50 (Diomedes); *AE* 1980.846 (Bassus); *AE* 1983.930 (Zabdas).

33. *MAMA* 4.293.

34. J. G. C. Anderson, "An Imperial Estate in Galatia," 19.

35. Smyrna 23.1.225 (*CIG* 3382; *IGR* 4.1477). The two men may be said to be *her* sons because they are illegitimate, that is, his sons but not recognized as such under law because of his slave status. But slaves do not always follow the legal niceties of familial terminology in inscriptions. In other cases, they do not hesitate to call their children just that. For that reason, it is possible that these two males are her sons by a different father from Telephoros Joulianos.

36. *TAM* 2.1044. Note he says specifically that he himself bought the tomb.

37. *TAM* 2.967.

38. *TAM* 2.338. The whole question of the threptoi in these inscriptions is not settled. They may have been slaves—in some cases they certainly were—but they are so numerous in the inscriptions of Asia Minor that one wonders if they were always slaves. I have not included them in my accounts of slaves from Asia Minor because I believe their exact status is still disputable. If they were slaves, their ubiquitous presence in the inscriptions of certain areas (Termessus, for example) indicates a remarkable integration into the normal family structures of the free populace. This very ubiquity, however, has led me to doubt that they were, for the most part, slaves. For a discussion of the threptoi, see Cameron, "*Threptoi* and Related Terms in the Inscriptions of Asia Minor"; see also Nani, "*Threptoi*."

39. *TAM* 3.357.

40. *TAM* 2.1020. "Olympene" indicates, I assume, that Hermes is a citizen of Olympus.

41. A similar situation occurs in *TAM* 3.663, in which a male slave of a woman provides a sarcophagus for himself "by permission of the mistress." It seems that the slave later had the name of a free or freed man added to the inscription. That man may have been related in some way to the slave, but there is no indication from the names that such is the case. It is possible, therefore, that the free or freed man is socially dependent in some way on the slave. In this case, as in many others of Asia Minor, the slave gives the name of his father as well as that of his owner.

42. *IGR* 4.921. The master is Ti. Claudius Paulinus (*hypatikos*, indicating consular rank?).

43. Knife and bed makers: Lionel Casson, *Ancient Trade and Society*, 39. Shoemakers and linen workers: ibid., 59 n. 21; Aeschines 1.97. Workers on the Erechtheum: *IG* 1².374; see Randall, "The Erechtheum Workmen;" Casson, 61 n. 31. Banking: Casson, 46; see Davies, *Athenian Propertied Families*, 433; Kirschenbaum, *Sons, Slaves and Freedmen*, 157–158. The upper class in ancient Greece used both slaves and freedmen to conduct banking operations. For classical Athens, see Garlan, *Slavery in Ancient Greece*, 67; for Greece under the early

empire, Pleket, "Urban Elites" 137. Roman laws also refer to slave bankers (*Digest* 14.3.19.1). According to Hippolytus (second century C.E., Rome), Callistus had been a managerial slave in charge of a banking operation set up by his master (*Refutation* 9.12.1ff.).

44. Book publishing and business: Cornelius Nepos *Atticus* 13.4; business and clerical: C. A. Forbes, "Education and Training," 328; medicine: Forbes, 346; *AE* 1929.215; *IGR* 1.283 is an inscription to a doctor, who seems to be an imperial freedman; slave philosophers: Gellius, *Noctes Atticae* 2.18; Macrobius, *Saturnalia*, 1.11.41–44.

45. Temple maintenance: Tod, "Epigraphical Notes," 17–18, for a study of an inscription from Delphi, about 94 B.C.E., which records the gift of some slaves to Delphi and lists their jobs. Temple maintenance of different sorts seems to be one of them. Constables: Chariton, *Chaereas and Callirhoe*, p. 43 (3.4.7); p. 62 (4.5.6). (For the Greek text of Chariton, see Charitonis Aphrodisiensis, *De Chaerea et Callirhoe Amatoriatum Narrationum*.) Note also the *eirēnarchēs* from Hadrianopolis: *MAMA* 7.135. Pliny (*Epistle* 10.19) mentions public slaves serving as prison guards. English equivalents for Greek and Latin terms, especially for occupational names, are at best approximations.

46. Barbers: C. A. Forbes, "Education and Training," 333. Mirror makers: Dessau 1779. Goldsmiths: Dessau 7710. Cooks: Columella, *On Agriculture* (1 praef. 5) talks about schools for cooks. Architects: Cicero, *To Quintus*, 2.2. See Forbes, 334, for lists of occupations.

47. Dessau 7479 (*CIL* 3.14206 [21]); see Varro, *On Agriculture*, 1.2.23 for slave innkeepers. Ulpian (*Digest* 14.4.5.2) speaks of a slave woman *negotiatrix*; see also *Digest* 14.3.8 for boys and girls as managers of *tabernae*.

48. See Casson, *Ancient Trade and Society*, 108–110, and the discussion later in this chapter for treatment of some of the documents from Pompeii. For slave agents living in cities apart from masters, see Treggiari, "Urban Labour in Rome"; Kirschenbaum, *Sons, Slaves and Freedmen*, 111.

49. The two articles most used here are Treggiari, "Household of Livia," and "Domestic Staff at Rome." See also "Jobs for Women"; "Women Domestics"; and "Lower Class Women."

50. Treggiari, "Household of Livia," 54, 57.

51. Ibid., 63, but see also Chantraine, "Freigelassene und Sklaven kaiserlicher Frauen," 389–416. Chantraine provides lists of freed and slave jobs of dependents of certain *female* members of the imperial families (396–398) and points out that, according to the evidence of these inscriptions, slaves of women in the imperial household (as opposed to slaves of men) seem to have had less chance for social improvement.

52. Lewis, "Attic Manumissions"; "Dedications of Phialai at Athens"; Tod, "Epigraphical Notes"; Aristide Calderini, *Manomissione* 424ff. I have some doubts about whether or not these lists are in fact manumission records. They nowhere explicitly name the persons as ex-slaves, and the legal language of the inscriptions is ambiguous. It seems to me at least possible that these are metics (resident aliens) who have been acquitted of some legal responsibility to other persons, but that does not necessarily mean that they are freedpersons and that the other persons mentioned are their former owners.

53. Tod, "Epigraphical Notes," 16. E. M. Wood, from the Demosthenic and pseudo-demosthenic speeches, claims to have counted conservatively over fifty references to slaves that give a job. Managerial and clerical jobs are numerous, second only to domestic jobs in number; agricultural jobs are few, though this might be due to the nature of the source (Wood, *Peasant-Citizen and Slave*, 45).

54. Tod, "Epigraphical Notes," 17–18.

55. See table H in the Appendix.

56. Litter bearer: *IG* 2–3.13224 (Athens, third to fourth century C.E., named Primos); *aleiptēs: IG* 2–3.7155 (Athens, first century C.E., Antiochos).

57. *Oikonomoi:* L p. 23 (*IG* 5.1.40, lines 6–7 and *CIG* 1276) (Sparta, no date, Philodespotos, public slave); *IG* 5.1.1235 (*CIG* 1498) (Taenarum, third century C.E.?, Eutyches). *Vilicus/oikonomos: IG* 2–3.11492 (Athens, second century C.E.?, Philetus). *Demosioi: IG* 2².1335.58 (Athens, 101 B.C.E., Agathokles); *IG* 2².502 (Athens, 302–301 B.C.E.?, Antiphates); *SEG* 27.42 mentions three inscriptions related to the public slave Philodespotos (Sparta, ca. 100 C.E.): *IG* 5.1.153 (*CIG* 1239B); *IG* 5.1.146 (*CIG* 1249 I); *IG* 5.140 (*CIG* 1257, 1276).

58. Public slave: *IG* 9.2871 (Larisa, Thessaly, no date, Hyacinthus). Slave of *comes: IG* 10.338 (Thessalonika, ca. fifth century C.E. or later, Philoxenos). *Oikonomos:* L p. 22 (Philo——).

59. E.g., *IG* 10.150 (Zosimos the *oikonomos*); *IG* 10.409 (Zosimos the *pragmateutēs*).

60. Gaius Ioulios: *ArchEph* 1910, pp. 354–61, no. 6 (Thessaly, before 16 C.E.). Aulos Kaprilos Timotheos: *SEG* 28.537 (Amphipolis, Macedonia; most scholars date the inscription to around the end of the first to the beginning of the second century C.E.). For discussion of this slave dealer, see Finley, "Aulus Kapreilius Timotheus"; Duchêne, "Sur la stèle d'Aulus Caprillus Timotheos, *sōmatemporos.*"

61. Slave shepherds: Robert 10 (1953): 31; *MAMA* 4.297. For a few references to agricultural slaves in Asia Minor after 300 C.E., see MacMullen, "Late Roman Slavery," 362. Gladiator: *TAM* 5.140 (Saittae, no date, Maternos); craftpersons: *MAMA* 6.170 (Davas, Phrygia, 120–35 C.E.; P. Aelios Parthenokles; Aelios gives his profession as *heimatistēs*, which may be tailor or, on the other hand, may mean that he was a clothes merchant); weaver: Raffeiner no. 39 (Nicea, first century C.E.?, Myrmex; Greek *histōn* is Latin *textrina*); public slaves: *MAMA* 1.418 (Baghlija, no date, Joulianos); *IGR* 4.914 records the recapture of 107 escaped public slaves (*dēmosioi douloi*, probably of lower status and not managerial slaves) at Cibyra in the first century C.E.; *eirēnarchēs: MAMA* 7.135 (Hadrianopolis, no date, Kosmion). We also encounter a *palaistrophylax* (guard of the palaestra): Raffeiner no. 40 (Patara, first century C.E., Ammonios). A slave in Tomi, Thracia, calls himself a *kynēgos*, which may indicate that he was a huntsman in the Amphitheater.

62. *Arcarii: TAM* 5.692 (Julia Gordus, first c. C.E.?, Stephanos); *TAM* 5.713 (Julia Gordus, 110–111 C.E., name unknown). *Tabularii: MAMA* 4.53 (Synnada, 54–68 C.E., Hyacinthus). *Kankellarius: IGR* 3.256 (Laodicea, no date, Seleukos). *Tabellarius: IGR* 4.1221 (Thyatira, no data, Pollion).

63. Oikonomos: Anderson (Galatia, 161–180 C.E., Eutyches); *TAM* 2.437 (Patara, second century C.E.?, Zosimos). *Dispensator: TAM* 5.745 (Julia Gordus, no date, Crescens). Dispensator/oikonomos: IGR 4.235 (Chios, no date, Genealios). Prostatēs: *IGR* 4.530 (Dorylaeum, no date, Kerdon).

64. Oikonomoi: *SEG* 28.1033; L p. 48 (Sagaris). Pragmateutai: *TAM* 2.1020, 2.59; *MAMA* 5.185; *BCH* 5 (1881): p. 346, no. 8; *IGR* 4.152, 4.1576; *SEG* 28.1242; *TAM* 5.442. These counts do not include thirty inscriptions of persons of uncertain status, many of whom are probably slaves, including twenty-one oikonomoi and nine pragmateutai. See tables I and J in the Appendix.

65. Procurators: *TAM* 2.459; *IGR* 4.749; *IGR* 3.243; *IGR* 3.75. Assistants to the procurators: *IGR* 4.1317. Vice procurator: *TAM* 2.459. *Grammateus: IGR* 4.1347. *Tabularius: IGR* 3.168. *Instrumentarius tabularorum: MAMA* 7.524. According to Kirschenbaum, in the Ro-

man legal texts, *"Procuratores* were generally freedmen; rarely slaves. *Institores* [managers of shops, etc.] were often slaves; seldom freedmen" (*Sons, Slaves and Freedmen*, 144, see also 150–153; see 144–145 for comparison of the two jobs and status significances).

66. Oikonomoi: *TAM* 4.276; *TAM* 3.258. Pragmateutai: *TAM* 3.123; and Robert *EA* 241 (P. Anterota).

67. Table H in the Appendix lists different known professions of slaves and freedpersons from eastern inscriptions. I make no pretense of completeness but give it in order to illustrate the preponderance of managerial positions among inscriptions that record a slave's or freed-person's job.

68. This is also borne out of Flory, "Family in *Familia,*" 80.

69. Garnsey, "Slaves in Business," 105.

70. Inn managers: Varro, *On Agriculture,* 1.2.23; Barrow, *Slavery in the Roman Empire,* 106–114; see also Dessau 7479 for the sixteen-year-old slave boy who managed an inn for his "owners/parents." For the Pompeii documents, see Casson, *Ancient Trade and Society,* 104–107.

71. Athenaeus *Deipnosophists,* 1.1.

72. Landvogt. See also Reumann, "Use of *Oikonomia."* Some results of Reumann's disser-tation are more readily available in his *"Oikonomia* as 'Ethical Accommodation.'"

73. L p. 16.

74. Ibid., pp. 8, 13; for discussion of the Ptolemaic period, see pp. 11–14.

75. Ibid., p.32 (Kern no. 99).

76. L p. 12.

77. An inscription from Priene, first century B.C.E., mentions "the *oikonomos* of the city, whoever it is at that time" (L pp. 37–38). See also *Inschriften von Priene,* no. 99, lines 13–99 (also in Landvogt 37), with the same phrase. *Inschriften von Priene,* no. 107, line 45 mentions "the one about to serve as *oikonomos*" (also in Landvogt 38; Priene, about 130 B.C.E.?).

78. Of a council *(boulē):* L p. 44 *(CIG* 2811) (Aphrodisias, dated by Landvogt to the Roman period); of a tribe *(phylē):* L p. 45 *(Mitt Ath* 15 [1890]: 268) (Mylasa, Caria, second century B.C.E.).

79. L p. 25.

80. Deciding from an inscription who is and is not a slave or freedperson is sometimes difficult when an explicit status is not stated. See the introduction to the Appendix below for a discussion of how I decided status in such cases.

81. The point is made repeatedly: Smyrna, p. 386; L. Robert, *Op. Min.* 2.883–885; 1.296; *BCH* 52 (1928): pp. 412–413; Robert *EA,* 240–243; ibid., p. 263; "Les honneurs que leur décernaient les villages montrent assez l'influence locale des intendants des grands domaines" (Naour, "Tyriaion en Cabalide," 112; *intendants* is Naour's French translation of *pragmateutēs*); MacMullen says slave bailiffs were "great folk locally" ("Late Roman Slavery," 363 n. 23).

82. There are many examples of pragmateutai (even using the Greek term) in the West as well. See, for example, the inscription of Phaustinos, the pragmateutes, at Rome *(IGR* 1–2.359). I have included, however, only examples from the eastern part of the empire.

83. *TAM* 5.687 *(tois par' hēmin pragmateuomenois Rhōmainois).* See also *IGR* 4.248 (Assus, Asia Minor, first century C.E.); *IGR* 4.903, 905, 913, 916, 917, 918, 919 (all from Cibyra); *IGSK* 19.2 (Sestios, probably first century C.E.); Hatzfeld, *Les trafiquants italiens dans l'orient hellénique,* 114.

84. Robert *EA* p. 241; I think he is a freedman because he shares the first name of the man whom he serves as pragmateutes.

85. *TAM* 3.123. For the same patron and patroness, leading figures in town, see also 3.122 and 3.58.

86. Ibid. 2.1020.

87. Senatorial: *BCH* 5 (1881): p. 346, no. 8; *CIG* 2831. Consular: *IGR* 4.1576 (*CIG* 3104). *Primipilus: IGR* 1–2.627; 3.1434. Note also *SEG* 28.1242: the slave pragmateutes of an important family from Balboura is also important, as the editors point out.

88. Slave of the "thrice asiarch": *MAMA* 6.222; Agathopous: *TAM* 2.59 (*IGR* 3.544).

89. Some scholars seem to think that managerial slaves such as pragmateutai were used almost exclusively on country estates. This would seem to be L. Robert's view in Robert *EA* 241.

90. Note also that slave agents often conducted business in cities separate from those of their masters. Laws from the first century c.e., for example, mention slave agents conducting business in Rome for their owners who live in the provinces; see Kirschenbaum, *Sons, Slaves and Freedmen*, citing *Digest* 5.1.19.3, among other texts. For slave agents in Jewish households, see the evidence from the Mishnah analyzed by Flesher, *Oxen, Women or Citizens?* 38, 127–131.

91. Tablet 15. Texts of 6 of the tablets are found in Casson, *Ancient Trade and Society*, 108–110; he discusses them on 104–107. See Bove, "Tab. Pomp. 27," 329–331, for a list of the first 54 of the 70 tablets and bibliography.

92. Tablet 7, Casson, *Ancient Trade and Society*, 109.

93. Casson, *Ancient Trade and Society*, 106.

94. Tablets 17 and 18, Casson, *Ancient Trade and Society*, 109–110.

95. Public slaves at menial tasks: Aristotle, *Constitution of Athens*, 50.2, 54.1. Cibyran slaves: *IGR* 4.914; cf. L. Robert, "Documents d'Asie Mineure," 408. For slaves as state accountants and registrars, see *IG* 2.1.403, lines 36–52 (Athens, 221–220 b.c.e.); *IG* 2.1.476, lines 37–49 (Athens, ca. 102 b.c.e.); both translated in Wiedemann, *Greek and Roman Slavery*, 156–157. See also the public slave bureaucrats at Pergamum: Macro, "Imperial Provisions for Pergamum."

96. The phrase is from the Pseudo-Aristotelian *Oeconomicus* 1.5.2. Slaves did occupy different status levels in classical Greece (see Garlan, *Slavery in Ancient Greece*, 145–148); the phenomenon is even more widespread and differentiated in the Roman Empire.

97. *Digest* 47.10.15.44. See also Buckland, *Roman Law of Slavery*, 81 and 239.

98. *Digest* 47.10.15.45. A humorous example of this mentality (that the slave is an extension of the owner) is furnished by Plautus (254?–184 b.c.e.). In his comedy *Casina* a husband and wife conduct a conjugal fistfight by having their respective slaves beat up one another (see lines 404ff.).

99. This common sense was enshrined in the laws. Callistratus, a jurist from the Severan period (193–235 c.e.), writes, "It is especially important to examine the status of each man, to see whether he is a decurion or a commoner; to ask whether his life is virtuous or marred by vice, whether he is rich or poor (for poverty might imply that he is out for gain), and whether he is personally hostile to the man against whom he is witnessing or friendly to the man whose cause he is advocating" (*Digest* 22.5.3; quoted in Garnsey, "Legal Privilege in the Roman Empire," 145–146). Aelius Aristides, the second-century rhetor, claimed that all

people were equal under Roman imperial justice (*Oration* 26.39; 26.59). But the legal sources contradict his lip service to egalitarianism; see Alföldy, *Social History of Rome*, 109–110; Garnsey, *Social Status and Legal Privilege*, 234–236; Lacey, "*Patria Potestas*," 124, 133–137.

100. Artemidorus, *Interpretation of Dreams*. For the Greek text, see *Artemidori Daldiani Onirocriticon Libri V.* In citing Artemidorus, I give first the book and section number from the Greek edition, then, in parentheses, the page number from Robert J. White's translation.

101. Ancient horoscopes also sometimes provide insight into lower-class attitudes; see MacMullen, "Social History in Astrology"; Lynn Thorndike, "A Roman Astrologer."

102. Artemidorus *Interpretation of Dreams*, 2.53 (White, p. 127). But cf. 4.49 (p. 205), where crucifixion may signify good even for a wealthy man.

103. The term (*pepisteumenoi*) is from ibid., 4.15 (p. 192).

104. Oikonomos: ibid., 1.74 (p. 55); oikonomia: ibid., 2.30 (p. 109); *diōkonomeō:* ibid., 4.61 (p. 211). Those "held in trust" or "having many possessions": ibid., 2.9 (p. 89).

105. See the Greek at ibid., 1.35 (p. 35, *en pistei onti*); 2.9 (p. 89, *hoi en pistei ontes*); 2.49 (p. 126, *ōn en pistei*); cf. 2.30 (p. 109); 2.47 (p. 125).

106. As reflected in the laws: Kirschenbaum, *Sons, Slaves and Freedmen*, 127–140, 142, 157. For the ambiguity of slave status even in classical Greece, see E. M. Wood, *Peasant-Citizen and Slave*, 76. This continuity in the everyday lives of persons moving from slave to freed status is also borne out by the fact that freedpersons in Roman society often remained in a dependent state, even, for example, continuing to live in the house of the former owner after manumission; see Robinson, "Slaves and the Criminal Law," 244–246; and Rawson, *The Family in Ancient Rome*, 13.

107. On the difficulty of distinguishing Roman slaves by physical appearance alone, see A. Watson, *Roman Slave Law*, 9; Appian, *Civil Wars* 2.120; *Digest* 18.1.4–5. Keith Bradley disagrees, saying, "A correlation did exist at Rome between the slave's physical appearance and his social inferiority" ("Roman Slavery and Roman Law," 481 n. 16). Bradley's statement constitutes no legitimate objection, however, because it does not say much about slavery per se—only about the social inferiority of slave to master. The point is that one could also take a poor, laboring, free person to be a slave due to social inferiority manifested in dress. It is the social inferiority that is discernible, not the actual status of slavery.

108. Kirschenbaum, *Sons, Slaves and Freedmen*, 128, 133–140. Interestingly, according to Paul Flesher, in Jewish legal traditions, reflected in the Mishnah, the freedperson's legal status is not linked to the legal status of the former owner. The Mishnah, as compared to Roman law and custom, limits the master's control over a freedman (Flesher, *Oxen, Women or Citizens?*, 38, 140–141; see also Urbach, "Laws Regarding Slavery," 58). But see also Robinson, "Slaves and the Criminal Law," for changes through time in Roman legal restrictions on freedmen.

109. A good review of the history and varieties of patron-client relations can be found in the Introduction to Badian, *Foreign Clientelae*. See also Saller, *Personal Patronage under the Early Empire*, and the review of Saller's book by D'Arms, *Classical Philology* 81 (1986): 95–98. For purposes of comparison with modern systems of patronage, see Eisenstadt and Roniger, "Patron-Client Relations" 77; *Patrons, Clients and Friends*.

110. See, for example, the satirical scene in Juvenal, *Sixteen Satires*, 1.102ff. Horace implies what clients might expect from their patrons: food (*Epistles* 1.17.12, 13–15), clothes (1.17.25–32), and gifts (1.17.43–51).

111. *CIL* 3.656, no date.

112. J. G. C. Anderson, "An Imperial Estate in Galatia," 19.

113. Pliny *Ep.* 10.5, 6, 10. In these letters Pliny also requests citizenship for clients of friends of his. Elsewhere, he asks the same favor for family members and clients of his clients (10.11; see also 10.104, 105, 106, 107).

114. A recent dissertation by Alan Mitchell examines the legal systems in the Greek East during the early Roman Empire, concentrating on Corinth and the early Christian community there. His research confirms the strong influence of the patronal system and ideology in the courts. See A. Mitchell, "I Corinthians 6:1–11"; for the dominance of patronage in the courts of the Republic, see May, *Trials of Character.*

115. Saller, *Personal Patronage,* 152; see also Ste. Croix, "Suffragium," 42–45.

116. On the offensive nature of patron-client language and the substitution of friendship language to mask patron-client relationships, see Saller, *Personal Patronage,* 11–15; D'Arms, Review of Saller, *Classical Philology* 81 (1986): 95; Nicols, "*Tabulae patronatus,*" 544. For examples of friendship language in patron-client inscriptions, see *TAM* 3.110 (Termessus, 223–224 C.E.); *TAM* 5.433 (183–184 C.E.); Kos 83 (Sicyon, first century C.E.); see also Kirschenbaum's discussion of such language in Cicero's letters (*Sons, Slaves and Freedmen,* 175). For an interesting discussion of the way "friends" bound themselves to one another through the asking and giving of favors in the patronal society, see Saller, *Personal Patronage,* 24–25. He notes the letter of Pliny (*Ep.* 7) in which Pliny speaks of binding another person to himself by means of favors.

117. Eric R. Wolf notes that patron-client reciprocity in modern cultures, in this case Spain, shows similar forms: the client usually receives tangible assets from the patron, while the patron receives esteem, loyalty ("information on the machinations of others"), and political support ("Kinship, Friendship, and Patron-Client Relations," 16–17).

118. Chariton, *Chaereas and Callirhoe,* 1.12.6 (p. 14 in Blake's translation); 2.3.3 (p. 24). On the *salutatio* see Martial *Epigrams* 3.7, 8.42; Saller, *Personal Patronage,* 128; Mohler, "The *Cliens* in the Time of Martial," 246–248.

119. *TAM* 3.123; see *TAM* 3.122 and 3.58 for the same patron and patronness. Often the council and demos of a city voted honors for a person, and that person's freedpersons provided the inscription and/or statue. See *TAM* 3.87, 117, 125, 129 (all from Termessus, no date); *IGR* 4.749 (Phrygia, second century C.E.).

120. Free and freed dedicants: *TAM* 5.245 (Kula, 145–146 C.E.), a long list is given of persons setting up an inscription to a ten-year-old male; among the dedicants are six slaves.

121. *TAM* 5.702 (Julia Gordus, Asia Minor, 36–37 C.E.).

122. According to Roman laws, owners may even be considered in debt to their own slaves, for a variety of reasons; see Kirschenbaum, *Sons, Slaves and Freedmen,* 78.

123. Eutychides: *IGR* 3.168. Eutyches: J. G. C. Anderson, "An Imperial Estate in Galatia," 19. Aurelios Herodes: *IGR* 1–2.673; note that the slave has two names. Usually, but not always, slaves identify themselves with only one name.

124. E. M. Staerman makes this point also for slavery in North Africa, though pointing out that slaves and freedpersons in North Africa had less chance for social mobility than in other provinces of the empire: see "Die Sklaverei im den afrikanischen Provinzen," in Staerman et al., *Die Sklaverei in den westlichen Provinzen,* (Stuttgart: F. Steiner, 1987), 1–37, esp. 21; see also, in the same volume, V. M. Smirin, "Die Sklaverei im römischen Spanien," 102. Garlan, *Slavery in Ancient Greece,* 77–78, also makes a connection between slave-master and patron-client structures for Greece just before Roman times.

125. Saller, *Personal Patronage*, 37–38.

126. See Seneca *De ben.* 2.21.5. Seneca is making the point that one should not receive gifts from someone considered morally inferior to oneself. But the distinction between moral and social inferiority was seldom maintained in the minds of upper-class Romans (see Saller, *Personal Patronage*, 127). For further discussion of the function of gifts in patron-client relations, including the observation that the gods were thus understood as patrons, see Mott, "The Power of Giving and Receiving"; Kirschenbaum, *Sons, Slaves and Freedmen*, 164–177.

127. Xenophon, *Oeconomicus*, 5.16; see also 15.1. See 9.16–17 for Xenophon's conviction that slaves have no actual share in a master's property.

128. Columella, *On Agriculture*, 1.8.13; see Garlan, *Slavery in Ancient Greece*, 148–153.

129. Columella, *On Agriculture*, 11.1.14–17, 19, 23. Of course, imitation (*mimesis*) in patronal ideology has an implicit function of maintaining traditional hierarchy; see Castelli, "Mimesis as a Discourse of Power in Paul's Letters," 81, 90.

130. Dessau 1949; See D'Arms, *Commerce and Social Standing*, 103–104.

131. Dessau 7694; trans. D'Arms, *Commerce and Social Standing*, 103.

132. Philodespotos: *IG* 5.1.153; *IG* 5.1.147, lines 16–18; *TAM* 3.747 (Termessus, no date); see also A. Spawforth, "The Slave Philodespotos." For the master-loving man: *MAMA* 4.336 (Ishikla second–third century c.e.). I interpret *philodespotos* and *philokyrios* as active (master-loving) rather than passive (loved by the master) on analogy with the name *Philotheos;* see Dodds, *The Greeks and the Irrational*, 35; Merrit, "Greek Inscriptions," 62, col. 1, line 4. For examples of philodespotos as an insult: Herodotus 4.142; Josephus, *Jewish War*, 4.175.

133. *SEG* 28.1033. Philokyrios: *TAM* 2.466 (Patara, no date).

134. D'Arms, Review of Saller, *Classical Philology* 81 (1986): 95–98. See also the relevant passage in Saller, *Personal Patronage*, esp. 141. Garlan insists that, for classical Athens also, slaves accommodated themselves to the structure of slavery and produced, as far as we can tell, no counterideology (*Slavery in Ancient Greece*, 197–200).

135. Dio, *History*, 52.26.5. Other authors, such as Plutarch and Pliny, also recognized the political importance of benevolence; see Mott, "The Power of Giving and Receiving," 71–72.

136. Boulvert, *Domestique et fonctionnaire*, 5.

137. Max Kaser makes this point based on a study of Roman laws of persons: "Under a sensible and well-to-do master, [a slave's] position could be equal to, or even better than, the conditions of free citizens belonging to the lower classes. . . . As a consequence of the law of *peculium* which placed a property at the slave's free disposal, and the 'adjectitious' liability under *actiones adiecticiae qualitatis* . . . , such slaves were able to move in daily life in a manner not much different from a free man's. . . . Accordingly, even the gift of freedom to the slave did not always ensure an improved social and economic position for him, especially when the patronal protection came to an end with the second generation" (Kaser, *Roman Private Law*, 85 [15.1.1]).

138. Aristotle, *Politics* 1.13, 1260a36–b6. See Ste. Croix's discussion of the passage, *Class Struggle*, 184–185.

139. See Oost, "The Career of M. Antonius Pallas."

140. Narcissus: Tacitus, *Annals*, 11.38.5. Epaphroditus: Weaver, "Social Mobility," 123. Crispinus and Licinius: Juvenal, *Satires*, 1.26 and 102. See also Weaver, "The Slave and Freedman Cursus"; *Familia Caesaris*. Note that the same situation is reflected in Jewish and Near Eastern sources: according to Gillian Feeley-Harnik, "Temple slaves in high positions

could achieve such eminence that they fell into the category of those to whom the saying was applied 'the King's slave is the King' (*Sebu.* 476)" ("Is Historical Anthropology Possible?" 112; see also Urbach, *Laws Regarding Slavery,* 33).

141. Finley, *The Ancient Economy,* 62; Garlan, *Slavery in Ancient Greece,* 83.

142. Pasion and Phormio: Ste. Croix, *Class Struggle,* 174, 558 n. 3; (Pseudo?) Demosthenes 45.71–75. Evangelus: Plutarch, *Pericles,* 16.3–5. Plutarch talks as if Pericles is doing all the activity, but it seems that Evangelus might have a larger role than the upper-class Plutarch gives him credit for.

143. Dessau 1949. See Ste. Croix, *Class Struggle,* 178. Other examples of upwardly mobile slaves are given by Suetonius, including Marcus Antonius Gnipho (*Grammarians* 7), Quintus Remmius Palaemon, who was a house slave of a woman, became a weaver, and then obtained an education by accompanying his owner's son to school (*Gram.* 23), and Lucius Voltacilius Pilutus, who, Suetonius says, was chained to the door as an old-fashioned doorkeeper but later helped his master in court cases (*Gram.* 27). Suetonius also tells of Asiaticus, a boy lover of Vitellius, sold to gladiator school, then rescued by Vitellius and later proclaimed a knight when Vitellius himself became emperor (*Vitellius* 12).

144. Kent, *Corinth,* no. 62. An important factor explaining the large number of freedpersons at Corinth was that, when it was refounded by the Romans in the first century B.C.E., it was settled by Roman freedpersons.

145. Ibid., 321.

146. See Balsdon, *Romans and Aliens,* 14.

147. Cook: Athenaeus, *Deiphosophists* 12.542f (Moschion, slave cook of Demetrius); writers and scholars: Terence (Seutonius *Life of Terence* 1); Publilius Syrus (Macrobius *Saturnalia* 2.7.6). Grammarians: Suetonius *On Grammarians;* Slave philosophers; Gellius *Noctes Atticae* 2.18 and Macrobius *Sat.* 1.11.41–44. See C. A. Forbes, "The Education and Training of Slaves."

148. J. L. Myers, *Dawn of History,* 98; as quoted in Barrow, *Slavery in the Roman Empire,* 197. See Wiedemann, *Greek and Roman Slavery,* 13: "Slavery served precisely as a method of integrating outsiders." For the same function in Jewish circles, see Urbach, "Laws Regarding Slavery," 48–49. According to John Demos, a certain kind of servitude in early New England had much the same function, working to incorporate outsiders into the dominant culture and society (*Entertaining Satan,* 25–26).

149. Artemidorus, *Interpretation of Dreams,* 1.31 (p. 32 in White's translation). Other dreams signifying manumission: dreaming that one is beheaded (1.35, p. 35); dreaming that one dies signifies freedom for lower-level slaves, but demotion for managerial slaves (2.49, p. 126); crucifixion (2.53, p. 127).

150. Ibid., 2.15 (p. 99). For other dreams signifying promotions to managerial positions, see 2.30 (p. 109), 2.31 (p. 111), and 2.47 (p. 125).

151. For an introduction to the romances, see G. Anderson, *Ancient Fiction;* Hägg, *The Novel in Antiquity;* Walsh, *The Roman Novel.* For the use of the novel by the social historian, see Millar, "The World of the *Golden Ass," Journal of Roman Studies* 71 (1981): 63–75.

152. Chariton, *Chaereas and Callirhoe,* 2.9.5 (p. 31 in Blake's translation); see also 2.4.8 (p. 26).

153. Pliny the Elder lists well-known, successful people who started out as slaves at Rome: *Natural History* 35.58 (199–201). In the second century, Lucian (*Conversations with the Dead,* 362) can also assume the plot: A rich, old man fools legacy hunters and leaves his

money to a recently bought, pretty slave boy; the characters proceed to discuss the probable social advance of the slave.

154. Statius (*Silvae* 3.3.46–49) emphasizes that Claudius Etruscus's slavery eventually brought such a good end because he had those of the highest status for his masters: "For you had no ordinary masters, but those to whom East and West alike do service. This is not something for you to be ashamed of—for what is there on earth or in heaven that does not have to obey; everything rules and is ruled in turn." For a picture of Publilius Satur's tombstone, with this interpretation, see Toynbee, *The Crucible of Christianity*, 159. For a similar example, see Dessau 7812.

155. For the Greek text of the "Life of Aesop," see *Aesopica*, vol. 1. This dating is that of Perry, *Life and Fables of Aesop*, 26. For an English translation, see Daly, *Aesop Without Morals*.

156. Dio Chrysostom, *Discourse* 15.22. The manuscripts have "lampmaker" (*lychnopoios*). Some editors suggest a change to *lychnophoros*, "lampbearer" (see Höistad, *Cynic Hero and Cynic King* 87 n. 2; and the Loeb edition, 164 n. 2). This translation is J. W. Cohoon's, except that I have substituted *lampbearer* where he took the liberty of supplying *vassal*. Cohoon was apparently not familiar with the tradition depicting Cyrus's slave origins.

157. An English version of Justin's history can be found in *Justin, Cornelius Nepos, and Eutropius*, trans. Watson. Justin Marcus Junianus probably wrote in the third century C.E. (*The Oxford Classical Dictionary*, 571). He seems to have abridged Trogus Pompeius's *Historiae Philippicae*. His account of Cyrus's origins, which may have been excerpted in part from Ctesias (Cook, *The Persian Empire*, 26), seems to borrow from Herodotus. The basic story is the same but with some interesting differences, one of which is that Cyrus is explicitly called a slave by Justin, though not by Herodotus (Justin 1.4). Furthermore, Cyrus's first act, according to Justin, is to free an oppressed Persian slave of a Mede and make him his companion in his revolt against the Medes (1.6).

158. See Schürer, *History of the Jewish People*, 1.28–32, and bibliography there cited. Most scholars believe that Nicolaus is following earlier sources, mainly Ctesias, a fourth-century historian (see Höistad, *Cynic Hero and Cynic King*, 86; Jacoby, *Fragmente* 2C.251; Cook, *The Persian Empire*, 21, 26). For the purpose of this study it is sufficient to note that these traditions were current in the first century C.E. The accuracy or antiquity of Nicolaus's account will not be pursued here. For the text of Nicolaus, see Jacoby, *Fragmente*, 2A.361–370, frag. 66.

159. Jacoby, *Fragmente*, frag. 66.4. *Sweepers* here (*kallynontes*) should probably be understood as general maintenance workers on royal property.

160. Nobility: ibid., 66.12; virtue: 66.45; prudence and courage: 66.6; high-mindedness: 66.12, 15. For justice and "truth" see frag. 67.

161. See ibid., esp. 66.33 and 66.12.

162. See footnote 157 above.

163. Petronius *Satyricon* 57. Other references to voluntary enslavement, in these cases as gladiators: *Satyricon* 117; Tatian, *Against the Greeks* 23; Manilius *Astronomica* 4.220–226; Seneca, *Letters*, 37.

164. According to Suetonius, the grammarian Gaius Melissus preferred slavery to Maecenas over freedom. His mother tried to prove his free birth and reclaim his freedom, but he desired to remain Maecenas's slave. He was repaid for his loyalty, says Suetonius, by being freed anyway and being eventually placed in charge of the library in the Portico of Octavia (Suetonius, *Grammarians*, 5.21).

165. Cassiodorus, *Letters*, 8.33. I quote Cassiodorus's statement, though it is much later than the early empire, because there is no reason to believe that this aspect of slavery had changed much from the early imperial times. Another sixth-century example is provided by an Egyptian woman named Martha who, though probably free-born, takes on slave status for the sake of some benefits (Reinhold, "Usurpation of Status," 299).

166. See further Alföldy, *Social History of Rome* 138–139, 141; *Digest* 1.5.51; Dio Chrysostom *Discourse* 15.22–23; Ramin and Veyne, "Droit romain et société"; Ramin and Veyne note that upper-class Romans could very well treat their slaves better than poor, free-born persons (497). For voluntary self-enslavement in Jewish sources, see Urbach, "Laws Regarding Slavery," 9.

167. But see Cambiano, "Aristotle and the Anonymous Opponents of Slavery"; cf. Garlan, *Slavery in Ancient Greece*, 121–126. Urbach ("Laws Regarding Slavery," 94) insists that for Jewish sources also, antislavery sentiments in literature do not signify any suggestion of the abolition of actual slavery.

168. When Athenaeus's "Sophists at Sup" try to imagine life without slaves, they can only imagine a world in which utensils move automatically, bread bakes itself, and fish voluntarily season and baste themselves, flipping themselves over in the frying pan at the appropriate time (*Deipnosophists* 6.267); see also Garlan, *Slavery in Ancient Greece*, 119, 128–133.

169. See Reinhold, "Usurpation of Status," 275: "In the imperial period, under the influence of the socio-political philosophy of Augustus, the Romans developed the highest degree of diversity of formal social stratification, and at the same time the highest incidence of social mobility in antiquity." Referring to classical Athens, Garlan insists that the "increasing heterogeneity" of slavery does not indicate the weakening at all of slavery itself or of the "statutory hierarchy" of the society (*Slavery in Ancient Greece*, 148).

170. For definitions and discussions of status inconsistency, see Meeks, *The First Urban Christians*, 22–23, 54–55, 215 n. 24; Lenski, "Status Crystallization," 405–413; Goffman, "Status Consistency"; Hornung, "Social Status."

171. See Reekmans, "Juvenal's Views on Social Change." The term *middle-class* is not really appropriate for Roman society, but there is no other that is better. Juvenal was not a laborer, and he was obviously a member of the leisured class. On the other hand, he was not independently wealthy either and so was always dependent on patrons.

172. See Juvenal, *Satires*, 1.26, 102, 111; 2.58; 3.81ff., 131, 189; 7.14ff.

173. For instances in which status problems sparked Martial's wit, see *Epigrams* 3.29; 4.46, 67,78; 5.13; 8.16; 9.73; 11.37. These are only a few examples; there are many others. For Horace, see his *Sermones*, 1.6 (the entire poem is about class distinctions and the problems of upward mobility); 2.7; see also *Epistle* 1.14. Gilbert Highet (*"Libertino Patre Natus"*) points out that Horace's biting satire against slaves and upward mobility reflects his own status problems and his sensitivity concerning his father's past as a slave.

174. Pliny, *Ep.* 10.11, 104, 105, 106, 107. Note how Pliny congratulates himself and friends on their liberality in freeing slaves and advancing their careers (*Ep.* 7.32; 8.16). His liberality, of course, does not completely dissuade him from the typical aristocratic belief that a man surrounded by his slaves is thereby living amid perils no matter how kind he is to the ruffians (see, for example, *Ep.* 3.14). This is quite similar to Seneca's advice that masters be kind to their slaves (*Ep.* 47.17), though on another occasion he lets slip his observation that a master's life is in the (sometimes not too merciful) hands of those people he owns (*Ep. Mor.*

[*Moral Epistles*] 4.8). The theme was common among slave-owners, probably because to some extent the fear was, too (see Bradley, *Slaves and Masters in the Roman Empire*, 30–31).

175. Seneca, *Ep. Mor.*, 47.17. This quotation is from a letter in which Seneca advocates kindness toward slaves. This kindness, however, carefully maintained the social structure of the slave's inferiority (Watts, "Seneca on Slavery," 184–190). Kindness is fine, but everything in moderation.

176. Plato, *Republic*, 6.495c–6a. For a discussion of this and other relevant passages, see Ste. Croix, *Class Struggle*, 412. See Plato, *Gorgias*, 518; *Sophist*, 226b for Plato's comments on weaving and the other crafts. But see also E. M. Wood, *Peasant-Citizen and Slave*, 171–172, for the ideological context of Plato's antibanausic and antidemocratic philosophy; for the connection between working for one's living and being a slave, ibid., 51, 133–134.

177. Aristotle, *Rhetoric* 1.9,1367a21–27; see also Ste. Croix, *Class Struggle*, 116f. For the remarks on long hair, see Aristotle, *Politics*, 8.2, 1337b19–21. On the social and class meanings of *kalos*, see Boer, *Private Morality in Greece and Rome*, 161–162.

178. According to a character in Xenophon's *Memorabilia*, even work as an overseer or bailiff is shameful for a free man, because it puts him constantly at the disposal of another person (*Mem.* 2.8.3–4). Demosthenes calls labor *doulika kai tapeina pragmata*, "slavish and humble activity" (Demosthenes 57.45). Cicero lists vulgar and illiberal occupations, meaning different kinds of manual labor, and notes that Greek democracy failed because it was controlled by "uneducated men," that is, craftspersons, merchants, and other "dregs of the state," rather than by leisured aristocrats (Cicero, *Pro Flacco* 17–18; see also 58; *De Officiis* 1.150; and Finley, *Ancient Economy*, 41). Later, Athenaeus, that storehouse of commonplaces, makes the same assumptions: "Indeed to have pleasure and luxury is a mark of the freeborn (*eleutheroi*); it eases their minds and exalts them; but to live laborious lives is the mark of slaves and men of low birth; hence their very natures become contracted" (*Deipnosophists* 12.512–513). Plutarch expresses the standard upper-class view in an attempt to modify it somewhat (*Moralia* 830D). Upper-class Jews of the period held the same prejudices: see Philo, *On Dreams* 1.7. The attitude was, of course, not limited to the literary circles. Laws of the later empire likewise assume that labor is not proper for upper-class persons and forbid persons of certain statuses from engaging in labor or business. See *Codex Justinianus* 10.31.34; 4.63.3; Ste. Croix, *Class Struggle*, 182. See also *Digest* 38.1.34, which says that if a freedwoman who agreed to continue providing services for her patron (performing prescribed *operae*) attains to a social position in which it would be unseemly for her to do the work, she is absolved of her responsibilities. *Digest* 38.16.1 says that a freedman's services should be suitable to his age, rank, and "mode of life" (see also 38.38.1; 38.50). See Hock, *The Social Context of Paul's Ministry*, for a study of the many negative and the few positive attitudes toward manual labor.

179. On the linen workers: Dio Chrysostom *Discourse* 34.23. See *Discourses* 14 and 15 for Dio's views of slavery and freedom. Philostratus tells us that Dio performed menial tasks during his exile period, planting, digging, carrying water for baths and gardens (*Lives of the Sophists*, 488). If Philostratus's account is historically accurate, we should nevertheless take Dio's activity as representing Cynic "toils" along the lines of the labors of Heracles. These toils are not the same as if he had actually become a craftsperson by trade.

180. Ste. Croix, *Class Struggle*, 274.

181. *IG* 1².1084. For other examples see Ste. Croix, *Class Struggle*, 274, which is the source of this translation, slightly modified. For lower-class views of manual labor, see

Pleket, "Technology in the Greco-Roman World," 9–12, and n. 18; Drinkwater, "The Rise and Fall of the Gallic Iulii," 835–838, 841–843; Thorndike, "A Roman Astrologer as a Historical Source," 426–427; E. M. Wood insists that the alleged Athenian contempt for manual labor is that of the upper-class opponents of democracy, not of the general population, and that the antibanausic concepts are linked to antidemocratic ideology of the upper class (*Peasant-Citizen and Slave*, 22, 28, 134; see esp. 137–145 for the several ideological functions of antilabor rhetoric in classical Athens).

182. Burford, *Craftsmen in Greek and Roman Society*, 27.

183. Artemidorus, *Interpretation of Dreams*, 1.2 (p. 16); see also 1.79 (p. 61), where dreaming that one has face-to-face sexual intercourse with one's mother is auspicious for laborers in the exercise of their craft.

184. See ibid., 1.53 (p. 43); 1.54 (p. 44); 3.62 (p. 174) for fear of unemployment.

185. The term *philodespotos* occurs in Josephus signifying slavish depravity (*Jewish War* 4.175; cf. Theognis *Elegies* 1.849).

186. *SEG* 27.42 (*IG* 5.1.153; *IG* 5.1.40). Note the *actor* Philodespotus, who may be a slave, in Apuleius, *Metamorphosis*, 2.26.2 (*The Golden Ass*, trans. Robert Graves [New York: Farrar, Straus and Giroux, 1951], 46).

187. *IG* 2–3.13224 (Athens third–fourth century c.e.?). *Verna: MAMA* 4.55 (Synnada, second century c.e.); see also Dessau 394, 5338, and the index, p. 283. *Doulos* as proper name: *TAM* 3.224; 3.421 (both Termessus). *Doulis* as feminine name: *TAM* 3.764 (Termessus). *Doulion: TAM* 3.444 (Termessus).

188. In several cases persons erected an inscription by permission of the master or mistress, though not explicitly calling themselves slaves: *TAM* 2.636; 3.269; 3.346; 3.762; 3.811 (all Termessus, no date but probably second–third century c.e.). Sometimes a person provides a dedicatory inscription "for his masters": *MAMA* 5.185 (Kuyucak, no date). Sometimes names give away a slave's status, as in *SEG* 28.1242 (Tyriaion, Lycia, mid-second century c.e.), where Phlegon alone has only one name and everyone else in his family (wife, children) has more. He is called, "Phlegon, pragmateutes of Marcia." In other cases, no explicit status is given, but certain terminology shows that the person is a slave, as when a man is honored "for his industrious slavery" (*SEG* 28.1033, Nicaea, first century c.e.). See also *TAM* 2.696 (Cadyanda, no date) which contains the terms *hypēresiēs heneken kai amempheos ergou . . . despousunō*. The man is obviously a slave though his status is not explicitly stated.

189. The status of the public slave Philodespotos (Sparta, ca. 100 c.e.) is explicitly given in *IG* 5.1.153 (*CIG* 1239) and *IG* 5.1.147 (*CIG* 1249 I) but not in *IG* 5.1.40 (*CIG* 1257 and 1276). Aurelios Traianos is called an imperial freedman in *MAMA* 1.22a, but his name is given without status designation in *MAMA* 1.22 (*CIG* 3990b).

190. *CIL* 6.14697. See Flory, "Family in *Familia*," 87.

191. "Family in *Familia*," 80.

192. Ibid., 65; see also 57, 78, 120.

193. Ibid., 120, 105.

194. For the importance of status by association among the lower class, see also Flory, "Where Women Precede Men," 219.

195. Dio Chrysostom *Discourse* 14.1. Dio states the truism in order to refute it from a moral philosophical point of view. From that point of view, ignorance and immorality are the most wretched state and a slave could be, in some sense, noble. But the moral philosophical

view is, of course, the minority one. Dio begins this way precisely because it is the common view, at least of people of his class. The slave's tombstone: *CIL* 13.7119; Barrow, *Slavery in the Roman Empire*, 10 n. 2.

2. SLAVE OF CHRIST AND 1 CORINTHIANS 9

1. See Marshall, *Enmity in Corinth*, 73, 78, 316.

2. Compare Luke 16:1–9, where the oikonomos is not said to be a doulos, but his employer is called his lord (*kyrios*).

3. For the variety of uses of slavery in Hebrew scriptures, see Flesher, *Oxen. Women or Citizens?* 11–26.

4. Pleket, "Religious History," 154–155.

5. Chariton, *Chaereas and Callirhoe*, (Blake), pp. 90, 92. Chariton has well-born characters refer to themselves as "your slave" when addressing the Great King of Persia (pp. 63, 70).

6. Note in Martial the contrast between the "cheap slaves of the salt-seller" (1.41) and Martial's more respectful treatment of the freedman (he ran a bookshop) of the "learned Lucensis" (1.2).

7. Petersen, *Rediscovering Paul*, 26. I agree with Petersen's statement that Paul also portrays himself as "a father who is a slave to his children (1 Cor. 9:19, 3:21–23; 2 Cor. 1:24, 4:5)." The portrayal of the leader as enslaved to those whom he leads is the subject of the following two chapters.

8. For the connection of stigmata to slavery, see Philo, *Every Good Man Is Free*, 10; Dio Chrysostom 14.19; 15.11; see also Jones, *"Stigma."* Jones makes a persuasive case that *stigma* usually referred to tattooing. Interestingly, he points out that tattooing for religious reasons was a practice of the *eastern* parts of the Mediterranean in Greco-Roman times (Egypt, Syria, Assyria). For such easterners, tattooing did not necessarily imply degradation, whereas it did for Greeks and Romans (144–145). If this is correct, one can see that Paul's reference to his tattoos of Christ had two different connotations: possibly positive for easterners and negative for traditionally minded Greeks and Romans. For other interpretations of the stigmata, see Betz, *Galatians*, 324–325; Tabor, *Things Unutterable*, 43.

9. Malan, "Bound to Do Right."

10. Ibid., 127.

11. Ibid., 134.

12. Ibid., 135.

13. See Daube, *The New Testament and Rabbinic Judaism*, 268–284, for Jewish contexts of this language and its possible influence on early Christianity.

14. See also Lev. 25:42–55; Isaiah 42:19, 48:20, 49:1–3, 56:6; Deut. 15:15.

15. Bartchy, *Mallon Chresai*, 124, n. 449.

16. I will not deal with the exegetical problems of 1 Cor. 7:21, which has been studied exhaustively by Bartchy. I have little to add to his presentation of the problems and possibilities for the interpretation of that verse.

17. Conzelmann, *Commentary on 1 Corinthians*, 127.

18. Aloys Funk realizes that status is a way of talking about social position, which is always in relationship to other positions. See his *Status und Rollen in den Paulusbriefen*, 13.

19. Russell, *Slavery as Reality and Metaphor in the Pauline Letters*, 49.

20. Ibid., 50.

21. Paul's statement in 7:23, "do not become slaves of human beings," supports Bartchy's decision that Paul in 7:21 advises the slave to take advantage of any opportunity to become free. Verse 23 indicates that, ideally, Paul considers slavery to Christ and slavery to a human owner as mutually exclusive. He believes, however, that the less than ideal situation must sometimes be endured by the Christian slave. In that case, the symbolic reinterpretation of the situation takes over in order to mitigate the undesirable experience of slavery to a human owner.

22. Other scholars have suggested that Paul is depicting himself as a slave in verses 16–18: Lightfoot, *Notes on Epistles of St. Paul*, 319; Robertson and Plummer, *First Epistle*, 190; Barrett, *A Commentary on the First Epistle to the Corinthians*; Holmberg, *Paul and Power*, 90; Horsley, "Consciousness and Freedom among the Corinthians," 587.

23. Conzelmann, *Commentary on 1 Corinthians*, 152, seems to believe that Paul's apostleship is in question and that Paul therefore must defend it by defending his freedom.

24. The classic work from this perspective is J. Weiss, *Der Erste Korintherbrief*. In recent years new work has been done. Hans Dieter Betz, for one, has repeatedly put the Corinthian debate within the context of moral philosophy and especially the Socratic tradition. See his *Der Apostel Paulus und die sokratische Tradition; Paul's Apology; Paul's Concept of Freedom*.

25. See Murphy-O'Connor, "Corinthian Slogans in 1 Cor. 6:12–20"; Stowers, "A Debate over Freedom." For the "widespread concept of the *sophos*" as occurring also in Jewish, and specifically Rabbinic, sources, see Fischel, "Story and History," 447.

26. Hock, *Social Context*, 58.

27. Note, however, Matt. 10:8, which instructs the evangelist to preach without pay. Perhaps this also reflects some background of disagreement or discrepancy among practices of the early church.

28. Plato, *Laws*, 741e. See also Robertson and Plummer, *First Epistle*, 182; Aristotle, *Politics*, 3.5.

29. For a list of different suggestions as to why Paul refused support (and scholars associated with the different suggestions), see Holmberg, *Paul and Power*, 89–91. Hock realizes that Paul's manual labor made him appear weak and servile to some segments of the population (though Hock seems to suggest that it would make Paul appear so to all the population, which is questionable); but Paul wanted to maintain his independence, so he had to work to support himself (*Social Context*, 60–61). Josef Meili (*Ministry of Paul*, 132–133) closely follows Hock's interpretation. Holmberg, *Paul and Power*, 91, also says that "Paul supports himself by work of his hands but only when this is necessary."

30. Hock seems to believe that this is actually the gist of Paul's argument (*Social Context*, 60–61).

31. Isocrates, *Nicocles*, 3.45. Several aspects of Isocrates' speech are reminiscent of Paul's own way of talking about his ministry: the king is temperate and restrained in financial matters (3.31–35). He holds power temperately and, in order to be above reproach, has limited his own freedom (3.29, 37, 45). His behavior provides an example and model for his people (3.37). The king calls his subjects his witnesses of his past conduct (3.46). The king uses himself as an example in the introduction to the parenetic section (3.47). In this second half of the work, the king argues that the parts (members) of the body politic are to work together for the good of the whole and that greater honor goes to the more serviceable parts (3.48). The king urges his subjects to realize that, even if absent in body, he is present in mind (3.51). He urges them to abstain from the very appearance of evil (3.54). Pauline parallels to

these themes are readily recognizable. Dio Chrysostom also speaks of the philosopher-king who, though permitted to do anything, voluntarily exercises self-restraint (*Discourse* 3.4, 10; see also 3.83–85, where the good king is compared to an athlete who does not exercise in vain but attains his goals; cf. 1 Cor. 9:24–26.

32. Epictetus 1.6.32; 4.10.10; 3.26.31ff.; 3.22.57. For a discussion of these passages and a full analysis of the figure of Heracles in Cynic thought, see Höistad, *Cynic Hero and Cynic King*.

33. Dio Chrysostom *Discourses* 1.59–62; 8.35. See Höistad, *Cynic Hero and Cynic King*, 34. For the sage-slave as an element in Rabbinic sources, see Fischel, "Story and History," 451 n. 42.

34. I have argued for this interpretation, and against the other possibilities, in my dissertation, "Slave of Christ, Slave of All: Paul's Metaphor of Slavery and 1 Corinthians 9" (Ph.D. diss., Yale University, 1988), 109–112. For other interpretations, see Robertson and Plummer, *First Epistle*, 189–190; Hock, *Social Context*, 100 n. 133; Grosheide, *Commentary on the First Epistle to the Corinthians*, 210. For conditional sentences in Pauline rhetoric in general, see Winger, "Unreal Conditions in the Letters of Paul."

35. Epictetus 2.1.23; see also 4.1, and Dio Chrysostom *Discourses* 14.14. For "the power of self-action," see Pohlenz, *Freedom in Greek Life and Thought*, 137.

36. Philo, *Every Good Man*, 60 and 61, see also 96–97; Epictetus 1.17.27; according to Epictetus, 1.14.16, one should never do something unwilling (*akōn*) or be persuaded to do the "necessary" (*anagkaiai*). (The English translation supplied in the Loeb edition is here a bit misleading.)

37. Aristotle, *Nicomachean Ethics*, 3.1.12 (trans. H. Rackham); see also 3.1.1.

38. Philo, *Every Good Man*, 60; 37 (being bought); 36 (obeying another); 34–35 (servile tasks and manual labor). See also Xenophon, *Cyropaedia*, 8.1.4; Marshall, *Enmity in Corinth*, 300, and references listed there.

39. Philo, *Every Good Man*, 61. Note that the Greek shows much similarity to Paul's terminology in 1 Cor. 9: *akōn poiein, anagkazesthai, doulos, eleutheros*.

40. Ibid., 100ff.; 149, 154. For "necessary servile labors," see 142.

41. See also ibid., 96–97: one is unenslavable (*adoulōtos*) if one cannot be compelled.

42. For an exhaustive study of the term *oikonomia*, see Reumann, "Use of *Oikonomia*"; see also Reumann, "*Oikonomia* as 'Ethical Accommodation.'"

43. This is the conclusion of Landvogt 8 and 13, with which my research outlined in the previous chapter agrees. See also Reumann, "Use of *Oikonomia*," 269, 545. Reumann notes that pagan philosophers and church fathers alike avoid talking about the deity as an oikonomos, and this even though they speak of the divine oikonomia. He thinks the reason is that the term *oikonomos* carried connotations of menial labor and servile status.

44. Artemidorus, *Interpretation of Dreams*, 1.35 (35): the managerial slave is the "slave held in trust," *doulos en pistei*. Essentially the same phrase is used in 2.49 (126). In 4.15 (192) these slaves are designated simply as "those entrusted" (*pepisteumenoi*). See also the Greek of 2.30 (109), which uses the terms *oikonomia* and *pistis;* and 2.9 (89).

45. For example, the Revised Standard Version: Matt. 5:12, 46; Mark 9:41; Acts 1:18; 1 Cor. 3:14, etc. But also, for different translations, John 4:36; Rom. 4:4; 1 Cor. 3:8.

46. Jury duty: see Scholia on Aristophanes, *Vespae*, 299; Lucian, *In Praise of Demosthenes*, 25. Public office: Plato *Republic*, 345e. Mercenaries: Thucydides 4.124; 7.25; 8.83. Physi-

cians: Aristotle, *Politics*, 1287a36. Reward: Plato, *Republic*, 363d, for example, speaks of the rewards of virtue. See Ste. Croix, *Class Struggle*, 189.

47. Ste. Croix, *Class Struggle*, 189.

48. In (Pseudo) Xenophon, *Constitution of the Athenians*, 1.11, *apophora* seems to refer to slave earnings. But usually (e.g., Aeschines, *Against Timarchus*, 97) it refers to the money paid by the slave laborer *to* his or her owner out of the earnings from the labor for a third party.

49. Höistad, *Cynic Hero and Cynic King*, esp. 195–222.

50. Jean Héring, among others, claimed that the abrupt move from chapter 8 to chapter 9 necessitated the assumption of different sources and later editing (*First Epistle of Saint Paul*, xiii and 75). Hurd (*The Origin of 1 Corinthians*, 70–71) discusses chapter 9 as a digression but one that relates to Paul's overall argument in 8:1–11:1. See also 131–157 for Hurd's review of attempts to divide 1 Corinthians into originally different letters. Barrett, *Commentary*, 220, notes that chapter 9 looks like a rather abrupt digression if "the subject of chapter 9 is regarded as Paul's defense of his apostleship against attacks by the Corinthians."

51. Soden, "Sacrament and Ethics in Paul," 264; Conzelmann, *Commentary on 1 Corinthians*, 137–138.

52. Wuellner, "Greek Rhetoric and Pauline Argumentation," 177–188, esp. 178.

53. This is in opposition to the interpretation of Marshall, *Enmity in Corinth*, 174.

54. Willis, *Idol Meat in Corinth*, 274; Horsley, "Consciousness and Freedom among the Corinthians," 587.

55. These claims are argued in more detail below in chapters 4 and 5.

56. Homer, *Iliad*, 21.445, 450; Herodotus, *History*, 8.137; Xenophon, *Anabasis*, 2.5.14; on the status significances of receiving a misthos in classical Athens, see E. M. Wood, *Peasant-Citizen and Slave*, 77–78.

57. Epictetus 4.1.139. For Socrates, see Xenophon, *Apology*, 16; and Blank, "Socratics Versus Sophists on Payment for Teaching."

58. Lucian, *On Salaried Posts*, 23; note Lucian's use of servile terminology: *douloi* (7); *andrapodōdes* (8); *misthos* (19); *memisthōkenai* (25).

59. Dio Chrysostom uses this same rhetorical strategy to redefine slavery and freedom in *Discourses* 14 and 15. In *Discourse* 15, for example, the slave argues that one's birth, having to obey a master, "being thrashed," or being owned by another—in other words, all the normal ways of defining slavery—do not necessarily mean one is a slave (Dio Chrysostom 15.3, 19, 24). A. W. H. Adkins calls this "persuasive definition" and says that it is "a not uncommon rhetorical device; and the student of popular values should be on the watch for it, since it is an attempt to change the accepted usage of value terms" (Review of *Greek Popular Morality*, 147).

3. THE ENSLAVED LEADER AS A RHETORICAL TOPOS

1. For example, Dio Chrysostom says, "The ruler may also be said to submit to the gods, *his* superiors. That is, the ruler rules naturally because he is superior and stronger; therefore, he must submit to those superior to himself, the gods" (271). Philo speaks of parents as being "servants of God" (*On the Decalogue*, 119–120). For further references to slavery to the gods, see the Introduction above.

2. Plato, *Laws*, 6.762e; see also 4.715c–d; and Cicero, *Pro Cluentis* 146, which says that

all people, magistrates and jurors included, are slaves (*servi*) of the laws "in order that we may be free." Libanius (fourth century C.E.) praises Constantius II and Constans because even though they are "lords of the laws," they have made the laws their own masters (*Oration* 59.162). Later, in 385 C.E., he says to Theodosius I, "Not even to you is everything permitted, for it is of the very essence of monarchy that its holders are not allowed to do everything" (*Or.* 50.19; see Ste. Croix, *Class Struggle*, from whom this translation is taken).

3. Plutarch, *Alexander*, 52.3. Actually, in spite of Plutarch's disapproval here, there were others who did hold that the superiority of the good ruler extends to his superiority over the laws. Dio Chrysostom maintains that the ruler must be good because he is greater than the laws. Everything is permitted him (*panta exesti*), so he needs self-control; he is the one who saves all, so he must control himself (*Discourse* 62.3; cf. 3.10). Of course, this is common Stoic material. See J. Weiss, *Der Erste Korintherbrief*; Stowers, "A Debate over Freedom," 62–68.

4. Höistad, *Cynic Hero and Cynic King*, 177. The primary support for the idea that the leader would endure even servile conditions for the good of others comes initially from the Odyssean speech of Antisthenes. See *Socraticorum reliquiae*, 2.339–343, 3.231–237. For Heracles and Odysseus as examples of the Cynic slave king, see Höistad, *Cynic Hero and Cynic King*, 87ff., 92–102, 150. On the relation between these Cynic motifs and Paul see H. Funke, "Antisthenes bei Paulus"; Malherbe, "Antisthenes and Odysseus."

5. For a definition of topos in the way I use the term, see the Introduction and notes. The use of topos analysis in Pauline studies has been advocated by several studies; see especially Wuellner, "Toposforschung und Torahinterpretation"; Brunt, "More on the Topos as a New Testament Form."

6. For a discussion of identification in the sense used here, see Burke, *A Rhetoric of Motives*, 20–23; and Crocker, "The Social Functions of Rhetorical Forms," 61. Eckstein ("Polybius, Syracuse, and the Politics of Accommodation," 266–267) notes that traditional Hellenistic kingship theory presented the king as the benevolent patriarch ruling from a superior position of honor.

7. Höistad, *Cynic Hero and Cynic King*, 98, 115.

8. For the placement of benevolent patriarchalism in traditional Hellenistic political theory, see Eckstein, "Polybius, Syracuse, and the Politics of Accommodation."

9. The categorization of constitutions in this and similar ways was common in political theory and rhetorical practice. See Ferguson, *Utopias of the Classical World* 23–28; Adkins notes the occurrence of the three constitutions, in some form or other, in Pindar, Herodotus, Aeschines, and Isocrates (Review of *Greek Popular Morality*, 145).

10. Eric Havelock's discussion of these analogies (*The Liberal Temper in Greek Politics*, 308–326) is illuminating, whatever one may think of his thesis in general. For a critique of Havelock's thesis, see Momigliano, Review of *The Liberal Temper*; and Finley, "Athenian Demagogues," 9.

11. Aristotle's own bias comes through clearly in his discussion of benefactors and recipients. He assumes that the benefactors are morally superior because they love those they benefit. The recipients, however, care only for what they get (*Nicomathean Ethics* 9.7.1).

12. Aristotle explicitly rejects this model in *Nic. Eth.*, 7.3.2, among other passages.

13. This is argued especially in *Politics*, 4.7, where Aristotle manifests the notion (typical for ancient authors) that democracy has little to do with elections per se. It is rather government by the lower class in the interests of the lower class.

14. Note that Aristotle realizes that the demos might take its leader from the upper class (*ek tōn gnōrimōn*) and that the demos will think of this leader as its protector (*prostatēs*, 5.5.3).

15. Theoretically Aristotle, like Plato, means "best" with regard to virtue. Virtue may, therefore, cross class lines, and Aristotle insists that anyone may be virtuous. But *Politics* 4.6.2ff (1293b32–40), among other texts, shows that Aristotle realizes that his idea of virtue, which is dependent on good education and good birth, is more likely to be found among the upper class. Aristotle would naturally be opposed to the voluntary self-abasement discussed above, as he makes clear in *Rhetoric*, 2.6.13. Anything that brings dishonor or reproach, such as failing to receive the honors due one from one's station, cannot be countenanced.

16. In *Discourse* 3.45, which compares kingship primarily with tyranny, Dio outlines three basic good and three corresponding degenerate forms of constitution. Plutarch knows the tradition also (*Moralia* 826a–827d).

17. 3.5. Dio also puts himself forward at times as the philosophical political leader in the benevolent-father mold (see, for example, *Discourses* 48.12–14 and 49.3).

18. In Dio's view the ruler will submit to the gods (*Discourse* 2.71), but the ruler will struggle so as not to seem inferior to any other person, even the best persons (2.77).

19. Already in the oration Dio has linked serving to demagogues and has contrasted them to counselors (*symbouloi*) who save the people by means of their policies (*Discourse* 38.2). Dio places himself in this last class and insists that he is not a demagogue. For similar arguments, see *Discourse* 4.44, 124, 131. Dio's rhetoric shows several parallels to Philo's. The rapid change of leaders, noted in Philo's discussion of democratic leadership in *On Joseph* above, also occurs in Dio (34.34, 37). In 66.12–13 the triplet of demagogues, sophists, and *xenagoi* occurs as it does in 4.131. Here also is an interesting parallel to Philo's *On Joseph*, 35. Like Philo, Dio says that to be a slave is bad enough, but to be a slave of many diverse masters, as are demagogues, is much worse. Such a person is a "public slave."

20. See editor's note on Horace *Satires* 2.5.3 by Fairclough, *Horace*, 198; Philo, *On Joseph*, 34; Plato, *Republic*, 557c, 561e; Plato, *Hippias Minor* 365a–b; Detienne and Vernant, *Cunning Intelligence*, 18–23, 27–48.

21. Stanford, *The Ulysses Theme*, 5, 91, 94, 112, 259 n. 6; Detienne and Vernant, *Cunning Intelligence*, 39, 313–317.

22. Horace, *Satires*, 2.5.3 (note footnote by Fairclough).

23. From Euripides, *Iphigeneia*, frag. 197; trans. C. B. Gulick, Athenaeus, *Deipnosophists* (Loeb) 12.513d.

24. Stanford, *The Ulysses Theme*, 94; see Farnell, *The Works of Pindar* 1:207, 216; see also Pindar, *The Nemean Odes*, 7.20–24; 8.19–27.

25. Euripides, *Rhesus*, 715, 498, 503, 894; Euripides, *Hecuba*, 132, 245, 251, 257.

26. The ambiguity comes from the phrase *heterois hypēretein existamenon* (Philo, *On Joseph* 34). Does it mean that, though the leader will undertake dangers, when it comes to mere labor he will "stand aside and leave others to serve him" (the translation of F. H. Colson [Loeb])? Or should it be taken that he will outstrip others in enduring dangers, but that when the prospect is labor he will "change himself in order to serve others"? The Greek seems to allow either interpretation. The former interpretation allows for an upper-class bias that permits leaders to endure dangers but not common, servile activity such as manual labor. The latter interpretation takes *labors* (*ponoi*) in the ethical, Cynic meaning, signifying hardships that the sophos endures in order to benefit others. For the latter, see Höistad, *Cynic Hero and Cynic King*, 92.

27. 4.69. See M. Smith, *Clement of Alexandria*, 54–55, for a discussion of the philosophical debate over accommodation and its parallels in Paul (1 Cor. 9:22) and other early Christian literature. Smith provides further references.

28. For a complete study of accommodation as philosophically justified, see Reumann, "Use of *Oikonomia*" esp. 384, 595; and "*Oikonomia* as 'Ethical Accommodation,'" 370–379.

29. Hobein, *Maximi Tyrii Philosophumena, Oration* 1.

30. Taylor, *The Dissertations of Maximus Tyrius* 2:177.

31. See, for example, the taunts against Bion, who was called *polytropos* and *poikilos* by Diogenes Laertius, *Lives* (4.77); Kindstrand, *Bion of Borysthenes* 134.

32. Maximus of Tyre 14.7 (my translation). Hyperbolus was often linked with Cleon in tradition as a famous demagogue. A fragment of Andocides (quoted by the scholiast on Aristophanes' *Wasps*, 1007) derides Hyperbolus as a "foreigner, barbarian and lamp maker" whose father was a "branded slave."

33. Plutarch, *Moralia* 52e. Note that, for Plutarch, Odysseus is usually an example of a frank and wise friend.

34. Euripedes, *The Suppliant Women*, lines 433–438, in *The Complete Greek Tragedies*. The person who obtains power in a democracy does so although he is nothing (*ouden*, line 425). The weak (*asthenēs*, line 433) is the group opposite the rich (line 434). Note also the link of democracy with freedom and equality, as in Plato. For Plato, democracy was the constitution that had too much freedom and equality. See *Republic*, 558b, 562b, 563a; *Epistle*, 8 (354d–e).

35. Yavetz, *Plebs and Princeps*, esp. 51, 98, 139. See also Cicero, *Pro Sestio*, 139 (*leves*) and 141.

36. Dio Cassius, *History*, 40.58.2ff. Note that the Greek words translated here as *deference* and *deferential* are explicitly servile terms (*therapeia* and *therapeuein*). The term for *upright* is *agathos*, also a word with class significance. See also Plutarch, *Cato Minor*, 49.2 for the same portrait, also with the use of the term *therapeuein*.

37. Plutarch, *Galba*, 11: *philanthrōpos, dēmotikas*. Plutarch elsewhere links *philanthrōpia* and *ta dēmotika* when talking about the populist: see *Publicola*, 4.5; H. Martin, "Concept of *Philanthropia*." Plutarch also presents Crassus as more of a populist leader than Pompey because Crassus's behavior was *to koinon kai to philanthrōpon* (to the benefit of the common people and humanitarian) in contrast to Pompey's austerity (*semnotēs; Crassus*, 7.4).

38. Note that "to be a demagogue" is practically equivalent to "catering to the many"; Plutarch, *Gaius Gracchus* (9.4).

39. In *Gaius Gracchus* 10.1, Plutarch notes that the proof offered that Livius was "well-disposed towards the people and honest" was that he never *seemed* to propose anything "for himself or in his own interests."

40. Cicero, *Pro Sestio*, 110. The image of the tyrant-demagogue from Plato is similar (*Republic* 566): he goes about grinning at everyone in a pretense of friendliness. The self-lowering of one politician would as a matter of course be questioned by another as insincere flattery or as revealing a truly servile nature.

41. Connor, *New Politicians*, 152. See also Ste. Croix, *Class Struggle*, 124ff.; Arnheim, *Aristocracy in Greek Society*, 144.

42. See Arnheim, *Aristocracy in Greek Society*, 144.

43. Aristophanes, *The Knights*, discussed later in this chapter.

44. Plutarch, *Moralia*, 806f–807a. Babbitt's translation (Loeb), modified by Connor.

45. *Scholia Aristophanica* 2: 2. The word translated here as *magistrates* (*stratēgoi*) may refer

to generals; it has wider applications. In post-classical Greek, for instance, it is used as the Greek equivalent to *duumvir* (Theissen, *Social Setting*, 79). The scholiast, therefore, is probably saying that Cleon slandered the other leaders, not necessarily the generals. This is the translation chosen by Rutherford.

46. Note the reference above to Euripides' *Hecuba* and the quotation from Stanford, *The Ulysses Theme*, 112. Odysseus turns away from his friends and toward the masses; this is one of his demagogic traits. Aristotle says that, for the most part, tyrants arise from among the common people and the demos. They gain by "calumniating the notables" (*Politics*, 5.10, 1310b9–16).

47. Yavetz, *Plebs and Princeps*, 106. See also Connor, *New Politicians*, 174–175; Arnheim, *Aristocracy in Greek Society*, 144.

48. Finley, "Athenian Demagogues," 5. I would modify Finley's statement only to point out that the theme extended well past Aristotle, as Plutarch himself, among others, shows. Finley's concern was with earlier traditions about demagogues. On gain as the traditional goal of the demagogue, note the passage from Euripides, *The Suppliant Women*, line 413, quoted above, where the term for gain is *kerdos*. For the traditional link of *kerdos* to the changeableness of the wily Odyssean character, see Detienne and Vernant, *Cunning Intelligence*, 17, 23 n. 3. The semantic link is so certain that *kerdē* itself often is translated *tricks*.

49. For further discussion of the populist as "patron of the common people" (*prostatēs tou dēmou*) see Connor, *New Politicians*, 111, n. 40; he provides further references. The scholiast on Aristophanes, *Knights*, 1128 takes *dēmagōgos* and *prostatēs tou dēmou* as synonyms.

50. Volkmann, *"Endoxos Douleia"*; see also his "Die Basileia als *Endoxos Douleia.*"

51. Claudianus Aelianus, *Varia Historia*, 2.20, p. 27; my translation. F. E. Adcock's claim that Antigonos did not mean "that he was subject to his people's will" is correct in that Antigonos's kingship was not a constitutionally or democratically limited monarchy (Adcock, "Greek and Macedonian Kingship," 173). But it is misleading in that it ignores that the statement is in a context of concern for status. The story as told by Aelian is a *chreia* meant to illustrate democratic, gentle rulership in which the king does not act arrogantly toward his subjects.

52. Goodenough's analysis of this tension in Philo is very interesting and, I think, generally correct (*The Politics of Philo Judaeus*, 51, 69–85).

53. Later in the treatise Philo denies that the true politician will be enslaved to the masses (*Joseph*, 67). Yet the section is still there in which Philo seems to allow it as a necessary evil of leadership, in the same way he allows for changeableness in a politician.

54. In *Discourse* 47, Dio defends himself against the accusation that he has acted like a tyrant (see especially 47.18, 24–25). According to his enemies, at least, Dio has no real concern for the poor and merely flaunts his power and high political connections. This oration is puzzling if it was delivered in the Assembly, because elsewhere Dio appears able to assume his popularity with the demos (as in, for example, *Discourse* 48). But it makes perfect sense if the charge has come from within the Council and if that is the arena in which Dio must defend himself (cf. § § 14 and 19). In that case, Dio's exercise of his own personal power, especially if he bypassed the proper channels for political activity via the Council, would have appeared tyrannical.

55. Throughout this discussion it must be remembered that the Council (*boulē*) and the Assembly (*ekklēsia*) were often at odds (see Jones, *The Roman World of Dio Chrysostom*, 80). The traditional way of presenting the conflict was that the Council reflected the interests of the

upper class and the Assembly the lower class. This is, of course, simplistic, but will hold true generally and, at any rate, was the way the ancients usually thought about the situation.

56. According to Jones's interpretation, "There must . . . have been some disturbance in which Dio had done as the wealthy were sometimes tempted to do, and had sided with the commons against his own class; later, he tried to make amends with his peers and recover his own lost influence" (*The Roman World of Dio Chrysostom*, 101). An attempt to block the convening of the Council or by-passing the Council by appealing directly to the people for ratification of a proposal was considered demagogic and may have been illegal (ibid., 97).

57. Augustine says that the bishop is the "slave of the many" (*servus esse multorum*) (quoted in Meer, *Augustine the Bishop*, 256; quoting section 32.1 of Codex Guelferbytanus 4096). Libanius praises the good ruler as the shepherd who is a "good slave" (*doulos agathos*) to the sheep (*Oration* 25.55–56). Indeed, Libanius says that rulers do not mind being called the slaves of their subjects, if they pursue the subjects' interests, just as good fathers do not mind being called slaves of their children, as they seek the welfare of these children (ibid., 25.54). For Theophylact, see Theophylactus Simocatta, *Historiae*, 1.1.18; English translation: *The History of Theophylact Simocatta*.

58. Höistad, *Cynic Hero and Cynic King*, 92–102, 177; Malherbe, "Antisthenes and Odysseus," 150 n. 35, 164, 172; H. Funke, "Antisthenes bei Paulus."

59. *Cyropaedia* 1.1.1. Xenophon is bemoaning the instability of governments in general, but I take his words about masters having no control even in their own homes to be antidemocratic rhetoric. Other antidemocratic indications in the *Cyropaedia* include 1.3.16 (Cyrus's decision on the tunics reflects the traditionally antidemocratic emphasis on private ownership against redistribution of wealth) and 1.3.10 (equality of speech [*isēgoria*], recognized as a democratic slogan, is ridiculed by Cyrus as drunken loudness).

60. See also ibid., 1.5.12 for Xenophon's traditional, aristocratic view of *philotimia*: "Lovers of praise must for this reason gladly undergo every sort of hardship [*ponos*] and every sort of danger [*kindynos*]."

61. See Herodotus, *History*, 1.108–116, esp. 114: *doulos*. Herodotus seems to know a tradition that Cyrus was a slave or of lowly origins. He holds that Cyrus was of noble birth but was reared by slaves of the king and was, therefore, considered by some a slave.

62. Xenophon uses the commonplace that the king, here Cyrus, is the good shepherd (*Cyropaedia* 2.14). Significantly, however, he does not speak of this relationship as the enslavement of the shepherd to the sheep, contrary to the way the commonplace occurs in Sophocles, Plutarch, and Libanius. This accords with Xenophon's strict benevolent patriarchal ideology.

63. Ibid., 8.1.44. The clause in brackets is not my editorial addition; it is given in brackets in some Greek editions.

64. The account of Cyrus in Justin is also very interesting and represents an independent account that preserves several of the traditions found in Nicolaus (see Justin, *Justin, Cornelius Nepos, and Eutropius*). Nicolaus's account, therefore, should not be thought idiosyncratic but as representing a different line of tradition from that of Xenophon.

65. For the texts see *Socraticorum reliquiae*, vol. 7; or *Antisthenis Fragmenta*, 24–28.

66. See Aristophanes, *Wasps*, esp. lines 590–602, for the antijury sentiment implied in Aristophanes' plays. That the Ajax-Odysseus debate is spoken as if before a jury is borne out by "Ajax" 7, in which Ajax again accuses his hearers of knowing nothing. He speaks of the irony of judges (*kritai*) and jurors (*dikastai*) knowing nothing.

67. It is fruitful to compare the second person plural constructions in Ajax's speech with the predominately second person singular constructions in Odysseus's. Odysseus, craftily, concentrates his attack on Ajax; Ajax fulminates against everyone, even the very people who will decide the case.

68. This phrase, along with the epithets Odysseus appropriates for himself at the end of the speech—*polytlanta, polymētin, polymēchanon* ("Odysseus" 14)—may well reflect the chameleon motif already examined in this chapter. Odysseus was the traditional representative of the many-mannered politician.

69. See Theissen, *Social Setting*, 70–73; Marshall, *Enmity in Corinth*, 215.

70. Antisthenes, some evidence indicates, may have found the popular politics more to his liking. It seems that he was despised by some because of his birth and background outside proper society at Athens (Diogenes Laertius, *Lives*, 6.1, 4). On the other hand, there is little indication that Antisthenes really approved of the demagogic leadership in Athens (ibid., 6.8). He may have sympathized with the more populist politicians without ever throwing in his lot with them or without ever actually approving of their politics. At any rate, like most of the Socratics, he seems for the most part to have avoided actual political involvement. See Höistad, *Cynic Hero and Cynic King*, 112, 114–115 for discussion of Antisthenes' political views.

71. See Euripides, *Hecuba*, 132, 254ff.

72. *Dēmos* is usually translated as "the people," but in Greek literature it meant the *common* people; in fact, it usually means the poor. (See Fox, *Pagans and Christians*, 51.) For that reason, I have often used the transliteration "demos," as the translation "the people" does not carry for moderns the class connotations of the Greek term.

73. I have slightly altered the translation by Rogers, *Aristophanes* (Loeb).

74. Note, for example, the anti-intellectualism of participants at "Trimalchio's Banquet" (Petronius, *Satyricon*, 58). Thucydides also has Cleon make anti-intellectual statements: "Lack of learning combined with sound common sense is more helpful than the kind of cleverness that gets out of hand. . . . As a general rule states are better governed by the man in the street than by intellectuals" (Thucydides, *History*, 3.36.3, trans. Rex Warner, quoted in Connor, *New Politicians* 166). On the alleged anti-intellectualism of the demagogues see Connor, *New Politicians*, 95, 163–168.

75. I have slightly altered Rogers's translation.

76. *Wasps* was produced in 422 B.C.E. It clearly reflects the same social and political situation as that of *Knights*.

77. The question of Aristophanes' own politics has been much debated. Obviously, even if he never sympathized with any oligarchic faction, he had no warm feelings for the demagogues, though he may have scorned Cleon more than the other populist leaders. How much of this scorn was due to personal grudges (Connor mentions this possibility: *New Politicians*, 168 n. 55) and how much to political views we will probably never know. On Aristophanes' upper-class point of view, see Dover, *Greek Popular Morality*, 35–37; E. M. Wood, *Peasant-Citizen and Slave*, 174.

78. The "haves": Plato, *Republic* 565; 566a; the rich: ibid., 564e. For the rich and the poor as the two basic classes of the polis, see ibid. 423. See also Plato, *Epistle* 8, which deals with tension between the two classes.

79. Though Plato differentiates tyrannies from democracies, his castigation of tyrants and demagogues is of a piece. Note, for example, how he lumps them together in *Republic*,

568c, when he accuses tragedians of promoting democracy: "They will hire loud and per-suasive voices to collect the crowds and move them closer to democracies or tyrannies." (Trans. Sterling and Scott.)

80. Trans. Sterling and Scott. For *pantodapos*, cf. ibid., 567c; note also *poikilos*, *pleistōn ēthōn meston*, and *tropōn pleista* in this context (561e), all of which have to do with the chameleon nature of the democratic leader and constitution.

81. The Greek is *prostatēs tou dēmou* (see ibid., 562d, 565c, and cf. Aristophanes, *Knights*, 1128).

82. Dio Chrysostom later echoed this characterization of tyranny, saying that tyranny wore, instead of a friendly smile, a "grin of false humility" (*tapeinon . . . hypoulon*, 1.79).

83. Plato, *Republic*, 569b. See also *Epistle* 8 (354e).

84. Plato, *Republic*, 395c, 396a. For Plato's attitude toward manual labor see ibid., 495d, 443c; *Gorgias* 518; *Sophist* 226b; Ste. Croix, *Class Struggle*, 412.

85. The quotation is from Plato, *Republic*, 434a, trans. Sterling and Scott. See also ibid., 443c.

86. It is true that Plato theoretically allows for the possibility that people from the lower class may be natural rulers and should therefore be educated to rule and brought into the ruling class. But he tips his hand in several places and reveals his upper-class bias against manual laborers, slaves, women, etc. (see *The Statesman* 289e–290a; *Republic* 396b, 443c, 495d, 563b). For Plato, rulers should be those who demonstrate "virtue" (*aretē*). But in Plato's world, as A. W. H. Adkins argues, "no *tektōn* [craftsperson] had *aretē* unqualified, for this was the mark of the traditional *agathos*, the man of wealth and social position" ("*Aretē*, *technē*, Democracy and Sophists," 11).

87. For the use of "the strong" as denoting the upper-class leaders, see Plato, *Republic*, 432. Compare Philo, *On Dreams*, 1.155. See Theissen, *Social Setting* 70–73, for discussion of *weak* and *strong* as social categories.

88. Plato includes the sophists among those who associate with the crowd in order to offer political service. In his opinion, by doing so they make the people their own lords (*Republic*, 493d). There is a sense in which Plato's benevolent guardians will lower themselves and labor among the citizens of the lower levels (ibid., 519d–520a). In the context of his cave analogy, Plato insists that the philosopher condescend to become involved in the city (ibid., 520). But the aristocratic leader does not actually take on the lifestyle of those below or attempt to identify with them. This is not social self-lowering at all but merely the condescension of one who, contrary to personal inclination, is persuaded to rule.

89. The image of voluntary self-enslavement occurs elsewhere in Plato. In the *Symposium*, the participants agree that voluntary slavery (*douleia hekousios*) is acceptable for lovers and those who bind themselves to someone in pursuit of virtue. "This willful slavery [*ethelodouleia*] is not at all shame or flattery" (184, my translation). The way the image is introduced shows that it was known as a political metaphor: the student who adheres to someone in order to learn from that person is not like those who enslave themselves for wealth, office, or influence.

90. The classic English monograph on Philo's politics is Goodenough, *The Politics of Philo Judaeus*. See also his "The Political Philosophy of Hellenistic Kingship." Jouette M. Bassler (*Divine Impartiality*, 94–97) offers a critique of Goodenough's views, but her comments have little bearing on Philo's general views of political constitutions or on the politics of *On Joseph*.

91. Goodenough, *The Politics of Philo Judaeus*, 48 n. 28, says about the connection be-

tween *oikonomia* and *politeia*, "I should guess that the comparison was a Greek commonplace." Goodenough's reticence to make an outright claim to that effect is unnecessary.
See Reumann, "Use of *Oikonomia*," 170–178, 207ff. Aristotle speaks of *oikonomikē basileia*
(*Politics*, 1285b32–34). Aristophanes speaks of political stewardship using the terms *epitropos*
and *tamias* (*Knights* 212, 948, 959).

92. The term is Philo's: *ho politikos ontōs*; see *On Joseph* 67.

93. For Philo's views on democracy, see Goodenough, *The Politics of Philo Judaeus*, 86–90.
Philo sometimes acts as if democracy is an admirable constitution, but his democracy is
nothing like that of the actual Athenian practice. He is really a monarchist in the Platonic
mold. Any actual democracy would probably look to Philo like mob rule. (This interpretation is contrary to the claims of Andrews, "Paul, Philo, and the Intellectuals," 160: "Philo's
ideal government is a democracy under a constitution that honors equality.")

94. Philo, *On Joseph*, 67, my translation. There seems to be a lacuna in the text. The
words in brackets are supplied to fill out the sense. See editors' suggestions in the Loeb
edition, 174 n. 2.

95. Ibid., 67–69. Philo uses several popular Stoic images: the true leader is a member of
the best citizenship, the world; others may control the body, but he alone controls his actual
person; because of his natural, inner freedom from any external compulsion, the noble leader
can be impartial, favoring neither rich nor poor; he will reject flattery and use only salutary
and beneficial words (*sōterios*, 73); he will use boldness of speech (*parrēsia*) but without
arrogance.

96. Note that in ibid., 76 the image of the physician is used to argue that the leader will
not swerve from harsh measures, even if the patient objects and the surgery is painful. In §33
the image of the physician was evoked as an example of one who *would* alter behavior
according to the physical condition of the individual. The topos is, naturally, flexible. Its
primary function is to stress that the physician's actions will be chosen solely with a view to
the patient's recovery, not to unimportant external factors, such as the wealth or poverty of
the patient.

4. SLAVE OF ALL IN 1 CORINTHIANS 9

1. For treatments of Paul's admission of chameleon behavior, see H. Chadwick, "All
Things to All Men"; Bornkamm, "Missionary Stance of Paul"; Moffatt, *The First Epistle of
Paul to the Corinthians*, 203–204; Ellison, "Paul and the Law." For Paul's use of *kerdainō* (gain),
see Daube, "*Kerdainō* as a Missionary Term"; *The New Testament and Rabbinic Judaism*, 352;
Barrett, *Commentary*, 211. For disagreement with Daube's interpretation, see Hock, *Social
Context*, 100 n. 114.

2. See, for example, Prior, *The Message of 1 Corinthians*, 162. Barrett, *Commentary*, 215;
Rauer, *Die "Schwachen" in Korinth und Rom*, 31; Black, *Paul, Apostle of Weakness*, 118.

3. Theissen, *Social Setting*, 121–143. Black is aware of Theissen's work, calling it "pen-
etrating" (*Paul, Apostle of Weakness*, 283 n. 33). Black realizes the class-specific meanings of
astheneia, especially in the context of the related terms in 1 Corinthians 1 ("powerful," "wise,"
"of noble birth"). Black does not, however, allow Theissen's observations to affect his exegesis or definitions of *weakness* in 1 and 2 Corinthians. Rather, he tends to speak of all
Christians as in one group with Paul: the weak. Black does not deal with conflict within the
Corinthian church between strong and weak as higher class and lower class. He correctly

calls his own definition of the weak in Corinth "ethical and soteriological," whereas Theissen wishes the analysis to include social or class-specific aspects of *weak* and *strong*.

4. I think it likely that the Erastus mentioned by Paul was the Erastus who was a city official in Corinth; see Romans 16:23 and Theissen, *Social Setting*, 75–83, 130. For the discussion of the social significance of *strong* and *weak*, see 70–73; Theissen's arguments are supported by the research of Black, see *Paul, Apostle of Weakness*, 13 and 98. For the cultic setting of meat-eating, see Theissen, *Social Setting*, 126–127.

5. As Theissen states, "Their more liberal attitude belongs primarily in the upper classes" (*Social Setting*, 138). Peter Marshall supports Theissen on this (*Enmity in Corinth*, 208–218, 284). For the Cynic and Stoic context of the arguments of the strong, see Stowers, "A Debate over Freedom."

6. Barrett, *Commentary*, 207; Grosheide, *Commentary on the First Epistle to the Corinthians*, 207–209; Schmithals, *The Office of Apostle in the Early Church*, 47; Pratscher, "Der Verzicht des Paulus," 295; Petersen, *Rediscovering Paul*, 150.

7. Taken alone, the phrase *exousia hymōn* in 9:12 could mean "authority *over* you" rather than "authority that is yours" (reading objective rather than subjective genitive). When Epictetus, for example, uses the phrase *echein mou exousian* (3.24.70), he means "to have authority *over* me." But Paul's use of *metechein* here, coupled with the parallel occurrence of *exousia hymōn* in 8:9 as subjective genitive, indicates that the phrase in 9:12 should be translated "to share in *your* authority." This also fits Paul's argument better, because in this section he is taking care to place himself among the strong in the possession of freedom and authority.

8. Dautzenberg, "Der Verzicht auf das apostoliche Unterhaltsrecht," 219. See also Rom. 14:13; 2 Cor. 11:29.

9. This is also the interpretation of Willis, *Idol Meat in Corinth*, 273 n. 15.

10. This point is made specifically by Murphy-O'Connor, *1 Corinthians*, 84, and more generally by Theissen, *Social Setting*, 137. See, for agreement, Malherbe, *Social Aspects*, 72, 81.

11. Bornkamm, "Missionary Stance of Paul," 203.

12. For the traditional connection of *exousia* and *eleutheria* in Greek literature, see Marshall, *Enmity in Corinth*, 285–294. Note that in Rom. 14:3 "those who eat" should not "despise" (*exoutheneō*) those who abstain; those who abstain should not "judge" (*krinetō*) those who eat. The two terms are juxtaposed again in 14:10. Why does Paul use two different words here, linking one with the position of the strong and the other with that of the weak? An obvious and probably correct explanation is that *exoutherneō* carried social status implications ("to look down on"). The weak can be told not judge the strong, but they can hardly be told not to "look down on" the strong because they, the weak, are of lower status to begin with. To make the point with a pun, one can only *exouthenein* when one has *exousia* (see, for example, 1 Cor. 6:12).

13. Horace calls his patron Maecenas *rex paterque* (*Epistle* 1.7.37–38). According to Gilbert Highet ("*Libertino Patre Natus*," 279), "*rex* at a later date was certainly the client's word for a rich patron." (See Juvenal *Satires* 5.14, 130, 137, 161; 7.45; 10.161.) Were some people at Corinth styling themselves "kings" as a claim to patronal position over others in the Corinthian church?

14. Robertson and Plummer, *First Epistle*, 224–225; see also Brandt, *Dienst und Dienen im Neuen Testament*, 100 n. 4.

15. Aristotle, *Nicomachean Ethics*, 9.10.6; 4.6.1; see Marshall, *Enmity in Corinth*, 73, 78, 316.

16. Romans 15, unlike 1 Corinthians 9, does urge mutual submission of the strong and the weak. But the letter to the Romans shows Paul in a completely different position vis-à-vis the addressees. In 1 Corinthians, Paul has a specific purpose in directing his criticism more to the strong. Furthermore, to Greco-Roman listeners, especially those of higher status, Paul's suggestion that they submit themselves to the weak, their social inferiors, was shocking. They would expect him to urge the submission of the weak to the strong. Therefore, the mutual submission of Romans 15 is actually more radical than it seems, if understood in its social historical context. This fact, coupled with the observation that in 1 Corinthians 9 Paul directs his call to submission primarily to the strong and not to the weak, highlights just how shocking Paul's suggestions in 1 Corinthians 9 really are. See Marshall, *Enmity in Corinth*, 290.

17. As Malherbe remarks, "Paul's attitude toward his labor is reflected by the fact that he lists it in a series of hardships (1 Cor. 4:12) and that he regards it as servile (1 Cor. 9:19) and an act of abasement (2 Cor. 11:7)" (*Paul and the Thessalonians*, 56 n. 83).

18. Hock, *Social Context*, 67.

19. Malherbe, *Paul and the Thessalonians*, 55.

20. See ibid., 56: "Paul was prepared to give up his social status in order to identify with manual laborers." Paul's education and other class indicators suggest a position of higher status for himself. See also Malherbe, *Social Aspects*, 29–59.

21. E. A. Judge realizes that "democratic ideology" was traditionally in tension with the normal patronal structures of the "republican" and "household" models of social structure (his terms). Patronal society did appropriate democratic ideology to some extent, but the two were essentially opposed in Greek and Roman tradition. See Judge, *Social Pattern*, 38–39.

22. Theissen, *Social Setting*, 139.

23. Ibid., 107. Theissen gives credit to Troeltsch, *The Social Teaching of the Christian Churches*, 69–89, for the definition and analysis of *love-patriarchalism*, admitting that Troeltsch does not use this particular term.

24. Theissen, *Social Setting*, 140. In the Greco-Roman world, as Marshall says, "Power and social predominance are closely linked with moral ascendancy. . . . The strong are superior in every way. Their blatant disregard for the weak, against which Paul so strongly reacts, is proper. In contradistinction, *asthenēs* not only denotes lowly status and worthlessness but also servility" (Marshall, *Enmity in Corinth*, 290).

25. See chapter 1 above; and Castelli, "Mimesis as a Discourse of Power in Paul's Letters."

26. Interestingly, changeableness was often seen to be the wily device of the weaker party in a conflict. As Pindar said, "The cunning of the weaker has taken the stronger by surprise and brought about his downfall" (quoted from the fourth *Isthmian* by Detienne and Vernant, *Cunning Intelligence*, 36). Paul's own polytropic behavior, therefore, appropriately identifies him with the weak at Corinth in their conflict with the strong. Paul's relatively high social status is seen in several factors: his letters indicate a rhetorical education of some sort; his own views of manual labor (that it is degrading) imply a position among the higher strata of Greco-Roman society; and there is some indication that he was a Roman citizen. This last factor may not be historical, as it is claimed not by Paul but by the author of Acts. It must be

taken into account as a possibility, however. The developing consensus is now that Paul came from the middle to higher (though not highest) strata of Roman provincial society. See Malherbe, *Paul and the Thessalonians*, 55–56; Meeks, *First Urban Christians*, 52; Marshall, *Enmity in Corinth*, 400–401.

27. Marshall correctly notes the status implications in Paul's call to the strong to give in to the weak: "It is not a question of compromise, which would have been unpalatable enough, but of accommodation of the strong to the weak. Such accommodation would mean the loss of freedom and respect" (*Enmity in Corinth*, 290–291).

28. Hock, "Christology."

29. Chariton, *Chaereas and Callirhoe*, 3.6.3–4. See Hock, "Christology," 8.

30. Xenophon *Ephesiaka*, 2.10.3–4.

31. Hock, "Christology," 10–11.

32. See Meeks, *First Urban Christians*, 180–182.

5. THEOLOGY AND IDEOLOGY IN CORINTH

1. Jameson, "The Symbolic Inference."

2. Ibid., 517. For further discussion of these ideas, see Jameson, *The Political Unconscious*, esp. 200.

3. Jameson's term for the ideological context in general is "subtext." See "The Symbolic Inference," 516.

4. Marshall, *Enmity in Corinth*, xii, 396–399. Note the status implications of giving and receiving in other cultures analyzed by anthropologists: Mauss, *The Gift*, 39–40; for the Roman situation, see 47–52.

5. As Judge points out, in the patron-client structure (or at least ideology) of Greco-Roman society, money was usually passed down the social scale. See Judge, *Rank and Status*, 26.

6. Letty Russell draws attention to a comparable rhetorical function of authoritative symbols in modern culture. She notes that in contemporary churches women pastors who are normally opposed to the use of hierarchical structures and symbols of authority some-times nevertheless must stress their own authority in order to gain a hearing for their message, which may in the end have a more egalitarian or antihierarchical goal. See Russell, "People and the Powers," 14; *Household of Freedom*, 80: "The new pastor does not realize that power is situation variable. She cannot decide to share power and work in a process of empowerment until her authority has been recognized as legitimate because she does not fit the accustomed father role."

7. See 1 Cor. 7:22–23, and chapter 2 above. Laub, *Die Begegnung des frühen Christentums*, 74–75. A recent study by Kyrtatas (*The Social Structure of the Early Christian Communities*) is largely devoted to showing that early Christianity, Paul included, did not challenge the structure of slavery. This main thesis is correct, whatever one may think of other aspects of Kyrtatas's study.

8. Epictetus 1.10.4.

9. See Havelock, *The Liberal Temper In Greek Politics*, 391ff., for a discussion of political uses of *interest* and *benefit*. The translation of *homonoia* is usually *concord*. Some scholars express dissatisfaction with any English translation, claiming that no English term fully captures the different nuances of the Greek (see, for instance, the dissatisfactions expressed

by Tarn in *Alexander the Great*). For the purpose of this study I will use *concord, unity,* and even the transliteration *homonoia* interchangeably. On *homonoia,* see Kramer, *Quid Valeat homonoia in Litteris Graecis;* Tarn, *Alexander the Great,* vol. 2, app. 25, pp. 399–449; Ferguson, *Moral Values in the Ancient World,* 118–132; P. Funke, *Homónoia und Arché.*

    10. Xenophon, *Memorabilia,* 3.5.16 (note *homonoēsousin*). Regarding the occurrence of "the advantageous" in deliberative speeches in general, Theon notes that anyone delivering a deliberative speech must use comparison (*sygkrisis*) in order to advise about the best choice (Theon, *Progymnasmata,* p. 61, lines 3–4).

    11. Isocrates, *On the Peace* 10, 11, 16, 26, 28.

    12. Ibid., 39; see also 35, 66, 70.

    13. Demosthenes, *Epistle,* 1.3.

    14. Ibid., 1.9–10. I am following the editors of the Greek texts who add *mē* before *tōn idiōn.* See the translation by Goldstein, *The Letters of Demosthenes,* 206, and his commentary on 255. Note the opposition in 1.10 of "private enmity" to "the common benefit."

    15. Aristotle, *Politics,* 5.8.6; *Rhetoric,* 1.8.2, 7. See K. Weiss, "*Sympherō,*" 9.69–78, for other references in Aristotle to *sympherein* and related words. Dio Chrysostom, *Discourse* 32.37, 70; 34.6, 17, 19, 22; 38 (38.50 especially points out that concord can be destroyed by small-minded persons acting selfishly). Plutarch, *Lycurgus,* 25.3. Lycurgus promoted unity and concord in Sparta by de-emphasizing private concern and emphasizing public: "In a word, he trained his fellow-citizens to have neither the wish nor the ability to live for themselves [*kat' idian*]; but like bees they were to make themselves always integral parts of the whole community [*tō koinō*]." Marcus Aurelius, *Meditations,* 6.54: the bee is the model for seeking not one's private benefit but the public good. This thought is followed in the text by the common analogy of the ship as representative of human community and the cooperation that is necessary for the salvation of the crew. For the function of the beneficial and edifying in deliberative speeches see D. Watson, "1 Corinthians 10:23–11:1 in the Light of Greco-Roman Rhetoric," 301–318, esp. 302.

    16. Epictetus 2.10.4–5, 7–9. For the occurrence of *sōtēria* as the ultimate benefit for the group see esp. Philo, *On Joseph,* 32–36; see also 63, 72–73, 75; Dio Chrysostom, *Discourses* 32.26; 38.10, 15; Isocrates, *On the Peace,* 39.

    17. An interesting exception to the general trend in the scholarship is the "hermeneutics of suspicion" practiced by G. Shaw, *The Cost of Authority.* Shaw's analysis, however, is not nuanced enough for my tastes.

CONCLUSION

    1. Space does not permit me to mention the many works that have influenced my thinking about the ideological function of religious language; I nevertheless must refer to the works of Mikhail Bakhtin: see especially Bakhtin/Medvedev, *The Formal Method in Literary Scholarship;* Voloshinov [Bakhtin?], *Marxism and the Philosophy of Language;* Bakhtin, *Speech Genres and Other Late Essays.* See also, for a good summary of Bakhtin's ideological criticism, Booth, "Freedom of Interpretation."

BIBLIOGRAPHY

Editions and translations of Greek and Latin authors are from the Loeb Classical Library unless otherwise indicated.

Adcock, F. E. "Greek and Macedonian Kingship." *Proceedings of the British Academy* 39 (1953): 163–180.

Adkins, A. W. H. *"Aretē, Technē,* Democracy and Sophists: Protagoras 316b–328d." *Journal of Hellenic Studies* 93 (1973): 3–12.

———. Review of *Greek Popular Morality in the Time of Plato and Aristotle,* by K. J. Dover. *Classical Philology* 73 (1978): 143–158.

Aelianus, Claudis. *Varia Historia.* Edited by Marvin R. Dilts. Leipzig: Teubner, 1974.

Aesopica. Edited by Ben Edwin Perry. Urbana: University of Illinois Press, 1952.

Alföldy, Géza. *The Social History of Rome.* Totowa, N.J.: Barnes and Noble Books, 1985.

Anderson, Graham. *Ancient Fiction: The Novel in the Graeco-Roman World.* Totowa, N.J.: Barnes and Noble Books, 1984.

———. *Eros Sophistes: Ancient Novelists at Play.* Chico, Calif.: Scholars Press, 1982.

———. *Lucian: Theme and Variation in the Second Sophistic.* Leiden: E. J. Brill, 1976.

Anderson, J. G. C. "An Imperial Estate in Galatia." *Journal of Roman Studies* 27 (1937): 18–21.

Andrews, Mary E. "Paul, Philo, and the Intellectuals." *Journal of Biblical Literature* 53 (1934): 150–166.

Antisthenis Fragmenta. Edited by Fernanda Decleva Caizzi. Milan-Varese: Istituto Editoriale Cisalpino, 1966.

Arnheim, M. T. W. *Aristocracy in Greek Society.* London: Thames and Hudson, 1977.

Artemidori Daldiani Onirocriticon Libri V. Edited by Roger A. Pack. Leipzig: Teubner, 1963.

Artemidorus. *The Interpretation of Dreams (Oneirocritica).* Translation and commentary by Robert J. White. Park Ridge, N.J.: Noyes Press, 1975.

Attridge, Harold W. *First-Century Cynicism in the Epistles of Heraclitus.* Missoula, Mont.: Scholars Press, 1976.

Austin, M. M., and P. Vidal-Naquet. *Economic and Social History of Ancient Greece: An Introduction*. Berkeley: University of California Press, 1977.

Badian, E. *Foreign Clientelae*. Oxford: Clarendon, 1958.

Bakhtin, M. M. *Speech Genres and Other Late Essays*. Translated by Vern W. McGee. Austin: University of Texas Press, 1986.

Bakhtin, M. M. / P. N. Medvedev. *The Formal Method in Literary Scholarship: A Critical Introduction to Sociological Poetics*. Translated by Albert J. Wehrle. Cambridge: Harvard University Press, 1985.

Baldwin, Barry. "Rulers and Ruled at Rome: A.D. 14–192." *Ancient Society* 3 (1972): 150–163.

Balsdon, J. P. V. D. *Romans and Aliens*. London: Gerald Duckworth, 1979.

Barrett, C. K. *A Commentary on the First Epistle to the Corinthians*. London: Adam and Charles Black, 1968.

Barrow, R. H. *Slavery in the Roman Empire*. New York: Dial Press, 1928.

Bartchy, S. Scott. *Mallon Chresai: First-Century Slavery and the Interpretation of 1 Corinthians 7:21*. Society of Biblical Literature Dissertation Series, no. 11. Missoula, Mont.: The Society, 1973.

Bassler, Jouette M. *Divine Impartiality: Paul and a Theological Axiom*. Chico, Calif.: Scholars Press, 1982.

Beare, F. W. *A Commentary on the Epistle to the Philippians*. New York: Harper, 1959.

Berger, Peter. *Rumor of Angels*. Garden City, N.Y.: Doubleday, 1969.

———. *The Sacred Canopy: Elements of a Sociological Theory of Religion*. Garden City, N.Y.: Doubleday, 1967.

Betz, Hans Dieter. *Der Apostel Paulus und die sokratische Tradition*. Tübingen: J. C. B. Mohr (Paul Siebeck), 1972.

———. *Galatians*. Philadelphia: Fortress Press, 1979.

———. *Paul's Apology: 2 Corinthians 10–13 and the Socratic Tradition*. Berkeley: Center for Hermeneutical Studies, 1975.

———. *Paul's concept of Freedom in the Context of Hellenistic Discussions about the Possibilities of Human Freedom*. Berkeley: Center for Hermeneutical Studies in Hellenistic and Modern Culture, 1977.

———. "The Problem of Rhetoric and Theology According to the Apostle Paul." In *L'Apôtre Paul*, edited by A. Vanhoye, 16–48. Leuven: Leuven University Press, 1986.

Biezunska-Malowist, Iza. "La vie familiale des esclaves." *Index. Quaderni Camerti di Studi Romanistici, International Survey of Roman Law* 8 (1978–79): 140–143.

Black, David Alan. *Paul, Apostle of Weakness*. New York: P. Lang, 1984.

Blalock, Herbert M., Jr. "Status Inconsistency, Social Mobility, Status Integration, and Structural Effects." *American Sociological Review* 32 (1967): 790–801.

Blank, David L. "Socratics Versus Sophists on Payment for Teaching." *Classical Antiquity* 4 (1985): 1–49.

Boer, W. den. *Private Morality in Greece and Rome: Some Historical Aspects*. Leiden: E. J. Brill, 1979.

Bömer, Franz. *Untersuchungen über die Religion der Sklaven in Griechenland und Rom*. 4 vols. Wiesbaden: F. Steiner, 1958–1963.

Booth, Wayne C. "Freedom of Interpretation: Bakhtin and the Challenge of Feminist Criticism." In *The Politics of Interpretation*, edited by W. J. T. Mitchell, 51–82. Chicago: University of Chicago Press, 1983.

Bornkamm, Günther. "The Missionary Stance of Paul in 1 Corinthians 9 and in Acts." In *Studies in Luke-Acts*, edited by Leander E. Keck and J. Louis Martyn, 194–207. Philadelphia: Fortress Press, 1980.

Bornscheuer, L. *Topik. Zur Struktur der gesellschaftlichen Einbildungskraft*. Frankfurt: Suhrkamp, 1976.

Boulvert, Gérard. *Domestique et fonctionnaire sous le haut-empire romain: La condition de l'affranchi et de l'esclave du prince*. Paris: Belles Lettres, 1974.

Bove, L. "Rapporti tra 'dominus auctionis,' 'coactor' ed emptor in Tab. Pomp. 27." *Labeo* 21 (1975): 322–331.

Bradley, Keith R. "Roman Slavery and Roman Law." *Historical Reflections/Réflexions Historiques* 15 (1988): 477–495.

———. *Slaves and Masters in the Roman Empire: A Study in Social Control*. New York: Oxford University Press, 1987.

Brandt, Wilhelm. *Dienst und Dienen im Neuen Testament*. Münster: Antiquariat Th. Stenderhoff, 1983.

Briscoe, John. "Rome and the Class Struggle in the Greek States 200–146 B.C." In *Studies in Ancient Society*, edited by Moses I. Finley, 53–73. London: Routledge and Kegan Paul, 1974.

Brockmeyer, Norbert. *Antike Sklaverei*. Darmstadt: Wissenschaftliche Buchgesellschaft, 1979.

Brown, Peter. *Society and the Holy in Late Antiquity*. Berkeley: University of California Press, 1982.

Bruce, F. F. *Paul, Apostle of the Heart Set Free*. Grand Rapids: Eerdmans, 1977.

Brunt, John C. "More on the Topos as a New Testament Form." *Journal of Biblical Literature* 104 (1988): 495–500.

Brunt, P. A. "Evidence Given under Torture in the Principate." *Zeitschrift der Savigny-Stiftung für Rechtsgeschichte, romanistische Abteilung* 97 (1980): 256–265.

———. Review of *The Slave System of Greek and Roman Antiquity*, by W. L. Westermann. *Journal of Roman Studies* 48 (1958): 165–168.

Buckland, William Warwick. *The Roman Law of Slavery: The Condition of the Slave in Private Law from Augustus to Justinian*. New York: A. M. S. Press, 1969.

Bünker, Michael. *Briefformular und rhetorische Disposition im 1. Korintherbrief*. Göttingen: Vandenhoeck und Ruprecht, 1983.

Burford, Alison. *Craftsmen in Greek and Roman Society*. London: Thames and Hudson, 1972.

Burke, Kenneth. *A Rhetoric of Motives.* Berkeley: University of California Press, 1969.

Calderini, Aristide. *La manomissione e la condizione dei liberti in Grecia.* Opera premiata dalla R. Accademia scientifico-letteraria di Milano col premio Lattes. Milan: U. Hoepli, 1908.

Cambiano, Giuseppe. "Aristotle and the Anonymous Opponents of Slavery." *Slavery and Abolition* 8 (1987): 21–40. Reprinted in *Classical Slavery,* edited by M. I. Finley, 22–41. Totowa, N.J., and London: Frank Cass, 1987.

Cameron, A. "Inscriptions relating to Sacral Manumission and Confession." *Harvard Theological Review* 32 (1939): 143–179.

———. "*Threptoi* and Related Terms in the Inscriptions of Asia Minor." In *Anatolian Studies Presented to W. H. Buckler,* edited by W. M. Calder and Josef Keil, 27–62. New York: Longmans, Green, 1923.

Caplan, Lionel. "Power and Status in South Asian Slavery." In *Asian and African Systems of Slavery,* edited by James L. Watson, 169–194. Berkeley: University of California Press, 1980.

Caragonnis, C. C. "*Opsonian:* A Reconsideration of Its Meaning." *Novum Testamentum* 16 (1974): 35–57.

Cassiodorus. *Letters of Cassiodorus (Variae Epistolae).* Translated by Thomas Hodgkin. London: Henry Frowde, 1886.

Casson, Lionel. *Ancient Trade and Society.* Detroit: Wayne State University Press, 1984.

Castelli, Elizabeth Anne. "Mimesis as a Discourse of Power in Paul's Letters." Ph.D. diss., Claremont Graduate School, 1987.

Chadwick, Henry. "All Things to All Men." *New Testament Studies* 1 (1954–55): 261–275.

———. "St. Paul and Philo of Alexandria." *Bulletin of the John Rylands Library* 48 (1965–66): 286–307.

Chadwick, W. Edward. *The Pastoral Teaching of St. Paul: His Ministerial Ideals.* Edinburgh: T. and T. Clark, 1907.

Chantraine, Heinrich. "Freigelassene und Sklaven kaiserlicher Frauen." In *Studien zur antiken Socialgeschichte,* edited by Werner Eck, Hartmut Galsterer, and Hartmut Wolff, 389–416. Cologne, Vienna: Böhlau, 1980.

Chariton. *Chaereas and Callirhoe.* Translated by Warren E. Blake. Ann Arbor: University of Michigan Press, 1939.

Charitonis Aphrodisiensis. *De Chaerea et Callirhoe Amatoriatum Narrationum.* Edited by Warren E. Blake. Oxford: Clarendon, 1938.

Clarysse, W. "Harmachis, Agent of the Oikonomos: An Archive from the Time of Philopater." *Ancient Society* 7 (1976): 185–207.

Coleman-Norton, Paul R. "The Apostle Paul and the Roman Law of Slavery." In *Studies in Roman Economic and Social History in Honor of Allan Chester Johnson,* edited by P. R. Coleman-Norton, 155–177. Freeport, N.Y.: Books for Libraries Press, 1951.

Connor, W. Robert. *The New Politicians of Fifth Century Athens*. Princeton: Princeton University Press, 1971.

Conzelmann, Hans. *Commentary on 1 Corinthians*. Philadelphia: Fortress Press, 1975.

Cook, John Manuel. *The Persian Empire*. London: J. M. Dent and Sons, 1983.

Corcoran, Gervase. "Slavery in the New Testament." Parts 1, 2. *Milltown Studies* no. 5 (1980): 1–40; no. 6 (1980): 62–83.

Cranfield, C. E. B. *A Critical and Exegetical Commentary on the Epistle to the Romans*. 6th ed. Edinburgh: Clark, 1975.

Crocker, J. Christopher. "The Social Functions of Rhetorical Forms." In *The Social Use of Metaphors: Essays on the Anthropology of Rhetoric*, edited by J. David Sapir and J. Christopher Crocker, 33–66. Philadelphia: University of Pennsylvania Press, 1977.

Crook, John A. *Law and Life of Rome, 90 B.C.–A.D. 212*. Ithaca, N.Y.: Cornell University Press, 1967.

———. "*Patria Potestas.*" *Classical Quarterly* 61 (n.s. 17) (1967): 113–122.

———. "Working Notes on Some New Pompeii Tablets." *Zeitschrift für Papyrologie und Epigraphik* 29 (1978): 229–239.

Dahl, Nils Alstrup. "Paul and the Church at Corinth." In *Studies in Paul*, 40–61. Minneapolis: Augsburg, 1977.

Daly, Lloyd W. *Aesop Without Morals*. New York: Thomas Yoseloff, 1961.

Danker, Frederick W. *Benefactor: Epigraphic Study of a Graeco-Roman and New Testament Semantic Field*. St. Louis: Clayton, 1982.

D'Arms, John H. *Commerce and Social Standing in Ancient Rome*. Cambridge: Harvard University Press, 1981.

———. Review of *Personal Patronage under the Early Empire*, by Richard P. Saller. *Classical Philology* 81 (1986): 95–98.

Daube, David. "Dodges and Rackets in Roman Law." *Proceedings of the Classical Association* 61 (1964): 28–30.

———. "*Kerdainō* as a Missionary Term." *Harvard Theological Review* 40 (1947): 109–120.

———. *The New Testament and Rabbinic Judaism*. New York: Arno Press, 1973.

———. *Roman Law: Linguistic and Philosophical Aspects*. Edinburgh: At the University Press, 1969.

Dautzenberg, Gerhard. "Der Verzicht auf das apostolische Unterhaltsrecht: Eine exegetische Untersuchung zu 1 Kor 9." *Biblica* 50 (1969): 212–232.

Davies, J. K. *Athenian Propertied Families, 600–300 B. C.* Oxford: Clarendon Press, 1971.

Deissmann, Adolf. *Light from the Ancient East: The New Testament Illustrated by*

Recently Discovered Texts of the Graeco-Roman World. 2d ed. New York: G. H. Doran, 1927.

Demos, John P. *Entertaining Satan: Witchcraft and the Culture of Early New England.* New York: Oxford University Press, 1982.

Demosthenes. *The Letters of Demosthenes.* Translated by Jonathan A. Goldstein. New York: Columbia University Press, 1968.

Detienne, Marcel, and Jean-Pierre Vernant. *Cunning Intelligence in Greek Culture and Society.* Atlantic Highlands, N.J.: Humanities Press, 1978.

Dewey, Arthur J. "A Matter of Honor: A Social-Historical Analysis of 2 Corinthians 10." *Harvard Theological Review* 78 (1985): 211–217.

Diakonoff, I. M. "Media." In *The Cambridge History of Iran*, edited by Ilya Gershevitch, 2:36–148. Cambridge: Cambridge University Press, 1985.

The Digest of Justinian. Translated by Alan Watson. Latin text edited by Theodor Mommsen with Paul Krueger. Philadelphia: University of Pennsylvania Press, 1985.

Dillon, George L. *Rhetoric as Social Imagination.* Bloomington: Indiana University Press, 1986.

Dodds, C. H. "Notes from Papyri." *Journal of Theological Studies* 26 (1924): 77–78.

Dodd, E. R. *The Greek and the Irrational.* Berkeley: University of California Press, 1951.

Dover, K. J. *Greek Popular Morality in the Time of Plato and Aristotle.* Berkeley: University of California Press, 1974.

Drinkwater, J. F. "The Rise and Fall of the Gallic Iulii: Aspects of the Development of the Aristocracy of the Three Gauls under the Early Empire," *Latomus* 37 (1978): 817–850.

Duchêne, H. "Sur la stèle d'Aulus Caprillus Timotheos, sōmatemporos." *Bulletin de correspondance hellénique* 110 (1986): 513–530.

Dudley, Donald R. *A History of Cynicism: From Diogenes to the 6th century A.D.* London: Methuen, 1937.

Duff, A. M. *Freedmen in the Early Roman Empire.* Oxford: Clarendon Press, 1928.

Duncan-Jones, Richard. *The Economy of the Roman Empire: Quantitative Studies.* Rev. ed. Cambridge: Cambridge University Press, 1974.

Eckstein, A. M. "Polybius, Syracuse, and the Politics of Accommodation." *Greek, Roman and Byzantine Studies* 26 (1985): 265–282.

Eisenstadt, S. N., and L. Roniger. "Patron-Client Relations as a Model of Structuring Social Exchange." *Comparative Studies in Society and History* 22 (1980): 42–77.

———. *Patrons, Clients and Friends: Interpersonal Relations and the Structure of Trust in Society.* Cambridge: Cambridge University Press, 1984.

Elert, Werner, "Redemptio ab hostibus." *Theologische Literaturzeitung* 72 (1947): 265–270.

Ellison, H. L. "Paul and the Law—'All Things to All Men.'" In *Apostolic History and the Gospel*, edited by W. Ward Gasque and Ralph P. Martin, 195–202. Grand Rapids: Eerdmans, 1970.

Emmerson, Richard Kenneth. *Antichrist in the Middle Ages*. Seattle: University of Washington Press, 1981.

Fairclough, H. Rushton. *Horace: Satires, Epistles, and ars poetica*. New York: G. P. Putnam's Sons (Loeb), 1926.

Farnell, Lewis Richard. *The Works of Pindar*. London: Macmillan and Co., 1930.

Fears, J. Rufus. "Cyrus as a Stoic Exemplum of the Just Monarch." *American Journal of Philology* 95 (1974): 265–267.

Feeley-Harnik, Gillian. "Is Historical Anthropology Possible? The Case of the Runaway Slave." In *Humanizing America's Iconic Book*, ed. Gene M. Tucker and Douglas A. Knight, 95–126. Chico, Calif.: Scholars Press, 1982.

Ferguson, John. *Moral Values in the Ancient World*. London: Methuen, 1958.

————. *Utopias of the Classical World*. London: Thames and Hudson, 1975.

Finley, Moses I. *The Ancient Economy*. 2d ed. London: The Hogarth Press, 1985.

————. *Ancient Slavery and Modern Ideology*. New York: Viking Press, 1980.

————. "Athenian Demagogues." In *Studies in Ancient Society*, edited by Moses I. Finley, 1–25. London: Routledge and Kegan Paul, 1974.

————. "Aulus Kapreilius Timotheus, Slave Trader." In *Aspects of Antiquity*, ed. M. I. Finley. 162–176. London: Chatto and Windus, 1968.

————. "Between Slavery and Freedom." *Comparative Studies in Society and History* 6 (1964): 233–249.

————, ed. *Classical Slavery*. London: Frank Cass, 1987.

————, ed. *Slavery in Classical Antiquity: Views and Controversy*. Cambridge, England: W. Heffer, 1974.

Fischel, Henry A. "Story and History: Observations on Greco-Roman Rhetoric and Pharisaism." In *Essays in Greco-Roman and Related Talmudic Literature*, edited by H. A. Fischel, 443–472. New York: KTAV Publishing House, 1977.

Fitzgerald, John T. "Cracks in an Earthen Vessel: An Examination of the Catalogues of Hardships in the Corinthian Correspondence." Ph.D. diss., Yale University, 1984.

Flesher, Paul V. M. *Oxen, Women or Citizens? Slaves in the System of the Mishnah*. Atlanta: Scholars Press, 1988.

Flory, Marlene Boudreau. "Family and '*Familia*': A Study of Social Relations in Slavery." Ph.D. diss., Yale University, 1975.

————. "Family in *Familia*: Kinship and Community in Slavery." *American Journal of Ancient History* 3 (1978): 78–95.

————. "Where Women Precede Men: Factors Influencing the Order of Names in Roman Epitaphs." *The Classical Journal* 79 (1983): 216–224.

Forbes, Christopher, "Comparison, Self-praise and Irony: Paul's Boasting and the Conventions of Hellenistic Rhetoric." *New Testament Studies* 32 (1986): 1–30.

Forbes, Clarence A. "The Education and Training of Slaves in Antiquity." *Transactions of the American Philological Association* 86 (1955): 321–360.

Foucault, Michel. *Language, Counter-memory, Practice*. Edited by Donald F. Bouchard. Ithaca, N.Y.: Cornell University Press, 1977.

Fox, Robin Lane. *Pagans and Christians*. New York: Alfred A. Knopf, 1987.

Fraser, P. M. *Rhodian Funerary Monuments*. Oxford: Clarendon Press, 1977.

Fredrich, Carl Johann, ed. *Inschriften von Priene*. Berlin: G. Reimer, 1906.

Freeman, Gordon M. *The Heavenly Kingdom: Aspects of Political Thought in the Talmud and Mishnah*. Lanham, Md.: Jerusalem Center for Public Affairs/Center for Jewish Community Studies, 1986.

Fuks, Alexander. "Plato and the Social Question: The Problem of Poverty and Riches in the Republic." *Ancient Society* 8 (1977): 49–83.

Funk, Aloys. *Status und Rollen in den Paulusbriefen: Eine inhaltsanalytische Untersuchung zur Religionssoziologie*. Innsbrucher theologische Studien 7. Innsbruck, Vienna, and Munich: Tyrolia, 1981.

Funke, Hermann. "Antisthenes bei Paulus." *Hermes* 98 (1970): 459–471.

Funke, Peter. *Homónoia und Arché: Athen und die griechische Staatenwelt vom Ende des peloponnesischen Krieges bis zum Königsfrieden (404/3–387/6 v. Chr.)*. Wiesbaden: Franz Steiner, 1980.

Gabba, Emilio. "Literature." In *Sources for Ancient History*, edited by Michael Crawford, 1–79. Cambridge: Cambridge University Press, 1983.

Galinsky, G. Karl. *The Heracles Theme*. Oxford: Basil Blackwell, 1972.

Garlan, Yvon. *Slavery in Ancient Greece*. Revised and expanded edition. Ithaca, N.Y.: Cornell University Press, 1988.

Garnsey, Peter. "Descendents of Freedmen in Local Politics: Some Criteria." In *The Ancient Historian and His Materials: Essays Presented to C. E. Stevens*, edited by Barbara Levick, 167–180. Westmead, Farnborough, Hants, England: Gregg International, 1975.

———. "Legal Privilege in the Roman Empire." In *Studies in Ancient Society*, edited by Moses I. Finley, 141–165. London: Routledge and Kegan Paul, 1974.

———. "Slaves in Business." *Roma* 1 (1982): 105–108.

———. *Social Status and Legal Privilege in the Roman Empire*. Oxford: Clarendon Press, 1970.

Goffman, Irwin. "Status Consistency and Preference for Change in Power Distribution." *American Sociological Review* 22 (1957): 275–281.

Golden, Mark. "The Effects of Slavery on Citizen Households and Children: Aeschylus, Aristophanes and Athens." *Historical Reflections/Réflexions Historiques* 15 (1988): 455–475.

Goldstein, Jonathan A. *The Letters of Demosthenes*. New York: Columbia University Press, 1968.

Goodenough, Erwin R. "Paul and Onesimus." *Harvard Theological Review* 22 (1929): 181–183.

———. "The Political Philosophy of Hellenistic Kingship." *Yale Classical Studies* 1 (1928): 55–102.

———. *The Politics of Philo Judaeus.* New Haven: Yale University Press, 1938.

Goodspeed, Edgar J. "Paul and Slavery." *Journal of Bible and Religion* 11 (1943): 169–170.

Gordon, M. L. "The Freedman's Son in Municipal Life." *Journal of Roman Studies* 21 (1931): 65–71.

Grant, Robert M. "Hellenistic Elements in 1 Corinthians." In *Early Christian Origins: Studies in Honor of Harold R. Willoughby*, edited by Allen Wikgren, 60–66. Chicago: Quadrangle Books, 1961.

Grayston, Kenneth. *The Letters of Paul to the Philippians and to the Thessalonians.* London: Cambridge University Press, 1967.

Grene, David, and Richard Lattimore, eds. *The Complete Greek Tragedies.* New York: Modern Library, 1956.

Grimaldi, William M. A. "The Aristotelian *Topics.*" In *Aristotle: The Classical Heritage of Rhetoric*, edited by Keith V. Erickson, 176–193. Metuchen, N.J.: Scarecrow Press, 1974.

Grosheide, F. W. *Commentary on the First Epistle to the Corinthians.* Grand Rapids: Wm. B. Eerdmans, 1953.

Hadas, Moses. *Three Greek Romances.* New York: Bobbs-Merrill, 1964.

Hägg, Tomas. *The Novel in Antiquity.* Oxford: Basil Blackwell, 1983.

Hargreaves, John. *A Guide to 1 Corinthians.* London: SPCK, 1978.

Hatzfeld, Jean. *Les trafiquants italiens dans l'Orient hellénique.* Paris: Ancienne Librairie Fontemoing, 1919.

Havelock, Eric A. *The Liberal Temper in Greek Politics.* New Haven: Yale University Press, 1957.

Heinen, Heinz. "Sklaverei in der hellenistischen Welt." Parts 1, 2. *Ancient Society* 7 (1976): 127–149; 8 (1977): 121–154.

Héring, Jean. *The First Epistle of Saint Paul to the Corinthians.* London: Epworth Press, 1962.

Highet, Gilbert. "*Libertino Patre Natus.*" *American Journal of Philology* 94 (1973): 268–281.

Hock, Ronald F. "Christology and the Conventions of Ancient Slavery: Looking Again at Phil. 2:5–11." Paper presented at the Western Regional meeting of the Society of Biblical Literature, 20–21 March 1986, at the University of Santa Clara, Santa Clara, California.

———. "Paul's Tentmaking and the Problem of His Social Class." *Journal of Biblical Literature* 97 (1978): 555–564.

———. *The Social Context of Paul's Ministry: Tentmaking and Apostleship.* Philadelphia: Fortress Press, 1980.

Höistad, Ragner. *Cynic Hero and Cynic King: Studies in the Cynic Conceptions of Man.* Lund: Carl Bloms Boktryckeri A.-B., 1948.

Holmberg, Bengt. *Paul and Power*. Philadelphia: Fortress Press, 1980.

Hopkins, Keith. *Conquerors and Slaves*. Cambridge: Cambridge University Press, 1978.

————. *Death and Renewal*. Sociological Studies in Roman History, 2. Cambridge: Cambridge University Press, 1983.

————. "Elite Mobility in the Roman Empire." *Past and Present* 32 (1965): 12–26.

Hornung, Carlton A. "Social Status, Status Inconsistency, and Psychological Stress." *American Sociological Review* 42 (1977): 623–638.

Horsley, Richard A. "Consciousness and Freedom among the Corinthians: 1 Corinthians 8–10." *Catholic Biblical Quarterly* 40 (1978): 574–589.

Horst, Pieter W. van der. "Chariton and the New Testament." *Novum Testamentum* 25 (1983): 348–355.

Humphreys, Sarah C. *The Family, Women and Death: Comparative Studies*. London: Routledge and Kegan Paul, 1983.

Hurd, John Coolidge. *The Origin of 1 Corinthians*. New York: Seabury Press, 1965.

Jackson, Elton F. "Status Consistency and Symptoms of Stress." *American Sociological Review* 27 (1962): 469–480.

Jacoby, F. *Die Fragmente der griechischen Historiker*. Berlin: Weidmann, 1926.

Jameson, Fredric R. *The Political Unconscious: Narrative as a Socially Symbolic Act*. Ithaca, N.Y.: Cornell University Press, 1981.

————. "The Symbolic Inference; or, Kenneth Burke and Ideological Analysis." *Critical Inquiry* 4 (1978): 507–523.

Jehn, Peter, ed. *Toposforschung: Eine Dokumentation*. Frankfurt: Athenäum, 1972.

Johnson, Alan F. *The Freedom Letter*. Chicago: Moody Press, 1974.

Jolowicz, Herbert F., and Barry Nicholas. *Historical Introduction to the Study of Roman Law*. 3d ed. Cambridge: Cambridge University Press, 1972.

Jones, C. P. *The Roman World of Dio Chrysostom*. Cambridge: Harvard University Press, 1978.

————. "*Stigma:* Tattooing and Branding in Graeco-Roman Antiquity." *Journal of Roman Studies* 77 (1987): 139–155.

Judge, E. A. "Cultural Conformity and Innovation in Paul: Some Clues from Contemporary Documents." *Tyndale Bulletin* 35 (1984): 3–24.

————. "The Early Christians as a Scholastic Community." *Journal of Religious History* 1 (1960): 125–137.

————. *Rank and Status in the World of the Caesars and St. Paul*. [Christchurch, New Zealand]: University of Canterbury, 1982.

————. "The Social Identity of the First Christians." *Journal of Religious History* 1 (1960): 201–217.

————. *The Social Pattern of Christian Groups in the First Century*. London: Tyndale Press, 1960.

Justin. *Justin, Cornelius Nepos, and Eutropius.* Translated by John Selby Watson. London: Henry G. Bohn, 1853.

Juvenal. *The Sixteen Satires.* Translated by Peter Greene. New York: Penguin Books, 1974.

Kaser, Max. *Roman Private Law.* 4th ed. Translated by Rolf Dannenbring. Pretoria: University of South Africa, 1984.

Kent, John Harvey. *The Inscriptions, 1926–1950.* Corinth; results of excavations conducted by the American School of Classical Studies at Athens, vol. 8, pt. 3. Princeton: American School of Classical Studies at Athens, 1966.

Kiley, Mark C. "Colossians as Pseudepigraphy." Ph.D. diss., Harvard University, 1983.

Kindstrand, Jan Fredrik. *Bion of Borysthenes: A Collection of the Fragments with Introduction and Commentary.* Uppsala and Stockholm: Almquist and Wiksell, 1976.

Kirschenbaum, Aaron. *Sons, Slaves and Freedmen in Roman Commerce.* Washington, D.C.: Catholic University of America Press, 1987.

Kramer, Hans. *Quid Valeat homonoia in Litteris Graecis.* Göttingen: Officina Academia Dieterichiana, 1915.

Kuch, Heinrich. *Der antike Roman: Untersuchungen zur literarischen Kommunikation und Gattungsgeschichte.* Berlin: Akademie-Verlag, 1989.

Kyrtatas, Dimitris J. *The Social Structure of the Early Christian Communities.* New York: Verso, 1987.

Lacy, W. K. "*Patria Potestas.*" In *The Family in Ancient Rome*, edited by Beryl Rawson, 121–144. Ithaca, N.Y.: Cornell University Press, 1986.

Lakoff, George and Mark Johnson. *Metaphors We Live By.* Chicago: University of Chicago Press, 1980.

Landvogt, Peter. *Epigraphische Untersuchung über den Oikonomos: Ein Beitrag zum hellenistischen Beamtenwesen.* Strasbourg: M. Dumont Schauberg, 1908.

Laub, Franz. *Die Begegnung des frühen Christentums mit der antiken Sklaverei.* Stuttgart: Verlag Katholisches Bibelwerk, 1982.

Leenhardt, Franz-J. *L'Epitre de Saint Paul aux Romains.* 2d ed. Geneva: Labor et Fides, 1981.

Lenski, Gerhard E. "Social Participation and Status Crystallization." *American Sociological Review* 21 (1956): 458–464.

——. "Status Crystallization: A Non-Vertical Dimension of Social Status." *American Sociological Review* 19 (1954): 405–413.

Levin, Harry. "Motif." In *Dictionary of the History of Ideas*, 3:235–244. New York: Charles Scribner's Sons, 1973.

Lewis, D. M. "Attic Manumissions." *Hesperia* 28 (1959): 208–238.

——. "Dedications of Phialai at Athens." *Hesperia* 37 (1968): 368–380.

Libanius. *Libanii Opera.* 12 vols. Edited by R. Foerster. Leipzig: Teubner, 1903–1927.

Liefeld, Walter L. "The Wandering Preacher as a Social Figure." Ph.D. diss., Columbia University, 1968.

Lietzmann, Hans. *An die Korinther I/II*. Ergänzt von Werner Georg Kümmel. Tübingen: J. C. B. Mohr (Paul Siebeck), 1969.

Lightfoot, J. B. *Notes on Epistles of St. Paul*. 1895. Reprint. Grand Rapids, Michigan: Baker Book House, 1980.

Liversidge, Joan. *Everyday Life in the Roman Empire*. New York: G. P. Putnam's Sons, 1976.

Loane, H. J. *Industry and Commerce of the City of Rome (50 B.C.–200 A.D.)*. Baltimore: The Johns Hopkins Press, 1938.

Longenecker, Richard N. *Paul, Apostle of Liberty*. New York: Harper and Row, 1964.

Lyall, Francis. "Roman Law in the Writings of Paul—Adoption." *Journal of Biblical Literature* 88 (1969): 458–466.

———. "Roman Law in the Writings of Paul—The Slave and the Freedman." *New Testament Studies* 17 (1970): 73–79.

———. *Slaves, Citizens, Sons: Legal Metaphors in the Epistles*. Grand Rapids: Zondervan, 1984.

Lyons, George. *Pauline Autobiography: Toward a New Understanding*. Atlanta: Society of Biblical Literature, 1985.

MacMullen, Ramsay. "Late Roman Slavery." *Historia* 36 (1987): 359–383.

———. *Roman Social Relations, 50 B.C. to A.D. 284*. New Haven: Yale University Press, 1974.

———. "Social History in Astrology." *Ancient Society* 2 (1971): 105–116.

———. "Social Mobility and the Theodosian Code." *Journal of Roman Studies* 54 (1964): 49–53.

Macro, A. D. "Imperial Provisions for Pergamum: *OGIS* 484." *Greek, Roman and Byzantine Studies* 17 (1976): 169–179.

Mactoux, Marie Madeleine. "Le champ semantique de doulos chewz les orateurs attiques." In *Schiavitù, manomissione e classi dipendenti nel mondo antico*, 35–97. Rome: "L'Erma" di Bretschneider, 1979.

Magie, David. *Roman Rule in Asia Minor*. 2 vols. Princeton: Princeton University Press, 1950.

Malan, F. S. "Bound to Do Right." *Neotestamentica* 15 (1981): 118–138.

Malherbe, Abraham J. "Antisthenes and Odysseus, and Paul at War." *Harvard Theological Review* 76 (1983): 143–173.

———. "Gentle as a Nurse." *Novum Testamentum* 12 (1970): 203–217.

———. *Paul and the Thessalonians: The Philosophic Tradition of Pastoral Care*. Philadelphia: Fortress Press, 1987.

———. *Social Aspects of Early Christianity*. 2d ed., enlarged. Philadelphia: Fortress Press, 1983.

Manning, C. E. "Liberalitas—The Decline and Rehabilitation of a Virtue." *Greece and Rome* 32 (1985): 73–83.

Marshall, Peter. "Enmity and Other Social Conventions in Paul's Relations with the Corinthians." Ph.D. diss., Macquarie University, 1980.

———. *Enmity in Corinth: Social Conventions in Paul's Relations with the Corinthians.* Wissenschaftliche Untersuchungen zum Neuen Testament. 2.23. Tübingen: J. C. B. Mohr (Paul Siebeck), 1987.

———. "A Metaphor of Social Shame: *Thriambeuein* in 2 Cor. 2:14." *Novum Testamentum* 25 (1983): 302–317.

Martin, Hubert Jr. "The Concept of *Philanthropia* in Plutarch's *Lives.*" *American Journal of Philology* 82 (1961): 164–175.

Martin, Ralph P. *Carmen Christi: Philippians ii.5–11 in Recent Interpretation and in the Setting of Early Christian Worship.* Rev. ed. Grand Rapids: Eerdmans, 1983.

———. *Philippians.* London: Oliphants, 1976.

Mason, Hugh J. *Greek Terms for Roman Institutions: A Lexicon and Analysis.* Toronto: Hekkert, 1974.

Mattusch, Carol C. "Corinthian Metalworking: The Forum Area." *Hesperia* 46 (1977): 380–389.

Maurer, Chr. "Grund und Grenze apostolischer Freiheit. Exegetische-theologische Studie zu I. Korinther 9." In *Antwort. Karl Barth zum siebzigsten Geburtstag am 10. Mai 1956.* Zürich: Zollikon, 1956.

Mauss, Marcel. *The Gift: Forms and Functions of Exchange in Archaic Societies.* London: Cohen and West, 1954.

Maximus of Tyre. *The Dissertations of Maximus Tyrius.* 2 vols. Translated by Thomas Taylor. London: R. H. Evans, 1804.

———. *Maximi Tyrii Philosophumena.* Edited by H. Hobein. Leipzig: Teubner, 1910.

May, James M. *Trials of Character: The Eloquence of Ciceronian Ethos.* Chapel Hill: University of North Carolina Press, 1988.

Meeks, Wayne. *The First Urban Christians.* New Haven: Yale University Press, 1983.

Meer, F. van der. *Augustine the Bishop.* Translated by Brian Battershaw and G. R. Lamb. New York: Sheed and Ward, 1961.

Meili, Josef. *The Ministry of Paul in the Community of Corinth as It Appears in the First Letter to the Corinthians.* Taiwan: Catholic Mission, 1982.

Meineke, Augustus, ed. *Fragmenta Comicorum Graecorum.* 2 vols. Berlin: G. Reimeri, 1841.

Mendels, Doron. "Perseus and the Socio-Eocnomic Question in Greece (179–172/1 B.C.): A Study in Roman Propaganda." *Ancient Society* 9 (1978): 55–73.

Mendelsohn, Isaac. *Slavery in the Ancient Near East: A Comparative Study of Slavery in Babylonia, Assyria, Syria and Palestine from the Middle of the Third Millennium to the End of the First Millennium.* Oxford: Oxford University Press, 1948.

Meritt, Benjamin D. "Greek Inscriptions." *Hesperia* 9 (1940): 53–96.

Millar, Fergus. "The World of the *Golden Ass.*" *Journal of Roman Studies* 71 (1981): 63–75.

Mitchell, Alan Christopher. "I Corinthians 6:1–11: Group Boundaries and the Courts of Corinth." Ph.D. diss., Yale University, 1986.

Mitchell, Stephen. "Requisitioned Transport in the Roman Empire: A New Inscription from Pisidia." *Journal of Roman Studies* 66 (1976): 106–131.

Moffatt, James. *The First Epistle of Paul to Corinthians.* New York: Harper and Brothers, 1938.

Mohler, Samuel L. "The *Cliens* in the Time of Martial." In *Classical Studies in Honor of John C. Rolfe,* edited by G. P. Hadzsits. Philadelphia: University of Pennsylvania Press, 1931.

––––––. "Slave Education in the Roman Empire." *Transactions of the American Philological Association* 71 (1940): 262–280.

Momigliano, A. Review of *The Liberal Temper in Greek Politics,* by Eric Havelock. *Rivista Storica Italiana* 72 (1960): 534–541.

Mott, Stephen Charles. "The Power of Giving and Receiving: Reciprocity in Hellenistic Benevolence." In *Current Issues in Biblical and Patristic Interpretation,* edited by Gerald F. Hawthorne, 60–72. Grand Rapids: Eerdmans, 1975.

Murphy-O'Connor, Jerome. *1 Corinthians.* Wilmington, Del.: Michael Glazier, 1979.

––––––. "Corinthian Slogans in 1 Cor. 6:12–20." *Catholic Biblical Quarterly* 40 (1978): 391–396.

Nani, T. G. "*Threptoi.*" *Epigraphica* 5–6 (1943–44): 45–84.

Naour, C. "Tyriaion en Cabalide." *Zeitschrift für Papyrologie und Epigraphik* 29 (1978): 91–114.

Nestle, Dieter. *Eleutheria: Studien zum Wesen der Freiheit bei den Griechen und im Neuen Testament, I: Die Griechen.* Tübingen: Mohr, 1967.

Nicolaus of Damascus. In *Die Fragmente der griechischen Historiker,* edited by F. Jacoby. Vol. 2A. Berlin: Weidmann, 1926.

Nicols, John. "*Tabulae Patronatus:* A study of the Agreement between Patron and Client Community." *Aufstieg und Niedergang der Römischen Welt* 2. 13, pp. 535–561. Berlin and New York: de Gruyter, 1980.

Niederwimmer, Kurt. *Der Begriff der Freiheit im Neuen Testament.* Berlin: Töpelmann, 1966.

Nisbet, Robert A. *The Social Philosophers: Community and Conflict in Western Thought.* New York: Thomas Y. Crowell, 1973.

Nock, A. D. *Essays on Religion and the Ancient World.* Edited by Zeph Stewart. Cambridge: Harvard University Press, 1972.

Ochs, Donovan J. "Aristotle's Concept of Formal Topics." In *Aristotle: The Classical*

Heritage of Rhetoric, edited by Keith V. Erickson, 194–204. Metuchen, N.J.: Scarecrow Press, 1974.

Oost, Stewart Irwin. "The Career of M. Antonius Pallas." *American Journal of Philology* 79 (1958): 113–139.

The Oxford Classical Dictionary, 2d ed. Edited by N. G. L. Hammond and H. H. Scullard. Oxford: Clarendon, 1970.

Perotti, Elena. "Una categoria particolare di schiavi attici: I *choris oikountes.*" *Rendiconti: Classe di Lettere e Scienze Morali e Stroiche*, Istituto Lombardo 106 (1972): 375–388.

Perry, Ben Edwin. *Studies in the Text History of the Life and Fables of Aesop*. Philological Monographs Published by the American Philological Association, no. 7. Haverford, Pennsylvania: The Association, 1936.

Petersen, Norman. *Rediscovering Paul: Philemon and the Sociology of Paul's Narrative World*. Philadelphia: Fortress Press, 1985.

Philemon. "Thebans." In *Fragmenta Comicorum Graecorum*, edited by Augustus Meineke. Vol. 4. Berlin: G. Reimeri, 1841.

Philip, E. D. "The Comic Odysseus." *Greece and Rome*, 2d ser., 6 (1959): 58–67.

Piazza, Thomas, and Charles Y. Glock. "Images of God and Their Social Meanings." In *The Religious Dimension: New Directions in Quantitative Research*, edited by Robert Wuthnow, 69–91. New York: Academic, 1979.

Pindar. *The Works of Pindar*. Translated by Lewis Richard Farnell. London: Macmillan, 1930.

Plank, Karl A. *Paul and the Irony of Affliction*. SBL Semeia Studies. Atlanta: Scholars Press, 1987.

Plato, *The Republic*. Translated by Richard W. Sterling and William C. Scott. New York: W. W. Norton, 1985.

Pleket, H. W. "Religious History as the History of Mentality: The 'Believer' as Servant of the Deity in the Greek World." In *Faith, Hope and Worship: Aspects of Religious Mentality in the Ancient World*, edited by H. S. Versnel, 152–192. Leiden: Brill, 1981.

―――. "Technology in the Greco-Roman World: A General Report." *Talanta* 5 (1973): 6–47.

―――. "Urban Elites and Business in the Greek Part of the Roman Empire." In *Trade in the Ancient Economy*, edited by Peter Garnsey, Keith Hopkins, and C. R. Whittaker, 131–144. Berkeley: University of California Press, 1983.

Pohlenz, Max. *Freedom in Greek Life and Thought*. Dordrecht, Holland: D. Reidel, 1966.

Powell, Benjamin. "Inscriptions from Corinth." *American Journal of Archaeology*, 2d ser., 7 (1903): 26–71.

Pratscher, Wilhelm. "Der Verzicht des Paulus auf finanziellen Unterhalt durch seine Gemeinden: Ein Aspekt seiner Missionsweise." *New Testament Studies* 25 (1979): 284–298.

Prior, David. *The Message of 1 Corinthians: Life in the Local Church.* Leicester, England: Intervarsity Press, 1985.

Raffeiner, H. *Sklaven und Freigelassene: Eine sozialogische Studie auf der Grundlage des griechischen Grabepigramms.* Innsbruck: Wagner, 1977.

Ramin, Jacques, and Paul Veyne. "Droit romain et société: Les hommes libres qui passent pour esclaves et l'esclavage volontaire." *Historia* 30 (1981): 472–497.

Randall, Richard H. "The Erechtheum Workmen." *American Journal of Archaeology* 57 (1953): 199–210.

Rankin, H. D. *Sophists, Socratics and Cynics.* Totowa, N.J.: Barnes and Noble Books, 1983.

Rauer, Max. *Die "Schwachen" in Korinth und Rom.* Freiburg: Herder, 1923.

Rawson, Beryl. "Family Life among the Lower Classes at Rome in the First Two Centuries of the Empire." *Classical Philology* 61 (1966): 70–83.

————, ed. *The Family in Ancient Rome: New Perspectives.* Ithaca, N.Y.: Cornell University Press, 1986.

Reekmans, Tony. "Juvenal's Views on Social Change." *Ancient Society* 2 (1971): 117–161.

Reilly, Linda Collins. *Slaves in Ancient Greece: Slaves from Greek Manumission Inscriptions.* Chicago: Ares, 1978.

Reinhold, Meyer. "The Usurpation of Status and Status Symbols in the Roman Empire." *Historia* 20 (1971): 275–302.

Reumann, John Henry Paul. "*Oikonomia* as 'Ethical Accommodation' in the Fathers, and Its Pagan Backgrounds." *Studia Patristica* 3 (1961): 370–379.

————. "The Use of *Oikonomia* and Related Terms in Greek Sources to about A.D. 100, as a Background for Patristic Applications." Ph.D. diss., University of Pennsylvania, 1957.

Rhodes, P. J. "Political Activity in Classical Athens." *Journal of Hellenic Studies* 106 (1986): 132–144.

Robert, Louis. "Documents d'Asie Mineure." *Bulletin de correspondance hellénique* 102 (1978): 395–543.

Robertson, Archibald, and Alfred Plummer. *First Epistle of St. Paul to the Corinthians.* New York: Charles Scribner's Sons, 1916.

Robinson, Olivia. "Slaves and the Criminal Law." *Zeitschrift der Savigny-Stiftung für Rechtsgeschichte, romanistische Abteilung* 98 (1981): 213–254.

Roland, Gayer. *Die Stellung des Sklaven in den paulinischen Gemeinden und bei Paulus.* Bern: Herbert Lang, 1976.

Rollins, Wayne G. "Greco-Roman Slave Terminology and Pauline Metaphors for Salvation." In *Society of Biblical Literature Seminar Papers 1987*, ed. Kent Harold Richards, 100–110. Atlanta: Scholars Press, 1987.

Rostovtzeff, Mikhail. *The Social and Economic History of the Roman Empire.* 2 vols. 2d ed. Revised by P. M. Fraser. Oxford: Clarendon Press, 1957.

Russell, Kenneth C. *Slavery as Reality and Metaphor in the Pauline Letters*. Ph.D. diss., Pontifical University, Rome, 1968.

Russell, Letty M. *Household of Freedom: Authority in Feminist Theology*. Philadelphia: Westminster Press, 1987.

──────. "People and the Powers." *The Princeton Seminary Bulletin*, n.s. 8 (1987): 6–18.

Ste. Croix, G. E. M. de. *The Class Struggle in the Ancient World from the Archaic Age to the Arab Conquest*. London: Duckworth, 1981.

──────. Review of *The Slave Systems of Greek and Roman Antiquity*, by W. L. Westermann. *Classical Review* 71 (1957): 54–59.

──────. "Suffragium: From Vote to Patronage." *British Journal of Sociology* 5 (1954): 33–48.

Saller, Richard P. *Personal Patronage under the Early Empire*. Cambridge: Cambridge University Press, 1982.

──────. "Slavery and the Roman Family." In *Classical Slavery*, edited by M. I. Finley, 65–87. London: Frank Cass, 1987.

Saller, Richard P., and Brent D. Shaw. "Tombstones and Roman Family Relations in the Principate: Civilians, Soldiers and Slaves." *Journal of Roman Studies* 74 (1984): 124–156.

Sampley, J. Paul. *Pauline Partnership in Christ: Christian Community and Commitment in Light of Roman Law*. Philadelphia: Fortress Press, 1980.

Sanday, William. *A Critical and Exegetical Commentary on the Epistle to the Romans*. Edinburgh: T. and T. Clark, 1958.

Sass, Gerhard. "Zur Bedeutung von *doulos* bei Paulus." *Zeitschrift für die neutestamentliche Wissenschaft* 40 (1941): 24–32.

Schmeling, Gareth L. *Chariton*. New York: Twayne, 1974.

Schmithals, Walter. *The Office of Apostle in the Early Church*. Nashville: Abbingdon Press, 1969.

Scholia Aristophanica. Edited and translated by William G. Rutherford. 3 vols. London: Macmillan, 1896.

Schumacher, Leonhard. *Servus Index: Sklavenverhör und Sklavenanzeige im republikanischen und kaiserzeitlichen Rom*. Forschungen zur antiken Sklaverei, 15. Wiesbaden: Franz Steiner, 1982.

Schürer, Emil. *The History of the Jewish People in the Age of Jesus Christ (175 B.C.–A.D. 135)*. 2 vols. Revised and edited by Matthew Black, Geza Vermes, and Fergus Millar. Edinburgh: T. and T. Clark, 1973.

Schütz, John Howard. *Paul and the Anatomy of Apostolic Authority*. London: Cambridge University Press, 1975.

Shaw, Brent D. "Latin Funerary Epigraphy and Family Life in the Later Roman Empire." *Historia* 33 (1984): 457–497.

Shaw, Graham. *The Cost of Authority: Manipulation and Freedom in the New Testament*. Philadelphia: Fortress Press, 1983.

Smirin, V. M. "Die Sklaverei in römischen Spanien." In Staerman et al., *Die Sklaverei in den westlichen Provinzen des Römischen Reiches im 1.–3. Jahrhundert*, 38–102. Stuttgart: F. Steiner, 1987.

Smith, Dennis. "Social Obligation in the Context of Communal Meals: A Study of the Corinthian Meal in 1 Corinthians in Comparison with Graeco-Roman Communal Meals." Th.D. diss., Harvard Divinity School, 1980.

Smith, Morton. *Clement of Alexandria and a Secret Gospel of Mark.* Cambridge: Harvard University Press, 1973.

——. Review of *Themen der paulinischen Missionspredigt auf dem Hintergrund der spätjüdisch-hellenistischen Missionsliteratur* by Claus Bussmann. *Catholic Biblical Quarterly* 35 (1973): 518–519.

Socraticorum reliquiae. Edited by G. Giannantoni. Collana Elenchos 6–7. Naples: Bibliopolis, 1983–85.

Soden, Hans Freiherr von. "Sacrament and Ethics in Paul." In *The Writings of St. Paul*, edited and translated by Wayne A. Meeks. New York: W. W. Norton, 1972.

Sokolowski, F. "The Real Meaning of Sacral Manumission." *Harvard Theological Review* 47 (1954): 173–181.

Solodukho, Yu. A. "Slavery in the Hebrew Society of Iraq and Syria in the Second through Fifth Centuries A.D." In *Soviet Views of Talmudic Judaism*, edited by Jacob Neusner, 1–9. Leiden: Brill, 1973.

Spawforth, A. "The Slave Philodespotos, *Syros Pot(e) Thenatas.*" *Zeitschrift für Papyrologie und Epigraphik* 27 (1977): 294.

Staerman, E. M., et al. *Die Sklaverei in den westlichen Provinzen des Römischen Reiches im 1.-3. Jahrhundert.* Stuttgart: F. Steiner, 1987.

Stambaugh, John E., and David L. Balch, *The New Testament in Its Social Environment.* Philadelphia: Westminister Press, 1986.

Stanford, W. B. *The Ulysses Theme.* 2d ed. Ann Arbor: University of Michigan, 1963.

Stanley, D. M. "The Theme of the Servant of Yahweh in Primitive Christian Soteriology, and Its Transposition by St. Paul." *Catholic Biblical Quarterly* 16 (1954): 385–425.

Steinmann, Alphous. "Zur Geschichte der Auslegung von 1 Kor. 7,21." *Theologische Revue* 16 (1917): 340–348.

Stowers, Stanley K. "A Debate over Freedom: 1 Cor. 6:12–20." In *Christian Teaching: Studies in Honor of Lemoine G. Lewis*, edited by Everett Ferguson, 59–71. Abilene, Texas: Abilene Christian University, 1981.

Swartley, Willard M. *Slavery, Sabbath, War and Women.* Scottsdale, Pa.: Herald, 1983.

Tabor, James D. *Things Unutterable: Paul's Ascent to Paradise in Its Greco-Roman, Judaic, and Early Christian Contexts.* Lanham, Md.: University Press of America, 1986.

Tarn, W. W. *Alexander the Great*. 2 vols. Cambridge: At the University Press, 1948.

Taylor, Lily Ross. "Freedom and Freeborn in the Epitaphs of Imperial Rome." *American Journal of Philology* 82 (1961): 113–132.

———. *Party Politics in the Age of Caesar*. Berkeley: University of California Press, 1949.

Theissen, Gerd. *The Social Setting of Pauline Christianity*. Edited and translated by John H. Schütz. Philadelphia: Fortress Press, 1982.

———. *Studien zur Soziologie des Urchristentums*. 2d expanded edition. Tübingen: Mohr, 1983.

Theon. *Progymnasmata*. In *Rhetores graeci*. Edited by Leonhard von Spengel. Leipzig: Teubner, 1894.

Theophylactus Simocatta. *Historiae*. Edited by Carolus de Boor. Leipzig: B. G. Teubner, 1887.

———. *The History of Theophylact Simocatta*. Translation and notes by Michael and Mary Whitby. Oxford: Clarendon Press, 1986.

Thorndike, Lynn. "A Roman Astrologer as a Historical Source: Julius Firmicus Maternus." *Classical Philology* 8 (1913): 415–435.

Tod, Marcus N. "Epigraphical Notes on Freedmen's Professions." *Epigraphica* 12 (1950): 3–26.

Toynbee, Arnold J. *Hannibal's Legacy: The Hannibalic War's Effects on Roman Life*. New York: Oxford University Press, 1965.

———, ed. *The Crucible of Christianity*. New York: World Publishing, 1969.

Treggiari, Susan. "Domestic Staff at Rome in the Julio-Claudian Peirod, 27 B.C. to A.D. 68." *Histoire Sociale* 6 (1973): 241–255.

———. "Jobs for Women." *American Journal of Ancient History* 1 (1976): 76–104.

———. "Jobs in the Household of Livia." *Papers of the British School at Rome*, n.s. 43 (1975): 48–77.

———. "Lower Class Women in the Roman Economy." *Florilegium* 1 (1979): 65–86.

———. "Questions on Women Domestics in the Roman West." In *Schiavitù, manomissione e classi dipendenti nel mondo antico*, 185–201. Rome: "L'Erma" di Bretschneider, 1979.

———. *Roman Freedmen during the Late Republic*. Oxford: Clarendon Press, 1969.

———. "Roman Social History: Recent Interpretations." *Histoire Social* 8 (1975): 149–164.

———. "Urban Labour in Rome: *Mercennarii* and *Tabernarii*." In *Non-slave Labour in the Greco-Roman World*, edited by Peter Garnsey, 48–64. Cambridge: Cambridge University Press, 1980.

Troeltsch, Ernst. *The Social Teaching of the Christian Churches*. New York: Macmillan, 1931.

Trummer, Peter. "Die Chance der Freiheit. Zur Interpretation des mallon Chresthai in 1 Kor 7,21." *Biblica* 56 (1975): 344–368.

Urbach, Ephraim E. "The Laws Regarding Slavery as a Source for Social History of the Period of the Second Temple, the Mishnah, and Talmud." In *Papers of the Institute of Jewish Studies*, Institute of Jewish Studies, vol. 1, edited by J. G. Weiss, 1–94. Jerusalem: Magnes, 1964.

Vanhoye, A., ed. *L'Apôtre Paul: Personnalité, style et conception du ministère*. Leuven: Leuven University Press, 1986.

Vernant, Jean-Pierre. *Myth and Society in Ancient Greece*. New York: Humanities Press, 1980.

Vidal-Naquet, Pierre. *The Black Hunter: Forms of Thought and Forms of Society in the Greek World*. Translated by Andrew Szegedy-Maszak. Baltimore: Johns Hopkins University Press, 1986.

Vittinghoff, Friedrich. "Soziale Stuktur und politisches System der hohen römischen Kaiserzeit." *Historische Zeitschrift* 230 (1980): 31–55.

Vogt, Joseph, *Ancient Slavery and the Ideal of Man*. Oxford: Basil Blackwell, 1974.

———, ed. *Bibliographie zur antiken Sklaverei*. Bochum: Brockmeyer, 1971.

Volkmann, Hans. "Die Basileia als *Endoxos Douleia*: Ein Beitrag zur Wortgeschichte der Duleia." *Historia* 16 (1967): 155–161.

———. "*Endoxos Douleia* als ehrenvoller Knechtsdienst gegenüber dem Gesetz." *Philologus* 100 (1956): 52–61.

Voloshinov, V. N. [M. M. Bakhtin?] *Marxism and the Philosophy of Language*. Translated by Ladislav Matejka and I. R. Titunik. Cambridge: Harvard University Press, 1986.

Walcot, P. "Odysseus and the Art of Lying." *Ancient Society* 8 (1977): 1–19.

Walsh, P. G. *The Roman Novel*. Cambridge: Cambridge University Press, 1970.

Warren, Austin. *Theory of Literature*. 3d ed. New York: Harcourt Brace Jovanovich, 1977.

Watson, Alan. *Roman Slave Law*. Baltimore: Johns Hopkins University Press, 1987.

Watson, Duane F. "1 Corinthians 10:23–11:1 in the Light of Greco-Roman Rhetoric: The Role of Rhetorical Questions." *Journal of Biblical Literature* 108 (1989): 301–318.

Watson, James L., ed. *Asian and African Systems of Slavery*. Berkeley: University of California Press, 1980.

Watts, William. "Seneca on Slavery." *The Downside Review* 90 (1972): 183–195.

Weaver, P. R. C. "Dated Inscriptions of Imperial Freedmen and Slaves." *Epigraphische Studien* 11 (1976): 215–227.

———. *Familia Caesaris: A Social Study of the Emperor's Freedmen and Slaves*. Cambridge: Cambridge University Press, 1972.

———. "The Slave and Freedman Cursus in the Imperial Administration." *Proceedings of the Cambridge Philological Society*, n.s. 10 (1964): 74–92.

———. "Social Mobility in the Early Roman Empire: The Evidence of the Imperial Freedmen and Slaves." In *Studies in Ancient Society*, edited by Moses I. Finley, 121–140. London: Routledge and Kegan Paul, 1974.

Weber, Max. "The Social Causes of the Decay of Ancient Civilisation." *The Journal of General Education* 5 (1950): 75–88.

Weiss, Johannes. *Der Erste Korintherbrief:* Kritisch-exegetischer Kommentar über das Neue Testament, no. 5. 9th ed. Göttingen: Vandenhoeck und Ruprecht, 1910.

Weiss, K. *"Sympherō."* In *Theological Dictionary of the New Testament.* 10 vols. Edited by Gerhard Friedrich; translated and edited by Geoffrey W. Bromiley, 9:69–78. Grand Rapids: Eerdmans, 1964–76.

Wellek, René, and Austin Warren. *Theory of Literature.* 3d ed. New York: Harcourt Brace Jovanovich, 1977.

Welwei, Karl-Wilhelm. *Unfreie im antiken Kriegsdienst.* Parts 1–3. Forschungen zur antiken Sklaverei 5, 8, 21. Wiesbaden: Franz Steiner, 1974, 1978, 1988.

Westermann, W. L. "Enslaved Persons who Are Free." *American Journal of Philology* 59 (1938): 1–30.

———. "The Freedmen and the Slaves of God." *Proceedings of the American Philosophical Society* 92 (1948): 55–64.

———. *The Slave System of Greek and Roman Antiquity.* Philadelphia: American Philosophical Society, 1955.

Wiedemann, Thomas. *Greek and Roman Slavery: A Source Book.* Baltimore: Johns Hopkins University Press, 1981.

———. Review of *Servus Index: Sklavenverhör und Sklavenanzeige im republikanischen und kaiserzeitlichen Rom,* by Leonhard Schumacher. *The Classical Review,* n.s. 35 (1985): 135–137.

Wilckens, Ulrich. *Der Brief an die Römer.* 3 vols. Zürich: Benziger; Neukirchen-Vluyn: Neukirchener Verlag, 1978–82.

Willink, M. D. R. "Paul, a Slave of Jesus Christ." *Theology* 16 (1928): 46–47.

Willis, Wendell Lee. *Idol Meat in Corinth: The Pauline Argument in 1 Corinthians 8 and 10.* Chico, Calif.: Scholars Press, 1985.

Winger, Michael. "Unreal Conditions in the Letters of Paul." *Journal of Biblical Literature* 105 (1986): 110–112.

Wittgenstein, Ludwig. *Philosophical Investigations.* 3d ed. Translated by G. E. M. Anscombe. New York: Macmillan, 1958.

Wolf, Eric R. "Kinship, Friendship, and Patron-Client Relations." In *The Social Anthropology of Complex Societies,* edited by Michael Banton, 1–22. New York: Frederick A. Praeger, 1966.

Wood, Ellen Meiksins. *Peasant-Citizen and Slave: The Foundations of Athenian Democracy.* New York: Verso, 1988.

Wood, Ellen Meiksins, and Neal Wood. *Class Ideology and Ancient Political Theory: Socrates, Plato, and Aristotle in Social Context.* New York: Oxford University Press, 1978.

Wuellner, Wilhelm. "Greek Rhetoric and Pauline Argumentation." In *Early Christian Literature and the Classical Intellectual Tradition: In Honorem Robert M. Grant,* edited by William R. Schoedel and Robert L. Wilken, 177–188. Theologie Historique, no. 53. Paris: Éditions Beauchesne, 1979.

———. "Paul as Pastor: The Function of Rhetorical Questions in First Corinthians." In *L'Apôtre Paul*, edited by A. Vanhoye, 49–77. Leuven: Leuven University Press, 1986.

———. "Toposforschung und Torahinterpretation bei Paulus und Jesus." *New Testament Studies* 24 (1978): 463–483.

———. "Where Is Rhetorical Criticism Taking Us?" *Catholic Biblical Quarterly* 49 (1987): 448–463.

Yavetz, Zvi. *Plebs and Princeps*. London: Oxford University Press, 1969.

Zucrow, Solomon. *Women, Slaves and the Ignorant in Rabbinic Literature*. Boston: Stratford, 1932.

INDEX OF

SCRIPTURAL

REFERENCES

GENERAL

INDEX

Accommodation, 92–95, 100, 141, 204*n*27, 204*n*28. *See also Levitas*
Adcock, F. E., 204*n*51
Adkins, A. W. H., 201*n*59, 208*n*86
Aelian, Claudius, 100
Aesop, 38–39
Agricultural manuals, 26–27. *See also* Household
Ajax, 93, 105–07, 112, 206*n*66, 207*n*67
Anaxandrides, 38
Andrews, Mary E., 209*n*93
Antisthenes, 92, 103–07 passim, 124, 207*n*70
Apuleius, Lucius, xv
Aristophanes, 98–99, 106–10 passim, 115, 207*n*77
Aristotle, 30, 44–45, 72, 89–90, 92, 99, 123, 144, 203*n*15
Artemidorus, 20–22, 32–35, 45–46, 74–75, 197*n*183
Athenaeus, 8, 15, 38, 43, 92–93, 195*n*168
Augustine, 103
Aurelius, Marcus, 144
Authority: in early church leadership, xxii, 52, 58; by association, 56; of slave of Christ, 56, 83, 134–47 passim; Paul's, xxi, 84, 85, 117, 118, 122. *See also Exousia*

Bakhtin, Mikhail M., 213*n*1
Barrow, R. H., 2
Bartchy, S. Scott, 198*n*16

Bassler, Jouette M., 208*n*90
Benevolent patriarchalism, 87–108 passim, 202*nn*6, 8, and 11, 206*n*62; ideological function of, 27, 29, 117, 127–28; Paul and, 125, 145; and other leadership models, 134, 137, 140; language of, in Paul's letters, 142; unity in, 148
Berger, Peter, 181*n*19
Betz, Hans Dieter, 199*n*24
Black, David Alan, 209–10*n*3, 210*n*4
Bömer, Franz, 179*n*6, 180*n*10
Bornkamm, Günther, 121
Bradley, Keith R., 181*n*1
Burford, Alison, 45

Calderini, Aristide, 186*n*52
Callistratus, 189*n*99
Castelli, Elizabeth Anne, 192*n*129
Chantraine, Heinrich, 186*n*51
Chariton, 11, 24, 39, 56, 130, 198*n*5
Cicero, 23, 45, 97–101 passim, 108, 116, 201–02*n*2
Cleon, 98, 102, 108–09, 115, 202*n*32, 205*n*45, 207*n*74
Cohoon, J. W., 194*n*156
Columella, 28
Concord. *See Homonoia*
Conzelmann, Hans, xvi, 64, 77, 199*n*23
Corinthians, First, 64, 69, 71, 78, 79, 128, 142, 144, 201*n*50, 209*n*3
Corinthians, Second, 120, 209*n*3

Cynics, 69–72 passim, 119, 125; and
Stoics, on suffering, 76; on enslaved
leader, 86–88; on heroes, 103, 105; on
the strong, 210*n*5
Cyrus, 39–42, 103–05, 206*n*59, 206*n*61

D'Arms, John H., 29
Daube, David, 198*n*13
Dautzenberg, Gerhard, 121
Deissmann, Adolf, xvi, xix, 63
Demagogues: bad, 125; Dio on, 203*n*19;
Plutarch on, 204*n*38; Plato on, 204*n*40,
207–08*n*79; Odysseus as a, 205*n*46
Demagogue topos, 86–116; enslaved lead-
er in, 134, 137
Democracy, 89–112 passim, 208*n*80,
211*n*21; and egalitarianism, 127–29; Ar-
istotle on, 202*n*13, 203*n*14; power in,
204*n*34; Philo on, 209*n*93
Demos, John, 193*n*148
Demosthenes, 144
Dio Cassius, 29, 96
Dio Chrysostom, 39, 41, 45, 70, 73–74,
90–91, 92, 100, 101–03, 108, 138, 144,
199–200*n*31, 201*n*59, 202*n*3, 203*nn*16,
17, 18, and 19, 205*n*54, 208*n*82
Dreams. *See* Artemidorus

Enslaved leader, 84; power and, 134; Philo on, 205*n*53; Libanius on, 206*n*57;
topos of, 115, 118, 139, 140, 202*n*4
Epicrates, 43
Epictetus, 31, 70–74 passim, 81, 143,
144, 200*n*36
Euripedes, 93, 95
Exousia (authority, right), 120, 121, 139,
210*n*7; Isocrates on, 70; and *eleutheria*,
210*n*12

Feeley-Harnik, Gillian, 192–93*n*140
Finley, Moses I., 99, 180*n*15, 205*n*48
Fishel, Henry A., 200*n*33
Flesher, Paul V. M., 190*n*108, 198*n*3
Flory, Marlene Boudreau, 2–3, 48

Foucault, Michel, 180*n*14
"Friendship," 23–24, 26, 138–39; Pliny
on, 191*nn*113 and 116
Funk, Aloys, 198*n*18, 199*n*21

Gabba, Emilio, 180*n*16
Galatians: slavery to Christ in, 60
Garlan, Yvon, 191*n*124, 195*n*169
Garnsey, Peter, 15, 189*n*99
Genesis: account of Joseph in, 113
"Gifts," 23–26, 138–139, 192*n*126
Goldstein, Jonathan A., 213*n*14
Goodenough, Erwin R., 205*n*52, 208*n*90,
208–09*n*91, 209*n*93

Havelock, Eric A., 202*n*10
Heracles, 70–71, 74, 86–87, 200*n*32
Héring, Jean, 201*n*50
Herodotus, 39, 103, 104
Highet, Gilbert, 210*n*13
Hock, Ronald F., 69, 123–24, 130,
199*nn*29 and 30
Höistad, Ragner, 86–88
Homer, 89–94 passim
Homonoia, 142–48 passim, 212–13*n*9,
213*n*15
Hopkins, Keith, 8, 184*n*27, 185*n*29
Horace, 43, 92, 195*n*173, 210*n*13
Household, 31, 137; structure of, 2–3,
12, 57, 59; hierarchy of, 34, 67; church
as, of Christ, 52, 58, 66, 137, 142, 149;
in parables, 56; democracy in, 89

Isocrates, 70, 143–44, 199*n*31

Jameson, Fredric R., 136
Jones, C. P., 198*n*8, 206*n*56
Joseph, 93, 113–14
Judge, E. A., 211*n*21, 212*n*5
Justin, Marcus Julianus, 39, 41, 194*n*157,
206*n*64
Juvenal, 31, 37, 43, 44

Kyrtatas, Dimitris, 212*n*7